From Pit
To Palace

Major Tom Godwin M.B.E

ISBN: 978-1-910205-42-6

First published in 2014 by
For The Right Reasons
(Charity no. SC037781)
Printers & Publishers
60 Grant Street, Inverness

British Library Cataloguing in Publication Data.
A catalogue record of this book is available
from the British Library.

INDEX CONTENTS

1

2

Palace Barracks. A Colonel Worth His Salt.
The Bangor Post Office Heist
The Guard's All Arms Wing. Surrey
6 Weeks of Bullshit

Mons Barracks and the RSM's Farewell

The Passing of my Father and the Family Funeral
The Presentation of New Colours to 1,2,3 and 4 Para.
Rushmoor Arena Aldershot 1974.
The Battalion Provost Sergeant and the Cockerill
Horbury Road Ossett, a change of Accommodation.
The Crown Hotel, Ossett
The Piscadors.
Walking. The Pennine Way
The 4th Battalion. Boxing, a way of Life.
Farewell to the 4th Battalion. Dining Out 1975
2 Battalion, The Parachute Regiment.
Regimental Sergeant Major.
The Ulster Tour with the Second Battalion 1976
The MV Balero. A South American Cruise Ship.
Farewell to 2 Para – A Surprise Posting.

Off Base at Home, Vine Close
Ballooning on Queen's Avenue.
A Surprise for Daughter Tanya. Trudy with the Red Devils
The Visit of HRH Prince Charles.

Colonel in Chief to the Regiment. Depot Para 1978
Her Majesty's Jubilee Medal 1977
A laugh over a Pair of Briefs
Depot Mess Nights. " The League of Gentlemen"

Selected, Dining Out and Posted to 1 Para as MTO
Roadside interview with Brigade Commander.
Instant Promotion.
U.S.A. Fort Campbell. Kentucky/ Tennessee 1979
The Tennessee Walking Horse.
Hopkinsville, The mayoral Invite.
The 101st Airborne Veterans and Clarkesville.

Posting as Captain Quartermaster
Charmandean. The Boarding School 1979-85.
Younger daughter Trudy.
Life With 2 UDR Armagh. Northern Ireland.
The Lighter Side of Ulster.
The Carrick – a – Rede Rope Bridge
The Officer's Mess 2 UDR
"Why not take some exercise Sir?"
Four Screws and a Barrel.

Attendance at a Courts Martial as a defending Officer
Aldershot. Soldier On!
Belize Central America 1982. Recce for six months tour.

The Quartermasters Staff at sea.

The battalion at War May-June 1982
Tuesday 1st June back in San Carlos Waters.
Homeward Bound Post War Falklands. The MV Norland
Reurn to Aldershot 1982. On leave in Yorkshire
Return to Armagh. Post war lecture

Who swam Alligators Creek?
Some reflections on life in Belize. Christine on holiday.
Reols "Rose Garden"
FORT LEWIS WASHINGTON STATE USA

. (Para Battle School)
"Sam" of Brecknock Labrador retriever.
Snowdonia – Beggelert – The Watkin Path
The Portmeirion Peninsula and village
Family happenings whilst at Brecon 84-87
And Brecon Friends
Godwin's walks in Wales.
USA: Holiday in America Christmas 1986

Quartermaster Headquarters Berlin and Signal Regiment
Berlin Headquarters. The Olympic Stadium.
"The Berliner" The British Military train
HM the Queen Annual Bithday Parade
The Berlin Wall 1961-1989
The Berlin Adventure Training Centre, Bavaria.
Charity Swim, Housefrau, Gurka visit
The Diary of our final year in Berlin

RE-SETTLEMENT AND INTO RETIREMENT 1990-1991
JOURNEY TO CYPRUS BY ROAD AND SHIP

The Alfa Hotel Athens
Into Cyprus and settling in

What a surprise! Telegram
from Prince Charles Colonel in Chief
Purchase of the village house "Kalo Chorio" Cyprus
Kalo Chorio Village, Limassol at 2.500 feet
Village Life
Easter in the village and the donkey race
Mr Vassilles – shopkeeper
The Agnes Martha, "A sailing Yacht.
New Years day lunch 1996
Over the Edge
Cyprus 1996
In and out. Scotland. Yorkshire. USA and Brecon.
Small village memories – The bat cave
Bay to bay swims
Orchid Hunting and Mountain walks

Now in retirement in Leavesden Hertfordshire –
having travelled a wonderful journey in the main
with my darling wife Chris and sixty years since
joining the parachute Regiment.

Dedication

This book is dedicated to my life companions, my darling wife Chris, my Regiment and my Labrador Sam.

'FROM PIT TO PALACE' by Major Tom Godwin MBE

Part 1

EARLY YEARS 1940 - 46

Gomersal near Leeds 1940 – 1946

Father was the Village Policeman here during those World War II years, and where Mum and Dad, sister June and brother Christopher and I spent a happy time. Christopher was born here in the year 1944.

The House

We lived in what had been a former Rectory, a dark place on the hillside of what was known as 'Lower Lane'. It had Gothic windows to the sitting room, flagged floors to the kitchen, gas lighting downstairs, the use of a gas poker to light the open fire grate in the kitchen and, as I recall, a gas pipe that was flexible and provided a flame to heat a large iron to enable Mum to iron clothes. We did not have a fridge but had a cold, dark cellar that always seemed to be freezing, even in summer. We used to take candles to bed in a holder if a light was required. There was no hot water in the house, only that which was heated on the stove. The house did not have a bathroom, we bathed in a large tin bath that was taken from a large hook in the scullery, usually on a Friday evening. The children were then all bathed in the same bath water!

The toilet or '**bog**' as we called it was some ten yards from the back door, built into a bank. It was a whitewashed brick room with a large hole in the floor. The hole was covered by a throne with a lid. The seat of wood was highly polished.

Looking down the hole there was what seemed to be a metal dustbin down below without a lid and a door behind that let the light in through the chinks. The door was opened once a week when the bin was removed to have its contents emptied.

The bin was pulled to the roadside where it was met by a marvellous machine with a flexi-hose that used to remove the contents. The bin was then returned to its underground hidey-hole.

Entertainment indoors was table tennis, cards and board-games such as ludo, snakes and ladders, draughts and marbles. We did have the luxury of a '**wireless**' or radio, powered by an electric accumulator that was changed weekly. This was provided by the Government, as our Police House was the headquarters of the local ARP/Wardens and some local army night patrols. We did have some kind of HMV record-player that played 'Gigli' records and choral records. We had a telephone! Government use!

We always kept chickens, ducks and rabbits. I used to take the odd duckling to school in my pocket. School was Hilltop Primary some two miles away, which of course we used to walk.

A posh neighbour once came to our house, a Mrs Thomson who had come to report her cat missing. Father knew where it was but didn't tell her as he had shot it with a twelve bore for killing our chickens!

Our house seemed to be open all hours, often it was difficult to sleep with the noise of people coming and going on nightly patrols and the wardens who enforced the 'blackout' throughout the village. All windows at night were covered so as not to show a light to enemy bombers on their way to and from Sheffield, Leeds and Hull. The only bomb the village suffered during the war was probably a jettisoned one and it landed on the cricket pitch and did NOT explode!

Although food was rationed during the war we never seemed to go short of the basics, though we grew most of our vegetables, potatoes, cabbages, carrots, turnips etc. We seemed to have an abundance of bacon, hams, eggs and fruit. Some apples came in barrels from Canada. Also clothing. I remember being togged out for school in knickerbockers. Very colourful they were too.

Father being the village 'Bobby' had the right kind of pals. Even after the war years they always used to meet up in the village pub 'The Wheatsheaf'. Even when I was into my late teens the wartime pals were having a drink and playing dominoes together. They were as I recall: publican - Ben Brown, the farmer – Harry Smith, the butcher – Alf Iveson, crisp and sweets manufacturer – 'TOFFEE' Smith, village shopkeeper – Josh Tetley. One can really see why we never went short of anything!

The Picnic

Some half a mile away living in Lower Lane was Peter Shepley, some two years older than me. We were the greatest of friends and in later years exchanged holidays and were always at each other's houses. We joined the army together during National Service years, and later on joined the West Riding Constabulary and were at Pannal Ash Police College, Harrogate, together.

On this occasion, at about six years of age, we took off from home on a picnic and to visit Peter's cousin at Spenborough some five miles away. On our way home during our return journey through fields and woods, we stopped at the side of a brook to have a paddle and eat our sandwiches. Whilst Peter was in the water I took out the sandwiches, tucked into mine and whilst doing so saw a large black beetle in the grass. I popped it into his sandwich and squashed it. We both finished our food, drank our lemonade, then foolishly I told him that he had eaten my squashed beetle! He was not best pleased.

As I had a head start I ran through the stream up the bank at the far side where I turned to see where he was. All I saw was a large lemonade bottle flying through the air. Well, it hit me! It shattered on my head and was the reason for six clips or stitches into my forehead once we had reached home and the doctor had been summoned. For years I had a perfect letter 'P' etched into my upper right forehead. Correct retribution...Eh? Served me right.

Morley: West Riding of Yorkshire

The Cycle Ride

I was taken to Morley Park as I recall. Morley being a small town to the west of Leeds City. Father was a Police Constable here as PC 664 of the West Riding of Yorkshire Constabulary. He and Mother, Alice, took me to the park to ride a three-wheeled tricycle.

I remember mastering this new toy, and, being somewhat adventurous and willful, insisted on being put on top of the flat-topped wall that encircled the Park. My wish was granted and all was fine and I went at best speed until...I ran out of wall! I was

11

taken to hospital by ambulance where they found that as a result of my fall, I had broken my right arm. I can remember the smell of the gas that was used to quell my pain and to put me to sleep. They called it 'Bunny Gas'. I have remembered the name to this day.

Always a walker, even as a six year old

My Grandparents on my mother's side lived at **Brighouse,** and to get there on a familiar bus route one had to go through **Cleckheaton**. Now and again we went there by pony and trap, then sometimes on to **Keighley** to see my other Grandparents who lived at No1 Myrtle View, Crossroads, off the Keighley to Halifax Road.

The route from Gomersal to Brighouse always seemed to stick in my mind, and I really loved my Grandparents, George and Mary Jayne Walton, who lived at 14 Camm Street, not far from a large cinema off the Bradford Road.

One bright morning I decided that sister June, one year younger than I, with myself as chief scout would walk to Brighouse to visit our Grandparents. I remember the route as: 'Through our village, top of the hill. Down steep hill into Cleckheaton, follow bus route straight up hill. Pub on crossroads straight on, over the MOOR - no houses. Downhill into Brighouse, turn right, past park to cinema. Go two streets'.

I remember that June and I had comfy sandals. The journey seemed to be OK as I recall. We arrived at Grandparents where a great deal of fuss was made. Grandfather made a telephone call to Father and we were returned by car that evening.

DISTANCE – six miles and a bit. I was asked never to take my sister walking again!

Grandfather and Grandmother Walton

Grandfather and Grandmother Walton died within six months of each other both in their 83rd year in 1976. Christine and I had a lovely relationship with them.

Grandfather was one of seven children and was the son of a farmer at Hartshead in between Brighouse and Cleckheaton. His working life was spent at Blakeborough Brothers of Brighouse; they made castings, heavy drain covers and all manner of metal parts. In his thirties Grandfather was a blacksmith in the engineering shop and operated a large steam hammer working molten metal. During one operation the molten metal splashed, hit his eye and came out of his mouth. Thereafter he wore a glass eye. He was transferred to the electrician's shop where he worked until retirement. Even so, just after the Second World War he drove a Standard 8 motor car for many years and went to and from work on a Villiers moped.

His favourite pub was 'The Stott's Arms' on the Wakefield Road. Always suited and booted he and his three pals would meet on Tuesday and Thursday evenings for 4 Gills, not a drop more! Unless in later years my Father and I called in on our way to see Father's cousin at 'The Stansfield Arms', Apperley Bridge.

Grandfather was set in his ways and would eat neither 'Fish nor Fowl'. Whereas dear Grandma Mary Jayne had cod and chips four times a week from the chippy at the end of Camm Street. Grandfather always had pork at Christmas. He was a mild mannered wonderful man and I never ever heard him raise his voice in anger.

Aunty Hilda, my mother's sister, married an ex-RAF pilot and navigator after the war - Uncle Stanley Newman – and she set up house in Wimbledon. Grandfather used to visit them annually by train and usually took me as a young teenager along with him. There I learned the delights of London: its museums, Petticote Lane, markets, jellied eels and the London underground. What a delight.

Grandfather had a couple of quirky party pieces. He could play the piano through his flat hat that he would throw onto the keys. He would also drop his false eye into his pint beer glass to look at you across the table.

When I finished the training at 18 years of age at Depot in Maida Barracks, Aldershot, dear Grandfather came to the parade as we passed off the Square. He was so proud afterwards to have met Brigadier Sir John Hunt of Everest fame, the mountain having recently been climbed for the first time. Sir John had organised the expedition and had been invited to be our reviewing officer of 40 Platoon in March 1955. We then went to Abingdon to complete eight jumps to earn our Wings.

What also tickled Grandfather was meeting the colonel of The Depot, one Colonel PINE-COFFIN.

During 1961 without fail, and weekly whilst in Bahrain, I used to send Grandmother 20 Park Drive cigarettes, out of packet, squashed and sent 'Airmail'. Mary Jayne loved her 'PARK DRIVE' cigarettes.

Gomersal: The Roman Wall and the 38 Pistol

At the Police House in Lower Lane within my parents' bedroom was a tall chest of drawers aptly named a 'tallboy'. It was off limits to small boys, in particular inquisitive ones. I knew that Father had a revolver but when looking within the forbidden 'tallboy' it was not to be found. In hindsight, thank God!

What *was* in there, was a muslin bag of BULLETS (every young boy's dream). I thought that a small handful to an eight year old would not be missed, as indeed it was proved to be... UNTIL, together with a few other interested pals, we went through the fields over the railway bridge and to the park near to Cleckheaton to the old Roman Wall, where I developed an interest in explosives. There we wedged the bullets within the cracks in the hard stone walls and threw stones at them. Well, there was a war on. The bullets exploded. The police were somehow sent for and I was taken home to Father (the Police Constable in the next village). A large belt was produced and I received a very painful hiding.

Father did get some bullets back!

Gomersal: Holiday by Pony and Trap

The year was 1946 and the ownership of a car to my parents was out of the question. Even had we had one, petrol was on ration. We had the use, however, of a pony and trap provided by one of Father's friends in the village. The horse was a spirited cob, the trap was sprung, with bench seats either side and the wheels were rubber rimmed. Father said the horse was a 'cob' cos it had no balls (and little boys remember things like that!).

Off we went one fine weekend. Father, Mother, Sister June and I, and brother Christopher in a pram in the centre of the trap. We went to Grandparents at Brighouse. The horse was put to grass in the field

14

to the rear of 14 Camm Street that Grandfather owned. On the Sunday only Father and I took off in the trap to Keighley whilst Mum, June and Chris stayed at Brighouse. From Brighouse we went over the Moors to join up with the Halifax to Keighley Road and I remember stopping at the **Raggles Inn** to give the horse a blow and to have something to eat. It was a hard journey even though we had a fit horse. We stayed the night at No.1 Myrtle View on the hillside west of Keighley, an end of terrace but four-storey building. I slept up in the attic. There was a skylight and a Po under the bed! Grandfather Godwin was in the same bed and there was barely any room.

Grandfather Thomas William Godwin was a large man and at that time in 1946 was in his fifties. He worked as a miller and part-time driver at the local corn mill some 600 feet below where he lived, down a flagged, paved snicket, dangerous to walk in wintertime. He was 22 stones in weight with a 22" neck. He used to take off the winged collar to his shirt and fasten it around Mum's waist for a laugh. He was the cricket umpire for the local Crossroads Team but, however did the bowler get past him? Or indeed see a wicket?

Whilst there, we went over the moor a couple of miles to visit John Andrews and his mother who ran a sheep and hen farm. Father had been to school with John Andrews at nearby Ingrow Junior School. On visiting, Father was always allowed to take home a hen or cockerel for the pot but.he had to catch it.

We spent a second night at Myrtle View and I remember climbing the ladder to the loft bedroom.

My Father's sister Margaret and hubby George lived with Grandfather at the time. Grandmother Mary had died and I remember nothing of her. Aunty Margaret had two boys Paul and Adrian, much younger than me. There had been another sibling of my age, Tony, but he had been taken ill on the moors and had died eating poisoned berries.

We were warned never to go off paths and tracks on the moors because of 'sink-holes'. It was said that a horse and cart vanished on **'Brown Moor'**. The village of Howarth, of Bronte fame, is not far away. Grandfather and, indeed, the Godwin and Allen family (uncle) are now buried within the Bronte Cemetery on that cold bleak moorside.

After a second night in Crossroads we retraced our steps to Brighouse and with a resting horse for one more evening we clip-clopped home to Gomersal. A lovely holiday, a horse and trap, Grandparents, sights to see, pubs, good food, moors, colours, birds and FREEDOM.

Bentley near Doncaster 1947 – 49

During 1946 Father was transferred as a Police Constable to Bentley, a mining village some three miles from Doncaster. We were housed at Bentley Police Station where there were two three - bedroomed houses as north and south wings.

I quickly formed friendships with the local lads Alan Little, Billy Mayes, Ivor Fox, George and Albert Dykes, and we all went to Bentley New Village School until those of us passed the eleven-plus and then went to the Percy Jackson Grammar School at Adwick-Le-Street. My form Master at the New Village School was Mr Turner and the headmaster was Mr Tomlinson. The Junior School was a sporty one and we were encouraged to play all manner of games, in particular in the school playground: 'British Bulldog', tag and a form of baseball.

Cricket was the main competitive game and in my second year and at ten years of age I was a part of the school team to win the Area Cricket Championships. We played Edlington and I took a super slip catch and took four wickets as a bowler. I have the form master, Mr Turner, to thank for my competitive and lifelong love of cricket.

As young boys did at our age we formed a 'Gang' and used to meet on Thursday evenings on the Police Station flat roof. We shinned up the cell bars covering the windows, up a fall pipe then onto the roof looking down on the trolleybuses on the main road below. Up there we used to keep biscuits, buns or sweets in tins for a weekly share out.

During the long, hot school holiday of 1947 the gang were forever out of doors and we used to walk miles to swim in the River Don and through the canal to the Orchards. The owner could never catch us of course, with cossies full of apples and pears, unless he was prepared to swim canal and river.

16

One of the gang, who shall be nameless, was an enterprising type and we would not have known how enterprising until he received three years detention at an Approved School or 'Borstal'. He had a Saturday job at a Greengrocer's next to the local cinema. Over a few weeks he removed wall bricks to gain entrance into the cinema sales kiosk. The thieving of sweets, crisps, cigarettes went on for weeks as well as cinema tickets and cash. The judge said that the deed was too well planned and executed to go unpunished without detention.

Winter of 1947 was harsh followed by a massive thaw in the spring, which led the River Don to burst its banks, and much of Bentley, Tollbar and Arksey was under water. Father was called out and I have a photo of him in an Army 'DUWK' (a motorised, wheeled boat) rescuing people from the upper windows of their terraced houses.

Two odd happy memories come to mind. When Father was on nights, 10 pm – 6 am, he used to bring home tubs of ice cream from Mazarella's ice cream factory and we had it for breakfast! Another memory was being taken by Father to Doncaster Races to see the Classic, 'St Ledger' Horse Race and to meet the tipster, 'PRINCE MONALULU'! A racing tipster, dressed as an African Prince, anklets, loincloth, head-dress – the lot, shouting 'I Gotta Horse.' Pay sixpence and you received a piece of paper with a supposed winning horse on it!

Sister June at ten years of age or so was into tap-dancing and used to attend ZENA MARSHALL'S Dance Academy. We used to go see her on the stage performing for the senior citizens.

Girls started to come into the equation as we went to a co-ed grammar school. One evening at a pal's house with parents out I discovered that my friend's 15 year old sister was as keen to see what was in my pants as for me not to find what was in hers. Needless to say that both sets of pants were down whilst reclining on the sofa when, in walked Mother! I was sent home, daughter chased upstairs. My Mother was approached the very next day and my pal's Mum gave her a book for me to read called, '*What Every Young Boy Should Know*'!

Doncaster at that time, the late forties, was the hub of the railway plant industry. The heavy locomotives were made and repaired there. It was a train spotter's paradise. The main lines used to split north after Doncaster and therefore there were two main lines through Bentley, their level crossings being about a mile apart. It was a dash to cycle from crossing to crossing to attempt to bag the best sighting of the Class A railway engines. We all had train spotter's guides and used to tick off those premier engines. The favourite was the 'Streamliner' or 'Streak' named **'Mallard'**; the one that was the fastest steam locomotive ever at 126mph. There were others that come to mind: 'Sir Nigel Gresley', Bushbuck, 'Reedbuck'. Some are now housed in the British Railway Museum at York but nothing can match what we experienced as these giants of the track thundered past at full speed, belching smoke. Here now, gone in a rattling, swaying blue flash.

I had a Saturday job delivering milk with the Dykes Brothers and Father had a liaison with the local squire at the Manor House at Arksey, and during the months of summer we would, as a family, take tea with Squire Crannage, play on his lawns, croquet even, and we were allowed to fish in his private lake.

Sometimes travelling into Doncaster by bus I would help Mum with shopping, and we would have tea and cakes at the 'DANUM' Café.

When Chipperfields Circus came to town annually the police families seemed to get premier seats and a good time was had by all. We used to go into Doncaster annually on the Wednesday evening to watch the professional wrestling with such notables as 'Tiger Woods'! Doncaster Rovers were the football team and at that time they were in the Third Division North! In fact in my memory they never ever got out of it. It was sixpence to get into the ground and the only soccer player that I can remember was Clary Jordan (I think that he actually played for **Sheffield**).

Summer holidays were fun. All home-grown entertainment and from dawn to dusk. Cricket, fishing, cycling, tree climbing, walking tracks and hedgerows for miles; train-spotting and making use of the excellent Bentley Miners Welfare Park that housed the normal swing parks, paddling and swimming-pools plus a Saturday theatre club. We had a local Ritz Cinema - 4p admittance, 6p upstairs - where Tarzan was the rage and Flash Gordon. (For June my sister, 'Lassie Come Home' all about a dog). No TV, no computers, no bullying.

Meals always at the table as a family. Church on Sunday twice, as I sang in St Peter's Church. From here, and then Doncaster, Grandfather Walton used to take me to London on the odd occasion. We usually regarded Doncaster as 'Down South', as one could grow tomatoes OUTDOORS.

Cudworth/Barnsley 1949 – 50

Father was transferred here from Bentley and late in our second year was promoted to Sergeant. He still kept the same police number, 664. It was here that we had our first motor car, a Morris 12 with running boards and a hydraulic jacking system that came from the car floor strongpoints to meet the road. The registration number was DKH 936. We were now able to go to the coast usually to Blackpool, through Brighouse, where we used to pick up Grandparents, George and Mary Jayne Walton. Petrol was on ration and as Grandfather had a car and moped we used his fuel also as a supplement.

We lived in a terraced police house in Manor Road, Cudworth, on the hillside, not far from the town police station. Two rooms downstairs with a small kitchen, three bedrooms and a family bathroom. A backyard with gate onto a back alley-way. No garden. We had a wireless, no TV. The 'Dick Barton' radio programme once a week was a must, as was 'ITMA' and Workers Playtime. The town boasted 'The Rock Cinema', a good enough library and a park with an exceptional outdoor swimming pool. The place seemed to me to be full of pubs and working men's clubs. We played an awful lot of table tennis, cards and Monopoly in our house during the winter months.

My friends were Brian Gallier who was an excellent pianist for 13 years of age. His solo piece that I loved to listen to was 'The Earl King'. Another soloist and pal was Brian Burton. He played a cornet in the local Sally Army Band. His passion was railway engines; his father worked on the railways. Fred Fieldsend lived off the main Barnsley Road and their house was backed by a disused quarry. A tall wall that we used to spend time climbing. Very tricky and not to be fooled with, much like Fred's sister who, at 16 years of

19

age, seemed to me to have bumps and curves in all the right places. She had absolutely no interest in me, even though I sang the song 'Irene, Goodnight Irene, I will see you in my dreams'! Which at that time was all the rage. I did for effect sing in St Peter's Church on a Sunday.

No effect – no Irene! Broke my heart.

In our spare time we used to go 'Spud Picking' in the potato fields. 2/6p for a full day's work 10am – 5pm., with a break. This was half a crown in pre-decimal money and there were eight to the £1.

As I had mentioned petrol was on ration, so I used to cycle to Grandfathers at Brighouse and there pick up 2 gallon cans i.e. one in each cycle pannier, and return with them for use in our family car. At evening time in summer, until Father whistled us in at 8pm, we used to play games around the local street gas lamp: 'Tag', 'Kick Can', 'Farmer Farmer'. In season there were whips and tops, roller skates, marbles or alleys, hoopla and kites. There was Bonfire Night and carol singing house to house. Hop-scotch, Knur and Spel, bows and arrows, catapults and of course various sports, soccer, cricket and rugby league.

School was Barnsley Holgate Grammar School a half-hour bus ride from where we lived. The almost two years there did nothing for me. An all-boys school with at that time a most bullying staff. The Headmaster one Dr Roche. He had a liking for the cane. Hand or bum made little difference to him. I visited his study twice, once for arriving at school late, the other for placing the waste paper basket on top of the half opened classroom door that dropped its Friday contents onto the lady cleaner. Six of the best both times. One hand. One bum.

Friday morning to me was a nightmare. We had mental arithmetic in the class of Mr Swift for 45 minutes, 'Godwin! What's seven squared?' No instant answer, picked up by the ears and cuffed. Or if you were at the back of the class – the hard blackboard rubber thrown with accuracy.

I took up boxing in the school gym to survive and remember once after school going to wasteland two streets from the Barnsley Road to 'Put 'em up'. One feint, one punch and I burst the lad's nose. Honour satisfied.

I did however learn something, 'The art of wanking by

20

demonstration'. We had a large affable lad in the class, over six feet tall, deep voice, large feet. At break time in the morning when most of us shot to the long, open urinal in the playground, the demonstrator would play with his Dick and show those who didn't know, how to make it hard and how to make it spit. He also used to smuggle 'Mickey Spillane' mucky boots into the English Lit lessons. Quite a lad our 'Titch'.

In my second year at Barnsley Grammar I was looking for a little light relief, and word went round that the Girls High School out of Barnsley, a mile or so away off the Huddersfield Road, were looking for some male actors to take part in Benjamin Britten's Opera, 'The Little Sweep'. I auditioned, could sing reasonably well, being church choir trained, and was chosen as one of 'The Twins'! Rehearsals were initially two early evenings a week, then later the addition of afternoons! (Sports afternoons). As it was out of the cricket season it suited me, as it stopped me being under the bullying Master Swift, and getting my head punched playing rugby league. The production went well and some weeks later into the dress rehearsal it was decided that we should play it for two paying nights over a Friday/Saturday.

Family and friends came along one evening and seemed to be impressed. In particular June, my tap-dancing sister. From here I had no great acting desires. One of our number, 'Stewart', from Barnsley Road, Cudworth did go on to become an actor. Whether or not he kept his name, 'Stewart Haig', I know not.

My other light relief whilst at Barnsley Grammar School was to represent the school at swimming, and diving off the five-metre board. There were medals somewhere.

We moved house during our second year to a modern semi at Sidcup off the Barnsley – Pontefract Road. I haven't much recall, only that it was near to the potato fields, adjacent to the Co-op grocer's shop and that we as a family were not there more than three months as Father had been promoted Sergeant and that we were on the move to **Ossett**.

Ossett near Wakefield 1950 -1954

During late 1950 Father was posted to Ossett as the Desk Sergeant at Ossett Police Station, then later as the Area Roving Sergeant, checking on male and female police officers on their beats. He was a fearsome man on duty, and he and his equally hard constable partner, PC Batey, used to rule the roost in town on Saturday nights.

There was a monthly dance at Ossett Town Hall. It was the Rock and Roll era, 'Teddy Boys' and all that, and Father and Batey used to take great delight in throwing drunken miscreants down the town hall steps at 'chucking out time!' The hard men, and there were always one or two fuelled by the booze, could never understand how they were knocked to the ground in one punch!

Father always carried a 4" lead filled rubber sap in his right hand and never had the need to draw the issue police baton. Miscreants and troublemakers were not usually arrested, they were just given a good hiding. 'One Punch' had such a reputation over the years and was welcome in the Conservative Club, Bowling Club and by the Town Fathers. Although he passed the police inspectors' written examination, he was never promoted.

One could understand why the local court reporter to the local newspaper, 'The Ossett Observer', was beside himself when Father appeared in court as a witness to his own assault. A woman was charged with assault on police and was fined ten shillings. She had crept up on Father whilst he was sorting her son out and dropped Father with her HANDBAG!

The family lived at, 'The Police House', Queens Drive, Ossett. A newly built detached house, with garage and extensive gardens to front and rear. Sitting room, front room for special occasions complete with roll-top desk and three-piece suite. We even had a scullery or wet room that housed a copper for boiling whites, a large mangle and a square washing machine for delicates, where one sat to one side and turned the inner paddles from outside by rotating them through the lid by means of a handle that one worked backwards and forwards. Boring stuff and hard work. One filled the square tub with hot water from the 'Copper', by ladle.

Our neighbour Mr Moss at 'Moslyn' was a town jeweller. In fact years later Father purchased my 21st birthday present from him: a

Roamer wristwatch. I still have it.

The close neighbours on the other side were Jack Wallace and his parents, who shared the house with him and his wife. Jack had a 650cc Gold Star motorcycle and used to roar off to work each morning at 7 o'clock. At that time as a 13 year old I would cut the lawn for Mr Moss each Saturday for 6d and do odd jobs for the Wallaces, such as cleaning old bricks of cement for future use.

Whilst at the Police House, although a few years forward, when I was in my 17th year, Mum gave us a great surprise by giving birth for the fourth time; a baby girl, my sister Melanie Jayne. Melanie was born at home in the 'Front Room', delivered by the local midwife. Father was out on police duties so after the successful birth with Mum propped up in bed, I was sent out for fish and chips.

With Father's new police mileage allowance, and as the Area Sergeant we were given assistance by the County Council to purchase a new car. An Austin Devon, one colour – grey. Father was a great tripper in his little time off, and evenings out and the odd day saw us in the Yorkshire Dales at Bolton Abbey, Kilnsey Crag, Kettlewell and Malam Tarn. Skipton and Keighley saw us as regular visitors as did the South Derbyshire Bakewell, Carver, the Ladybower Dam and the Blue John Mines. Each year without fail we visited the Blackpool Illuminations.

The School I attended was Ossett Grammar School, another change of uniform from the black and white of Barnsley Holgate, his time green with red piping. was a mixed school and we had some notable teachers, a different breed from that of Barnsley. Male and female; informative and pleasant. The Headmaster was Mr Axford (CANTAB). His wife also taught at the school. The History teacher was one, Loony Moore. He had poor eyesight, so bad that when the girls of the class had draped a pair of school green knickers over the light above his head, he never saw them!

Dear 'Annie' the Art Mistress only had one arm, the other was a false hand she tapped the desk with and the head of any unruly boy. She always insisted that my Christian name was GODWIN and always asked me for my surname! I had to remind her quite often. The Science Master Tom Clarke went to the local pub each lunchtime to place his illegal horse bet: 2/6p so we were informed.

23

Miss Lindley was out favourite. Young, *very* attractive and taught English Literature. Our form Master, who taught Mathematics, was Mr Atkinson. In his thirties, not to be fooled with and absolutely stank of cigarette smoke.

School was a pleasant experience in this environment. I played cricket and took up badminton and enjoyed the annual cross-country run. No great scholar, nevertheless I held my own, and the good school pal who I was equal to eventually became headmaster of Horbury Junior School. Derek Batey died in post in his forties through cancer, a great loss to the school and to cricket! He loved keeping wicket. Other pals were Alan Nicholls, Andrew Ockenden, Mike Stevenson, Joe Stacey and Duggie Brammer. Girls came into the equation but were clannish and at their age 13/14, were usually warned off the likes of inquisitive young boys.

Swimming was a passion and Wakefield Sun Lane Baths was a must on a Saturday: and diving from the five and ten metre board.

Cricket and cycling took pride of place and I had a touring cycle with a Sturmey Archer, three speed gear and panniers, and when I was not playing cricket on a Saturday afternoon I would take off to cycle to the Dales and the Wharfe Valley and to Brighouse to see my Grandparents. During school holidays I cycled further afield to Settle, York and Horton in Ribblesdale.

In 1951 the American Methodist Preacher came to the UK and I was asked to join a group to visit the Methodist College to go to see the famous 'Dr Billy Graham'. As with all the rest, I was taken in by the razzmatazz within the massive outdoor marquee, the choir, the hymns, the chanting, the preaching; the whole experience of mass hysteria. I was called forward, hands were laid on, 'I was saved'. The experience lasted about six weeks, during which time Mother thought that I was wonderful. Washing up, baby-sitting, any odd jobs done around the house without being asked. Methodist friends and I used to jump on public transport, take the upper deck to sing happy clappy hymns.

Then my long lost pal came over to stay from Gomersal, Peter Shepley, and off we went doing other things! He also smoked Capstan Full Strength cigarettes and wore cord drapes at 16 that were all the rage. Black drape jacket, velvet collar, blue trousers, suede creeper shoes. Mum bought me a maroon drape jacket and off we

24

went to the local cinema and to hang around the town centre looking 'cool'. We had a DANSETTE record-player and used to buy or exchange 45rpm records, Johnny Ray etc. At that time and for a few years afterwards, my friends and I used to walk to and from Dewsbury to attend the theatre to see, once a month, the Big Bands: Johnny Dankworth, Sid Phillips and the like.

I also, with the encouragement of June my sister and because she had a very attractive friend called Sheila Jenkins, took up Old Time Ballroom Dancing! Classes were taken at The Harry Lightowler School of Dance in Ossett. We became so proficient that we were entered for the Dance Examination in Sheffield and were 'Highly Commended'. Even I, with two left feet.

Norman Lockwood's Horse

Often on Saturday and Sunday mornings 6am to 12 noon and during much of the school holidays, I used to deliver milk in the South Ossett area with the local milkman and Town Councillor, Norman Lockwood. He owned a large modern bungalow down Queen's Drive and to the rear a two-acre field with hens and large hen houses, and a well-built brick stable to house a horse and sprung wheeled trap.

His pride and joy was a large bay gelding decked out in its finery as the Milk Horse. Norman regarded himself as a real, 'Hoss Man', leather gaiters to knee, brown smock and coaching whips various. The horse was suitably decked out when within the large trap shafts: collar, martingale, horse brasses resplendent.

One had to mount two cast iron steps to reach the milk float loading platform. We carried steel crates of pint bottles. Two large churns of milk, trays of eggs and often cabbages in season. I used to deliver the bottles to various addresses on the round and Norman would see to the loose milk ladling by measure, gills or pints into basins and jugs left on doorsteps.

The day started when we went to the farm about a mile away when we would watch the milk from the cows being riddled through a cooler, onwards to an inverted hopper affair with a control valve then squirted into cleaned and sterilised bottles to have their tops pressed on by us, by hand. We then loaded into the crates, the loose into the churn. During my second year this practice was discontinued as I believe by law all milk had to be pasteurised and the milk in bottles and sealed churns was delivered to us by Northern Dairies, in our case at about 7am. Thereafter to us, the milk never tasted the same! No cream!

I got into the habit of going from home to the stable to harness the horse, back him into the shafts having first put his collar on upside down. I would then lead him up the lane to the bungalow where we would start loading. The horse was 16 hands, was high-spirited and could really pull, even with a full load he was a handful. At the end of the morning and with an empty float and the horse stable-bound, we were a sight to see. Norman, feet braced, hanging over the back two hands of reins, me applying brakes to the wheels, the horse at full pelt to the lane turnoff. The 'Orse took a lot of convincing to stop, really he was underworked for his size and energy. To Norman he really was a show horse and he was the Gaffer.

It all went wrong one rainy day when the horse was tied up by his halter to a usual lamppost in Manor Road. We were about three quarters of the way through the round. Norman and I were on our way back from deliveries and about thirty yards from the rear of the milk float when a lady passing the horse on the pavement opened an umbrella as she passed his head! The horse reared up, snapped the halter and was off in a flash up Manor Road to pass the Co-op Clock Tower on the brow of the hill some 200 metres away. Norman and I running after the trap could not get near and watched the whole ensemble go over the brow of the hill.

Having arrived at the Clock Tower, we looked down the hill toward the Ossett to Horbury B road and to the T-junction. Neither the horse nor cart were to be seen.

The opposite side of the T-junction was bordered by a three-foot wall with a similar drop into a large field. When we arrived at the T-junction and were able to see over the wall we found a smashed cart, it having been bounced over the wall, the horse having jumped. The wheels were off, the shafts were crossed and the remains of crates, milk bottles, eggs, churns were scattered in the field. The horse was running, collar and braces still attached, tail erect and prancing like a show-horse.

After some time we were able to approach the horse, catch him by

26

the remains of the bridle and I walked him home to the stable about a mile away. He was quite uninjured. Norman, having called the vet, was amazed.

We had the debris in the field removed and carried on with the remaining deliveries that afternoon by borrowed vehicle.

One week later Norman bought a large van! Kept the 'orse though as a Show 'Orse.

ROUNDWOOD PIT OSSETT

First Employment: Roundwood Colliery, Ossett.

Just after my 15th birthday in 1952 and around Easter time I left Ossett Grammar School. Although in the 'A' form it was felt that I was in no way academic. Things were rather tight at home, employment generally was easy to be had through apprenticeships, so it was better for the family if I found work.

Father arranged for me to have an interview with the local colliery manager at 'Roundwood' Pit, Mr Hinchcliffe, at his colliery home. The 'Pit', about one mile from home, was sited at the eastern end of Queen's Drive, the road on which we lived. Where the drive met the Wakefield to Dewsbury Road at a T-junction the Colliery Cooling Tower, Pithead Baths, Winding Gear Towers and Slag Heaps could be seen on the ground to the right bordering the main road south towards Wakefield. The Colliery was served by its own railway that crossed the Dewsbury to Wakefield Road. A 'Flagman' was often to be seen, marshalling the light railway engine across the road.

A rather smart 'Holiday Inn' hotel is now on site, the pit and slag heaps having been closed years ago. Most of the waste heaps have been contoured to form playing fields and the M1 motorway runs through some of the old grounds. Now it looks rather rural.

I was offered employment as an apprentice until the age of 21 years and it was decided by Mr Hinchcliffe that I was to work three months in the Electricians' shop, three months with the Fitters and three months in the Surveyors' Department to see where I was best suited! After the three months trial in each department I would be asked which I preferred, then subject to the Departmental head's approval, there I would remain.

27

In the meanwhile and as a first choice I went to the Electricians' shop. The gaffer was Mr Jacky Crowther, a pleasant middle-aged man from Middlestown. He owned a Vauxhall Wyvern car, which was his pride and joy. I and another apprentice, Raymond Joinson, got to know it rather well, as we cleaned and polished it each Friday.

I was apprenticed to a Mr Jack Bedford, in his early thirties, a large bluff man who with myself had the patience of Job and looked after my wellbeing when down the pit extremely well. I was on the way to repairing switchgear above and below ground, jointing cables, repairing in situ coal-cutters, endless conveyor belt motors and installing cabling in the new winding house. The machinery that moved the cages up and down the two x 1000ft pit shafts was being converted from steam to 440V electrical power. Coal was hewn out of rock some 1000ft below ground from 4ft seams of coal from two main areas known as the 'Beeston' and 'Silkstone' Seams.

The miners really were something. In the main, smallish wiry men who worked on their knees for four hours or more in awful conditions at the immediate coal face hewing out their 'Stint', the area of black coal for the day measured out by the deputy or overman. The air was so thick with coal dust that one could hardly breathe and fine water was often sprayed to keep the dust down. As the coal was removed from the seam the roof would be shored up by the miners hammering in pit props. How they worked in this environment day after day God and they only knew. I could not get out of this forward hell-hole quick enough whenever we had to visit the coal face to repair machinery or extend cabling.

The other group of hard workers were known as 'Rippers'. They were the men who usually worked in teams during the night to drive or advance the roadways through which the conveyor belts passed to take the coal from the coal faces during the day. The fitters would be on hand to extend the sectionalised conveyor belts and metal supports. We, the electricians, would be called to install booster motors.

My other workmates who I recall were: Harry Bennet, Fred Lumb, Peter Kielty, Reg Williams and Donald Mulvey. Also Oliver Ward and Nash Mills, who worked shifts in the colliery power plant adjacent to the electricians' shop. Reg Williams was the early thirties 'Nut Case'. Forever running around naked in the pit-head

28

baths after work with his cock poked through a soapy sponge shouting, 'Get a load of this', as he wagged his erect member up and down. Little did he know that his apprentice, an older lad of minor years, 19, was seeing to William's wife at home whenever he worked extra shifts.

I was once working with Reg in the shop taking a five horsepower motor from its bed; we had a triangular frame above and a Stilson Jack that I was working by pulling on an endless chain. The motor was lifting but I felt the chain slipping, so I screamed, 'Look out'. Reg turned to me and said, 'Why kid?' The motor crashed back onto its bed and broke Reggie's BIG TOE!

My Guardian Angel

From the pit head to reach the shaft bottom some 1000ft below we used to travel with the miners in the pit cage during the 'Man Winding Hours'. At other times, when just coal was being moved up and down the shaft within its tubs, the winding was much faster and the landing harder.

It was rare for men and coal to be moved together but on an emergency or call to an unscheduled breakdown it did happen but normally the engine house would be notified 'Men on Board'. On one occasion only, Jack Bedford and I were travelling with the coal and we were within the bottom compartment of three. The upper two housed large tubs that were rammed out as the unloading level was reached. We heard them go, the cage moved up, settled on its side blocks then it was our turn to get out. The Banksman who met us opposite did not work the ramp and we were invited to step out onto the platform. Jack went first holding part machinery, I followed but turned to pick up a metal flange from the floor. I was halfway in and out of the cage when I felt it lifted from its blocks; it instantly plunged down, took my leather tool bag from my shoulder and this and the cage dropped 1000ft. Jack had the presence of mind to turn, grab me by the overalls and throw me onto the platform. He saved my life. He then grabbed the Banksman by the throat and gave him an old-fashioned message.

We had an instant sort out! The outcome was that the operator in the winding house had not been informed from the pit bottom that we

29

were on board. I was sent home from the electricians' shop to recover, soon got over it and looked upon Jack as a cracking fellow as indeed he was.

We used to visit old workings on the odd occasion to retrieve cabling and old junction boxes. The air supply was not good and we used to have the company of an experienced deputy with a DAVY lamp with the party to test for gas, methane or bad air.

In many parts of the old workings the rings holding the roof in place were sprung and we had to travel with caution. This particular day saw us retrieving cabling. The working gang had rolled things up and we were seated on an old sagging rubber conveyor belt having a break before returning to the pit bottom. It was Snaptime! Sandwiches from our tin boxes and a pint of cold tea! Never milk but lots of sugar.

I well remember 'Mark', an older member, who usually accompanied most parties into old workings as an advisor as he knew them so well. He was rather hampered and couldn't move fast as he always wore a truss. I was seated not far from him when he asked if I would mind getting his, 'Snap Bag' as he had left it some thirty yards away where we had been working. Being much younger and as he was already seated, I was pleased to do so. On my way back and not twenty yards away, there was a 'crack', a rumble then a whole cloud of dust as a section of the roof within two girders fell in and a 'Pottie', or large slippy stone, and other debris fell and crushed the old belt exactly where I had been sitting. Had I been there it would be doubtful that I would have survived. Talk about a 'Good Deed for the Day!' and my Guardian Angel.

The switchgear down the Pit had to be flameproof because of the risk of a spark igniting gas. There was of course a no smoking ban and miners were often searched to see that matches or lighters were not carried and taken underground. Many miners, to get their fix of nicotine, chewed plugs of tobacco.

Miners sometimes saw the fitters and electricians as necessary evils, as often when we were called to the coal face to extend cable or repair machinery we used to turn the power OFF. This would cost someone money or a later working shift.

We would lock the switch gear off, sometimes with chains and place notices - 'ELECTRICIANS WORKING' - sometimes hundreds of yards away before effecting repairs.

On one occasion I had done just this, opened up a motor housing, put a screwdriver in there and, for my pains, there was a 'Flash' and I was thrown across the tunnel. The screwdriver was welded to the frame. I was bruised but not hurt. Some bloody idiot had thrown a main switch 'On' so that he could work his piece of machinery. Now the whole lot was tripped. As for me? Thank God for insulated tools, rubber boots and gloves and for Jack Bedford's advice: 'Stick a screwdriver in first, lad!'

The mine was a dangerous place – thank you Guardian Angel.

I never, as an apprentice, moved to the Fitters' Shop or to the Surveyors' Department as was originally planned. I worked as an apprentice electrician within this very happy working environment, attended Night School for Mechanical Drawing and for my love of English. At the start of my third year I was interviewed by Mr Crowther, my boss and was asked to go to Manchester University on an HNC that would be financed by the National Coal Board. This would be a two-year course but I had to commit.

Over a couple of weeks I mulled over what this would entail and the real question was did I really wish to spend the rest of my life working underground? I thought not. This conclusion led me to leave Roundwood Colliery, not under a cloud, but to everyone's amazement.

I would go from working 1000 ft. underground to working 1000 ft. above ground.

Holiday in Blackpool Late 1954

During August I teamed up with my life long pal Peter Shepley, and we went off to Blackpool by bus from Ossett. Destination, Peter's Aunt's boarding-house in Central Blackpool, near to the Tower, the Ballroom and the Circus and lively pubs such as 'The Palatine': All-in charge for one week, seven pounds; three meals a day. We paid up front, which gave us an idea what was left to waste!

Peter was well into his 18th year. He smoked Capstan Full Strength cigarettes from morn till night. I smoked little but did sport a 'Calibre' cigarette lighter to hold, 'Passing Cloud' cigarettes. We were dressed usually in the evening in long, cord coats with velvet collar. Waistcoats run up by Mother of curtain material, sky-blue trousers, bootlace ties, crepe shoes and bright socks. 'Ducks arse' haircuts, swept back at the side and rear, quiff to the front. My God, what a package!! We drank dark and bitter beer mixed, 'Black and Tan', and were usually plastered on three pints. Destinations during the day were the Pleasure Beach, Blackpool Sands, under and onto the Piers. We made it to the 'Derby Baths' where my party piece was to execute a running Swallow Dive off the ten-metre diving board.

Two days into the holiday we found that our double room with twin beds had been invaded, and that hard dried peas had been placed under the bottom sheets of our beds. The third day saw us invade the room next door to drape toilet rolls around the room and light fittings, and to place condoms full of water in the sink. We had found out that the room was occupied by two sporty schoolteachers on holiday: Mother about forty years of age, daughter twenty years or so younger.

That evening we all went to the Tower Ballroom. Peter took Momma, I latched onto daughter. I could execute a passable quickstep and perform a, 'Bop' solo with part splits and a somersault. Peter could perform much the same.

After some dancing, drinking and horseplay it seemed natural to swap rooms back at the boarding-house. Unknown to Peter's Aunt, of course. The rest of the holiday was very enjoyable. I was taken apart by this randy, well-rounded school marm, who sent me off home with a 'Kiss Me Quick' hat.

I do remember arriving home in Ossett by bus with exactly sixpence in my pocket.

No complaints! Worth every penny spent.

The Impetuosity of Youth

Although happy at work at the Colliery, I always knew that there was something missing from my life, but I could not put my finger on it. I had not yet realised my desire to travel and my hidden urge for change. I had friends, hobbies, sports, even an auto-cycle that Grandfather had given up and allowed me to have. What was missing?

One Saturday evening my long-term friend Peter Shepley came to our house in Queen's Drive on the bus, as usual, from his home near Heckmondwyke. We were bound for 'the Dance' in Batley. This was held above Burtons the Tailors. The room was large and airy with square poles down the centre, mirrored if I remember, just the place to catch a glimpse of one's bryl-creamed DA haircut, as one took the bird around whilst executing the 'Leicester Bop'. This dance was quite a steamy affair, and the girl had rather to be up for it. It entailed her arms around your neck, your hands under and around her backside. Your feet at ten to two, her feet within and you shuffled to music clockwise around the ballroom. Whilst this was progressing you winked at your male friends similarly engaged by looking at the glass mirrors on the walls and uprights.

The Dance was 'dry', but one was allowed out during the half-hour interval to dash to the local pubs in the square for a couple of 'Black & Tans'. Back in, to secure a bird for the Last Waltz!

On this particular evening Father was kind enough to drop us off in Batley by car. The plan after the dance was to walk to Peter's home, some four miles, to stay the night in the company of whoever might be walking our way!

We never struck lucky with the birds, and so after the dance and into the pub for a swift half before closing time, saw us ready to walk home but gazing at a very large wall poster. One soldier on the poster was a military policeman in red peaked hat. The other soldier was a trooper flying through the air under a parachute. National Service was in vogue at the time and usually men of between 18 and 25 were called up by the Government to serve in the Army, Navy or Air Force for a period of two years. I was exempt as was Peter through being in restrictive trades, me at the National Coal Board, Peter at a metal wire drawing plant.

33

Things were about to change though as one could volunteer! In bravado and for that moment, whilst gazing at the poster Peter said, 'I am going to join them', pointing at Redcap. I said, 'You join them and I'll join *them*', pointing at the trooper.

One month later Peter was at the RMP Depot at Woking, I at the Depot at **Aldershot**. Our parents were not pleased!

THE PARACHUTE REGIMENT ALDERSHOT

Depot, Aldershot. Form Up 40 Platoon.
Maida Barracks 1955

Para training, sixteen weeks of it. My God it was hard. For a start it was winter, early January when 43 of us recruits, and all volunteers, formed up as 40 Platoon at the Regimental Depot. At the end of the training only 20 of us would leave the depot and go onto parachute training under the Royal Air Force instructors at RAF Abingdon in Oxfordshire.

Prior to 1953 all Airborne Recruits came as volunteers from all regiments of the army and as already trained soldiers. If successful they then took off their own headdress and insignia and were awarded the Maroon Beret and titles 'Parachute Regiment' on their shoulders, as well as the coveted, 'Pegasus' flash. They then joined 16 Parachute Brigade. They were then posted into 1, 2 or 3 Para Battalions if they were infantry, or supporting arms if they were Gunners, Signallers, Medics etc. (9 Squadron R.E.), (216 Signal Squadron), (Gunners 33 Lt Regiment Royal Artillery).

In 1953 the Regiment decided to recruit its own soldiers direct from civilian life. I was one such soldier. For the first two weeks we were not allowed out of barracks. In 12 weeks I went from a reasonably fit young 18 year old to one who could run two miles in 18 minutes in full kit, with rifle and under a helmet. Run, march then shoot, having done ten miles in one hour 45 minutes. Complete three timed circuits around a boggy, pit infested steeplechase course, jumping nine feet ditches, climbing six feet walls and running across up in the air ramps.

I survived the 'milling' in the boxing ring. Man against man, no quarter asked or given. No skills or finesse, just aggression and punch the man's lights out. If knocked down, GET UP. Punch away.

During the weeks we were physically honed to be able to tackle in the last two weeks the dreaded log race and the stretcher race. Long Valley tank tracks, out two and a half miles, back two and a half miles through cloying mud and water. We had such delights as 'The Water Assault Course', over and through the frozen Basingstoke canal. In between we shot various weapons, were taught field craft, camouflage and concealment: threw grenades, practiced First Aid and basic signalling.

Drill on the Square came into it and the culmination was a parade to 'Pass Off' the Square under the gaze of some high ranked guest, and family and friends. In our case the reviewing officer was Brigadier Sir John Hunt, of Everest fame. He had led the Expedition which the year before had climbed Everest for the first time.

In our penultimate week we went to Sennybridge Training Area in Wales, and there marched over the Black Mountains and Brecon Beacons in appalling weather. In actual fact our assault up Peny-ffan, the steepest slope, was called off by reason of high winds, snow and blizzard conditions.

Life as a 'CROW' Recruit

On arriving at Aldershot rail station and, after all, it *was* National Service days with dozens of recruits from a host of Regiments and Corps milling about, most units had their own transport to meet them in station trains. Not the Para! Pick up your suitcase, walk up Hospital Hill and TAB it to Maida Barracks, a victorian barracks on top of the hill overlooking Aldershot town, in sight of the military hospital: Distance, about a mile.

We were housed in old Victorian, brick built, T-shaped blocks, 12 squaddies to a room. 36 soldiers on the ground floor, 36 above on the first storey: showers, toilets, washrooms in the centre. Opposite the wet areas were double bunks where section corporals lived.

Each room had six beds either side of a main, heavy entrance door, a large coal bunker, a pot belly stove and one six foot table. Each bed had at its side one six foot steel locker. There was a bulletin board or notice board on the wall and two x 13 amp wall sockets in each room. No heating other than the pot belly stove. Dim, single 60 watt lamps, three to a room, hanging within a plastic cover.

The Company Officers were housed in wooden huts as were the stores between the main brick blocks. The most excellent thing about our block, 'I' block, was that we were adjacent to the minor barracks road that led direct to the Square, the Naafi and up the road some 600 yards to the WRAC or female soldiers' quarters, Mandora Barracks.

On arrival at the Depot and after kit issue at the quartermaster's stores on the next day, dressed in fatigue dress: cotton type overall trousers, shirt, pullover and wearing army boots and socks, the squad was marched off to meet the first depot delight! 'Paddy the Chop', the barber. All the fancy quiffed hairdos disappeared onto the floor as Paddy got busy with the regulation haircut.

All recruits thereafter ran or doubled everywhere, to and from meals, the Naafi, classes, the square, on the ranges. Civilian clothes were boxed to the company stores.

The Maida Gymnasium was notorious for its size and the severity of its staff, home grown but trained by the Army Physical Training Corps. We were issued with shorts PT blue plus one red, one white vest and one green towel. Shoes PT canvas. In there we were always in the 'Red' team or the 'White' team in competition. Wall bars, rope climbs, medicine ball exercises, stick games, mat work, burpees, sprints, murder ball. The gym sessions were two a day, each of 45 minutes with five minutes to change back into fatigue dress. The last class of the day stayed to clean the floor, and usually got the remains of and the dregs of the evening meal. On ration bully beef and pom potato 1000 ways.

40 Platoon: Staff and Personalities

The Parachute Depot CO was one Colonel Geoffrey Pine-Coffin. The Officer Commanding Major 'Willie' Corbould. The Regimental Sergeant Major 'Paddy' Pestell we thought a pig of a man with a manner of shouting into your face and spitting all over you in his wrath. Much later I was to find him a pleasant affable man with a great sense of humour, but by then of course he had been promoted

36

to Major (Quartermaster).

The Sergeants who were wartime old sweats were firstly Sgt Howells and then later Sgt Mackay. The senior corporal was 'Smudger' Smith. How they trained 40 Platoon as they did was truly remarkable. They had the patience of a saint and spent hours in the evenings, in their own time, showing raw recruits how to maintain equipment, dress correctly,how to execute drills with the rifle and they ran quizzes on the lessons that we had learned during the day: Wind and Elevation Tables, First Aid, Weapons Parts, Regimental History. Our destiny really was, of course, up to the performance and skills and knowledge of our platoon sergeants and corporals, and ours were first class.

I was fortunate to have the gift of being an above average shot and through the coaching of Sgt Mackay gained and was awarded Marksman's Badges on both the No.4 Rifle and on the Light Machine Gun.

We saw little of the Platoon Commander a Lieutenant. I think the Subalterns were shared out to more than one training platoon. He took centre stage at the 'Pass Off' Parade.

My personal pals who I formed a friendship with as recruits were Sid Dewey and Brian Day. We have known each other throughout the years, initially wewere in C Company 1 Para together and last met at Airborne Forces Day at Southsea in 2008. Terence Selby was my long term recruit pal as he served in Cyprus and at Suez in the same 7 Platoon, 1 Para as I, 1956 – 1957.

Most of the Platoon served their two or three years and then went back to civilian life. This was rather the norm during National Service days. Many volunteered for the Paras for the addition of PAY, as it was then 28 shillings a week, which was quite a substantial amount. I indeed served until 1957 and then left for civilian life having completed my signed three years engagement.

We did get a few T-shirts though on the way! 'Been there, done that!'

The Platoon was allowed out of barracks in uniform: Battle Dress and Boots or black shoes after the first four weeks. In actual fact we were awarded a 48 hour leave pass, Friday evening to Monday morning, where we could travel home by rail warrant, in uniform. I went by rail, home to Ossett. The second leave from Recruit

Training was after the 'Pass Off' Parade and before the movement under depot arrangements to the Parachute School at Abingdon. We were awarded a 72 hour pass, Thursday evening until Monday morning. Home again!

Parachute Training RAF Abingdon early 1955
Course 395

The Royal Air Force had better food, better accommodation, were more couth than we had been used to in our old Victorian Barracks. Women were also in Uniform! Impressed we were; with central heating within the barrack blocks, bread rolls freshly baked at the table and knives, forks and spoons on issue within the dining messes where we had always carried our own to and from meals at the double in Aldershot.

The Course 395 was a mixed bag of embryo parachuting and came from the Regiment Infantry, the RAF Regiment, the Royal Marines, the SAS/SBS, the Territorial Army, Overseas Students and some sneaky beaky Civilians.

One notable on the same course as me was Lt Mike Gray, later to be my CO as the Lt Col in 1 Para, my Brigade Commander as a Brigadier when I was commissioned into 16 Para Brigade and my Regimental Colonel when he dined me out at Depot Para in 1991, then as General Sir Michael Gray.

There were over a hundred of us on the four-week course and on the first working Monday we were broken down into small squads of six to eight students. We were then allocated a Sergeant, Royal Air Force Parachute Instructor or for short, a PJI. They were mostly drawn from the physical training wings of the Royal Air Force, and were all skilled parachutists in their own right, in both static line and free fall parachuting. The School Motto was and still is: 'Knowledge Dispels Fear'.

It was their job to inspire confidence to combat the fear of what was an unnatural act, leaping out into thin air under a parachute from 1000 ft. In the four weeks we would be expected to learn balloon and aircraft drills, the correct fitting of parachutes and equipment, how to make an exit from balloon and aircraft in a compact position. Safe flight drills whilst in the air, how to avoid entanglements and

38

safe compact landings whether forwards, sideways or to the rear. We marched from place to place, relaxed and full of confidence. Our instructor was Sgt 'Paddy' Foley, an Irishman with as soft a voice that ever kissed the 'Blarney Stone'. If he would have said that 'black could be white', you would have believed him. Dressed in one-piece, light blue overalls with rank insignia and his Royal Air Force Instructors Brevet under his soft blue beret, we hung onto his every word. He was to see that each of us carried out two balloon descents and six aircraft descents, (two with equipment, leg bags and one of these at night) all within the month.

The first two weeks were taken up within a large hangar, jumping off ramps, rolling on mats, swinging through the air on flight trainers in harness and learning how to land to distribute the shock of landing throughout the whole body. 'Feet and knees together lads, shoulders round. Chin on chest, watch the ground.'

At this time, 1955, we did *not* have a reserve parachute. They were issued during 1957 and thereafter. Flight drills therefore had to be spot on. With all the work within the hangar, on mats and in the air, we developed a core strength and used muscle groups that we thought that we never had.

After two weeks came the day of our first balloon descent at 'Weston-on-the-Green', the drop zone some 30 minutes from RAF Abingdon. A large, landscaped, short grassed area and with no obvious obstacles. An RAF Flight Lt would 'talk us down' by loud hailer once we had made exit from the balloon.

Well, there it was! A tethered World War II Barrage Balloon flying off the ground facing into wind with enough cable out to allow the cage suspended below to nestle onto the ground. It had an open front door through which four parachutists and one instructor were loaded or 'Emplaned' as the word was. Through this gap the exits would be made. In went the Paras in reverse order from making the exit from the balloon at 800 ft. Their strops or webbing and metal triangular hooks were passed to the dispatcher in order 4, 3, 2, 1 and he clipped the metal ends into a strong point situated in a block in the roof metal of the cage. He then passed a large pin through the four and made secure with a locking device.

The order was then given, 'Up 800, four men jumping'. The winch man on the ground repeated this order, let the brake off the cable drum and the cage and contents slowly lifted into the air like any other balloon. As the cable paid out a balloon crewman would clip on a material red and white sock to fly as a marker at every 200 feet. Once the cage had reached 800 feet the winch man would call out, '800 feet' and stop the winch. The balloon would settle, yaw about a little in the wind and then the dispatcher inside the cage would drop the bar covering the exit door and see that the winch cable below was clear. An instructor on the ground would wave a blue flag to signal that all was clear to dispatch the four parachutists one after the other.

The instructor in our case, Sgt 'Paddy' Foley, called, 'Dress forwards No1', he checked that our man's static line was connected to the frame in the centre of the cage, a quick check of the blue flag below had the man going out put his hands across his chest, shout 'Go' and the parachutist made a chest leading exit. The instructor then pulled in the empty parachute bag and strap dangling down below, put it behind him and went through the same drills for the next three men making an exit. All clear, then the winch started up again and the cage was hauled in to ground level ready for the next four jumpers.

The first two descents were monitored and it was seen if the parachutist had exited correctly, compact with feet and knees together and, God forbid, not dribbled over the edge of the cage: feet together on landing after carrying out all around observation drills in the air. The Flight Lt on the ground would debrief each student. If something was going wrong in the air, or the feet and knees were not correct for landing the student would be yelled at through the loud hailer.

In all two descents were made from the balloon, six other drops were made at Weston-on-the-Green including one carrying equipment strapped to the leg, with weapon, in a valise; and one performed in darkness at night, usually with 30 other parachutists, 15 in a Port stick, 15 from the starboard aircraft door.

After eight qualifying jumps all students were awarded the coveted Parachutists' Wings and the right of going on to serve within the Brigades, Regular or TA: The Maroon Beret.

It was fair to say that many parachutists hated the Balloon. Even trained Paras on continuation training. It was the silence of it all that got to people, and the initial drop of 200 ft. on exiting from the Balloon before anything seemed to happen to make the canopy inflate. Aircraft jumping was much different, it was noisy and the parachute was inflated as soon as you jumped out; it cleared the bag and was whipped away with you, in the slipstream. I was one of the exceptions! I liked ballooning and in particular later on as an instructor when I was able to assess the fears and delights of student jumpers.

The aircraft that we were trained to exit from under Sergeant Foley on our course 395 at Abingdon was the **Hastings**. Four noisy engines, prop driven. It was so noisy that conversation inside was difficult and we learned commands by using hand signals. It always seemed to stink inside and out of aviation fuel.

One boarded from the rear up some short, sturdy steps having run the gauntlet of the slipstream of two massive engines. There, from between 800 to 1200 ft, we were to exit from both port and starboard doors, one alternate jumper after another having seen the internal 'Red' then 'Green' jump lights. Within the aircraft on the shouted command, 'Action Stations', we shuffled down the aircraft, front to rear exit jumping doors in a long snake, one man immediately behind the other. We were then connected to a steel cable that ran high at the forward end of the aircraft to a stop at ground level at the exit door. Each parachutist was connected to this cable by his own strop that he held doubled in his hand. His own 'D' ring passed freely down this cable as he shuffled down to the door, before throwing his strop from him before making the exit. The folded webbing strop paid out as one left and was blown away by the slipstream. The parachute deployed from the bag attached to the strop until the Paras weight dropping below broke the final tie and the man was free. The strops and empty bags would be blown under to remain with the aircraft when they would be hauled in later after all the men had jumped. There was a retrieval winch for this, and, indeed, in rare cases to haul a parachutist back into the aircraft who had made a bad exit, twisting or somersaulting, and had tied up, not allowing his parachute to deploy.

Sometimes the strop or bag from the previous jumper would smack one in the face as one made the exit through the door, or if the jumper spun on exit or tripped to somersault the strop could wrap around or be pulled across the jumper's neck, causing a strop burn. Therefore, the last conscious thing we were taught to do by Sgt Foley before exiting the aircraft was to pull the smock collar right up off the jumping smock and tighten the Para helmet down, leaving nothing of the bare neck exposed.

Before emplaning, all parachutists were given a verbal warning by the Stick Commander or by the PJI: 'The Green light constitutes an ORDER to 'Go' and Exit the Aircraft. Failure to do so may result in your Court Martial.'

My favourite position, and later on in years when I was able to choose, was always to jump No1 Port. As well as being able to make a clean exit and with the aircraft doors open on the run in, one could always see the ground below and often the leaves on the trees.

During my time in Airborne Forces I parachuted from: the Hastings, Valetta, American C119, the Argosy, Beverley, Hercules and American Globemaster Aircraft as well as the Whirlwind and Wessex Helicopters.

After qualifying with our eight jumps we had completed the Course, and a proud Sgt Foley marched us onto the Parade Square at RAF Abingdon for the Station Commander to present each of us with our jump wings. To be sewn onto our battledress tunics, 1" under the title, 'Parachute Regiment' – ASAP.

Military Parachuting Recollections

It is fair to say that military parachuting was more of a trial than a pleasure. As far as I was concerned my one exception was jumping in 'Clean Fatigue', without equipment from the tethered balloon. Military parachuting differs so much from sport parachuting that many people are encouraged to take it up as weekend jumpers for charity etc.

The military parachutist is trained to arrive on the 'Drop Zone' in daylight or in darkness complete with equipment ready for battle. He has usually exited from an aircraft that has flown at low level from an airfield some hours away before levelling to dropping height between 450 and 1200 feet. Together with other parachutists in modern aircraft up to 90 strong they will carry main and reserve parachutes of over 60lbs in weight, and a body or leg bag carrying weapons, ammunition, food, water, signalling equipment of up to and often over 50 kilos. This parachuting is a means to an end, to deliver the fighting man onto or near to the battlefield.

During my 35-year service in Airborne Forces I carried out hundreds of descents during, both at home in the UK and overseas in Europe, within the Arctic Circle, in the Middle East and in America but was never called upon to parachute on operations. My only chance would have been at the Suez drop into Port Said but the 3rd Battalion was chosen to drop whilst 1 and 2 Para went by sea and at the time I was in 1 Para.

I was rather lucky over the years not to suffer too many injuries. With the weight of equipment one does not land like a feather. The landing is equivalent to jumping off an 18 ft. wall, forwards, sideways, and backwards at whatever the wind speed dictates. In training the parachuting is usually held at under 20 knots and the drop zone safety officer will usually cancel if the wind speed is above that.

I do recall however one drop onto Salisbury Plain in 1957 and because the complete battalion was dropped to demonstrate to dozens of high-ranking NATO Officers on how a Parachute Battalion could drop and rally into fighting formations. The 20 knot rule was ignored and the first three aircraft loads were dispatched into an over 25 knot ground wind by an over enthusiastic Drop Zone Commander, a Major. We in the aircraft on the run in, could not believe it when the green light above the exit doors came on. We had been given the ground speed. As a result, 32 of us from the three aircraft were carted off to hospital, all with upper body injuries. I was one such Para with a broken right scapula. The Royal Airforce safety officer on the ground had to make signal to the following aircraft, line astern, to cancel. There was an enquiry as there were some serious injuries, and the Army Major was reprimanded and lost two years' seniority.

I was only entangled once in the air with another parachutist. When one is about to come close to someone else in the air there is a drill to 'spread-eagle' one's arms and legs and to bounce off the

43

other Paras' rigging lines. On this occasion a chap above me came under my parachute canopy and into and through my rigging lines. He couldn't get out and we were entangled! One parachute canopy steals the air from the other in this situation and the air is spilt and then recovers.

When we hit the ground together, (and thank our lucky stars we were jumping without equipment on a mere training drop for RAF aircrew training,) I landed first and the miscreant above put one boot on my nose and face! The other on my chest. The next thing I remember was my nose being packed together and my Para smock being unzipped. The other Para who had tied himself up with me just happened to be our Battalion Medical Sergeant, Ken Dawes, and one of the lightest men in the battalion! Thank heaven for small mercies and for doing a great job on the Nose!

Parachuting Years later during 1983!

The battalion were there out in Belize, south of Florida for a year and during the tour Royal Airforce Hercules aircraft and instructors came out to enable the battalion to get in some parachute continuation training during summer. We were to drop onto quite a hard, sand baked drop zone called 'Barrell Boom'. I volunteered my soldiers on the quartermaster staff to parachute on a Saturday morning! We were busy during the week Monday to Friday supplying the battalion in the north and south with provisions, ammunition and equipment. Saturday seemed to me the best time for this without equipment 'Jolly'.

Being the Stick Commander of the Port Stick, as the senior officer I went out of the aircraft as No.1 leading my quartermaster's staff. The opposite door on the starboard side was led out by No.1, my good pal from OC Headquarters Company, Major Tom Smith. With doors open we had a pleasant flight 1000 ft. above an azure Caribbean sea and a level flight led us over the drop zone about three miles from our camp not far from Belize City.

I had a pleasant and compact exit from the aircraft and had Major Tom Smith in my sights. With about 200 ft. to go to landing all went wrong. I seemed to be spun like a top, was turned around in the air, came in for a backwards hard landing and was slammed into the

44

ground. I remember going into spasms with the pain. The Doctor, Steven Hughes, was with me quickly and I was given morphine and carted off to airport camp RAF hospital to lie on a board for a week with a broken vertebra. My bedside companion in hospital in our twin room was none other than Major Tom Smith. He was out of the game with concussion for two days! On landing we had been caught by a 'Sand-Devil', a mini whirlwind of hot dust and debris. We were the only parachutists injured! What do they say about not volunteering for anything? The QM's staff had a laugh – bless 'em!

Christine, my wife, had flown out from RAF Lyneham by VC10 on an indulgence flight to join me for a two-week holiday. Starting the very same day in the morning as I ended up in hospital.

My good pal, Captain Terry White, had the awful task of meeting Chris to tell her the news and to bring her to see me in the hospital ward. There was even talk by the RAF doctors of sending me back to the UK that evening on the same aircraft as Christine and some of the families had flown out on! We persuaded them not. It was most fortunate that a long serving pal of ours, Major Barry Andrews, was serving as Training Major with the Belize Defence Force and was in an adjacent barracks and in married quarters with his wife Ada who we had known for years. They arranged for Chris to stay with them in the meanwhile and for Barry to run Chris daily to visit me in hospital.

After a week I persuaded the RAF Surgeon that I was fit to travel and, subject to me not doing anything stupid, only a little gentle swimming, he agreed to me taking Chris to San Pedro Island and to The Paradise Hotel for the remainder of our two week holiday. We had a most marvellous seven days, helped by Barry and Ada who took us to the Belize Airport to board 'teeny-weeny' Airlines for the 20 minute flight and collected us afterwards and put Chris on the UK flight.

As I recall, I was only to suffer one more injury parachuting and that was in Aldershot, Hampshire on the Queen's Avenue Sports Ground and drop zone.

Whilst on my last posting in Berlin and away from the Parachute Brigade in my appointment as Major Quartermaster, Headquarters Berlin Brigade, I was obliged to carry out four parachute descents per year to retain my pay and to remain as being fit to parachute in the event of a recall. To achieve this I used to coincide my visits to the UK and to the Para Depot in Aldershot when the balloon training week was on, usually twice a year on the adjacent Queen's Avenue drop zone. There, I used to spend a week, complete my four balloon descents and help out as a parachute Balloon dispatcher on the ground and in the air, 'Up 800! Four men jumping!' There I would see the four men safely out.

On my last jumping day and on my fourth and last descent before returning to Berlin in three days hence, I was preparing to enter the balloon cage as last man, to be the first man dispatched at 800 ft. as we jumped in reverse order, when a 7RHA Gunner Corporal asked if he could jump No.1 as he had never done it. I agreed. We changed places, he to No.1, me to No.4.

When up in the air and with three other jumpers dispatched the balloon was much lighter and moved around in the air. When I went out of the balloon I was over the old runway where the Red Devils aircraft used to taxi and take off. The ground on landing was not like the rest of the green sport pitch cover. It was hard and compact, and I suffered a very hard stand up landing as there was little ground wind. I felt something 'go' down below. The other jumpers who had witnessed the hard landing came over to assist me off the drop zone. They packed up my parachute and reserve, and returned them to the Para stores vehicle. After waiting a while to recover I walked back to the Depot Para half a mile away and to the Officers' Mess.

On waking on the Friday morning after a cracking party in the Mess the night before I found that I had a highly inflated knee joint and a somewhat discoloured foot. The Depot Para 'lady' doctor was sent for, strapped my leg and had me wiggle my toes. The outcome was, 'painkillers and two days bed rest!' So, meals in bed! Excellent! Only one day in bed though as my return flight was Sunday.

On the Sunday I was most fortunate as my brother Christopher, who was serving in Aldershot at the time, arranged to drive me to Heathrow Airport to board the flight to Berlin as a disabled passenger. My wife Chris met me at Berlin Tegal Airport having been pre-warned. At home I was then confined to bed.

Come the Monday, I was expected to, and prepared to, go into work at Berlin Headquarters. I struggled into uniform, shirt sleeve

46

order thank God, and shoes but Christine insisted on taking me to the Berlin Military Hospital on Sick Parade. There I remember being the only person in the X-ray department and the X-ray operator, having carried out the X-ray, came to find me, pushing a wheelchair.

He said, 'Sit down, Sir, don't move to walk; you have a broken leg.' He then wheeled me off to a doctor surgeon I knew well, Dr Jackson. His surprise was as complete as mine. I had been walking around on a broken leg for four days. The break was complete and had snapped back exactly, so there was no decision to operate to have a look as now it would have started to 'tack' and heal itself. I was then encased in plaster from ankle to groin for six weeks. Jackson said that he had never witnessed anything like it and I had 'a fine pair of legs'. After this last Para episode though and at 53 years of age I gave up parachuting!

1st Battalion the Parachute Regiment 1955 – 1957

In 1955 the Battalion of 600 officers and soldiers were housed within Albuhera Barracks, the old Victorian red brick, double storey barracks in what was classed as the Aldershot Military Town. The Battalion was a part of 16 Independent Parachute Brigade. 2 and 3 Para in Aldershot were also a part as were the Gunners (33rd Light RA), Royal Engineers (9 Indep Sqn), Cooks, Medics, Signallers, Int. Corps, Drivers (63 Sqn RASC) and Ordinance Personnel. All were trained, therefore if needs be the battalion group could drop and fight as a self-contained Unit.

Having completed my Para Course at Abingdon I was then posted into 1 Para to join 7 Platoon, C Company. My Platoon Sergeant was the notorious 'Nobby Arnold', later to be RSM of 3 Para and to have a feature north of Aden named after him called 'Arnold's Spur'. The Company Sergeant Major was 'Cushy' Macdonald, an old War II Vet and anything else but 'Cushy'. The OC was also an old wartimer with a great history; a fine soldier and gentleman farmer, Major Don Fletcher M.C. The Company second in command was Captain Peter Chiswell, later to Command 3 Para as Lt Colonel then to be GOC Wales as a Major General. The Regimental Sergeant Major, the longest serving in that appointment within the Brigade, was WO 1 Tom Duffy MBE. Feared on the parade ground, but fair.

All young soldiers on joining the battalion were, at the earliest opportunity, to join an Instructional Cadre for two weeks under battalion sergeant instructors. We were instructed in signalling, drill, weapons training and tactics – battalion style.

Our instructors, as I recall, were Nick Carter MM and C/Sgt Bernie Hougham. Sgt Tom Foster from 'A' Company made up the trio.

Nick Carter was later to be RQMS Depot Para. Tom Foster was later to be RSM 1Para , then commissioned Capt. Quartermaster and awarded the MBE. C/Sgt Bernie Hougham was killed on a Para instructors course at Abingdon when the Hastings Aircraft he was in crashed some 47 seconds after take-off in 1962. The cause, metal fatigue affecting the ailerons.

During the Cadre, after a few days, one of our number and a recruit fresh from the training depot decided that military life was not for him. He refused to get out of pyjamas one morning, remained seated on his bed and, when the inspecting sergeant came into the room to carry out morning inspection, he, the soldier, informed the sergeant that he was Napoleon! He stood up, thrust a hand into his pyjama jacket and placed a pillowcase on his head as a hat! An ambulance was sent for and he was carted off to the Military Hospital, some half a mile away. Within three weeks he was out of the army, 'services no longer required'! Before leaving for home he came to see us! In effect 'Jock' had worked his ticket!

The Cadre having been completed I seem to have scored well on all tests, and coupled with being a marksman on weapons, was selected to attend a future Junior Non-Commissioned Officers Course.

Life within the company settled into somewhat of a routine of platoon then company formation field training followed by battalion overseas exercises in Denmark and Germany. We were kept fit by marching from training grounds and ranges back to barracks, even from Salisbury Plain after exercises.

I personally had one setback. The Battalion were 'locked into' a Camp at Ogbourne St George on Salisbury Plain to prepare for a battalion night drop. Hush, hush and Secret Squirrel stuff. During one afternoon we played sports, soccer, and I as goalkeeper came out for a ball and dislocated my knee joint. I was taken within six hours to Tedworth Military Hospital, there to spend two weeks and to suffer a knee operation.

In one respect this setback did me a favour. On returning to Aldershot I was given the appointment as Arms Storeman within the C Company Stores. It put me near to the administrative set up within the company headquarters and to the notice of the OC, the CSM, the stores chief CQMS and all who made the company 'tick' so to speak.

I kept the company weapons immaculate and would not take an unclean weapon into the stores from anyone of whatever rank and built up quite a reputation. As a result, and within a short time to give me some authority, I was made 'unpaid' Acting Lance Corporal! Oh the dizzy heights! I was on my way.

I slept within the stores in a private bunk alongside the weapons, together with the senior storeman and old soldier Cpl Taffy Reece.

The Battalion excelled at athletics and in particular cross-country running against many county regiments. We usually came out on top. We were certainly army athletics champions in 1957 and held the army cross-country title for eleven years.

My passion was cricket and I played for the Battalion and Brigade for more years than I can remember. During the summer months when in Aldershot we played local civilian teams in the evening at Tilford, Farnham, Haslemere and Farcham Police. Summer nights were spent in the nets with my cricketing pals, Bob Hunter and John Walker. I was usually first change bowler and always fielded second slip. Spanky Roberts ex-Para REME armourer was the wicket-keeper with whom I had a secret signalling system. Spanky loved the game so much he emigrated to Australia. Later on and whilst at Depot Para and with a different wicket-keeper, Glyn Grace, I signalled that I was about to bowl a 'Beamer' off a seven pace run. He took no notice and carried on hovering too near to the stumps. The fast ball fooled the batsman, hit the top of the off stump and bail and thereafter belted Glyn on the eyebrow! Result - laid out, brought round, hospital. Four stitches. We were playing the RAMC Medical Team, thank God.

During one summer evening 20 overs game, we took on Tilford Cricket Club. Tilford has the ideal setting. The Green surrounded by the Manor House, Cricket Pavilion, 'The Red Lion' pub, the church, a river and bridge. It is featured in the British Airways brochure.

We, as a young Para side, met the opposition, mostly old men in our eyes. Certainly well into their forties and one or two older. We skittled them out for under 80 and looked forward to a quick run chase and an early evening into the pub. The sloping pitch was our undoing. What we thought were two easy runs proved to be only one and they set the field to leave the sloping side open! We suffered six run outs! These old duffers could certainly field and throw down the stumps. We made 64 runs only.

Afterwards the teams made it into the pub where we were thrashed at skittles, introduced to 'Scrumpy Cider' and sent well on our way back to Aldershot by coach absolutely plastered, beaten all ends up, by 10.30 pm!

Time within barracks was interesting even whilst recovering from the knee operation and being within the company stores. The Company Quartermaster Sergeant had various moneymaking schemes, such as selling **free** one-pint china mugs to the Toms for 1/6d. He had me splitting thick leather bootlaces in half with a razor blade to sell at 6d a pair. Weapons cleaning material was sold and a levy on all was placed as 'Barrack Damages' for cracked windows, sink plugs taken from washrooms and stained mattresses on replacement.

With the Women's Royal Army Corps Barracks just up the road and ours an open barracks, the odd girlfriend or pub acquaintance was sometimes smuggled into the barrack blocks overnight on weekends. On one such Sunday morning the Duty Battalion Orderly Sergeant, the famed 'Nobby Arnold', chose to visit platoon C Company at 7 am to give a wake-up call by banging lockers with his stick and shouting as he thought funny, 'Who's for Church!' What he failed to spot when passing the foot of soldiers' beds and smirking 'Good morning' to each and all, were two bodies in one bed. Brian was laid on top of his girlfriend, she underneath him buried within the sagging mattress! Brian, blankets up to neck, head on two pillows, girlfriend head to one side, head under. He had the presence of mind and the cheek to say 'Good morning, Sergeant.'

On 'Nobby' leaving the room the bird was hidden in a six foot locker, then her breakfast produced from the cookhouse between two china plates before she was seen out of the door to join the pathway

50

and road past the barracks.

On another occasion the battalion cobbler saw fit to smuggle his London girlfriend into barracks for Saturday night, Sunday morning and had the use of an empty two-person bunk. Mid Sunday morning whilst they were still sporting in bed some wit threw into the room a 'Thunderflash' (a large banger type firework). The earth moved alright but all the small windows in the room were blown out! This cost all of the living-in members a levy of £40. A quite considerable sum in 1955.

Emergency Tour Cyprus 1956

Christmas 1955 was spent at home with the family in Ossett and with my long-term school girlfriend Mavis Binks. I remember joining carol singing groups and visiting mill owners' houses for the season's fayre. At that time, having dark hair, I was called on by elderly neighbours to go 'First Footing'. To be the first through the house door on New Year's Day, with a lump of black coal in hand and a cheery 'Happy New Year'. Usually one was given a sherry and a silver coin, usually a sixpence.

Returning to barracks in Aldershot on the 4th January we were in for a great surprise. We were informed that the whole Battalion would be in Cyprus within the month. We were sent to Cyprus in hindsight to be able to mount an operation from there into Egypt to stop President Nasser blocking the Suez Canal and taking over complete control of this international waterway. Nasser was also sucking up to the Russians and was threatening the stability of the Middle East. He was a pain in the backside to the interests in the West.

In the meanwhile, once in Cyprus, as well as training for operations we were made available to the guvnor Sir John Harding to seek out the insurgents within the hill villages, the mountain retreats and towns who were intent on murder and intimidation of Cypriots and the Turkish population to bring about 'Enosis', Union with Greece.

A retired Greek army colonel, George Grivas, had been smuggled on to the Island to set up this underground army to partition the island, kick out the ruling British and bring about direct rule of the

51

island from Greece. This would leave one third of the populace estranged as they were Turkish Cypriots.

The clandestine set up had the support of the Priesthood and of the Monasteries where EOKA gunmen sought solace. Those Greek Cypriots who opposed the EOKA movement were murdered, as were the police and Turks who supported continued British rule. There is no doubt that during 1956 to 1960 Cyprus was a divided island.

We, the Brigade, were often employed patrolling, cordon and searching in hills and towns to keep the peace between Greek and Turk, and to keep service families safe whilst within the main towns of Limassol and Nicosia. Murder of Royal Airforce families in supermarkets was carried out as intimidation. Policemen in Nicosia were shot in the head from behind by pistol, and even a WRVS lady in her vehicle was shot and murdered in the Kyrenia Pass.

For this battalion move to come about from the UK we were transported by air. The platoon that I was with, 7 Platoon C Company, boarded a Shackleton Coastal Command Aircraft. Never had one been so cold and miserable for so long. Thirty four of us with equipment were shoe-horned into the hold of this unpressurised thing, the unlucky ones even into the old gun turrets (holes 'an awl'). We had to block up the air holes to keep warm. Thank God on the way we did have a short stop at Malta. We had no sleeping bags in those days, just a lightweight blanket and poncho, battledress trousers, pullover and a smock.

January/February of 1956 saw the battalion in a holding camp at 'Wayne's Keep'. A tented, duckboarded camp south-west of Nicosia. Other units in the area were the North and South Staffordshire Regiments. Cyprus at this time of the year was cold and we suffered a hard, wet, miserable few weeks.

We then moved to an encampment, a flat plain of some size further west of Nicosia by about seven miles and a few hundred feet above the plain of Yeralacos Village. The area was large enough for the whole Brigade to construct and to build its own tented camps. Nicosia Airport, then an RAF station, was within sight.

Getting and keeping fit was the order of the day once the camp was built with 160lb four men tents for the 'Toms', Officers and Sergeants Messes, a canteen for each battalion and even outdoor cinemas. 'Wog' shops were set up where one could purchase 'egg

52

banjos' and soft drinks. Rows of tents were laid out in uniform fashion in company lines as the British Army had done for centuries. The main meal when in camp was usually an all-in stew cooked in Soya Stoves and various dishes boiled, stewed and braised using the old petrol No.1 burner.

The Company was often employed patrolling the Troodos and Kyrenia Mountain Ranges between February to October seeking out the insurgent gangs and killer groups, often with a fair amount of success. We often linked up in the Troodos hills with 45 Royal Marine Commando. We were often out ten days patrolling and setting up ambushes then returned to camp for four days.

In March 1956, within 7 Platoon, C Company I was promoted full corporal and therefore became responsible for the training, welfare and wellbeing of a section of men. One Bren Gunner, one L/Cpl 2i/c and six riflemen or 'Toms'. We were often formed into double section patrols, the Platoon Commander in command of one, the Platoon Sergeant the other.

Life within the tented camp outside Nicosia continued to improve. Generators and electric light were brought into canteens and messes as was ice for cold drinks. A NAAFI was set up where one could go for limited cans of beer. The camp area of course was ringed with barbed wire and patrolled by armed sentries. We did, as I recall, mount guard on Sir John Harding's official residence for a couple of weeks. My section spent two nights on the roof of the Ledra Palace Hotel overlooking the main prison in Nicosia whilst preparations were made to hang the 18 year old Greek Cypriot thug Karolis who was convicted of the murder of a policeman in town with a bullet from a pistol to the back of the head. We had a laundry within camp, a tailor and a swill and refuse collecting gang, usually employing local civilians of Turkish origin.

The Camp Krappa

One morning whilst in camp I was sent for by the Company Sergeant Major and was given six soldiers from within the Company, all proven to be ex-miners. I was told to report with them to the Quartermaster, a fearsome old bugger, World War II Vet with an MM. one Captain 'The Dog' Burns.

The brief was to dig out the battalion deep trench latrine, 'The Oasis'. It was to be 32ft x 12ft by 8ft. deep. When the hole had been dug it was to be capped with side-by-side toilet seats with lids and to have a timber and fly netting surround with a door at each end. 24 bog seats in all, 12 back to back, partition in the centre - half for Officers and Sgts, the other for Cpls and 'Toms'.

We were given a 27 $\frac{1}{2}$ KVA generator (my responsibility), pneumatics picks and timbers to shore up the sides as the pit was dug!

The Quartermaster ordered that we report each day Monday to Saturday inclusive 9am – 1pm. We were to be excused all other duties for two weeks, our deadline. Free coca-cola/orange juice on tap and first in the Q each day for lunch! We were to wear boots, puttees, shorts, PT shirts, sun hats, with a fresh supply of laundered clothing daily. We were untouchable! God declared it!

We completed and met the deadline. What a building it was. One could go in there, lift the lid. sit on the throne, chat to one's neighbour, no flies! Have a crap, read the paper. It had an apex roof and at both ends for all to see, the name: 'The Oasis'. The Quartermaster had an official opening, tape cut, Officers Only!

The 1 Para off duty soldiers were allowed in groups of four to go by unit transport and return to Nicosia to in-bounds bars, nightclubs and cafes! One of the group had to remain sober and be armed, usually with a Sten or later a Stirling sub-machine-gun. There were some good eating places, one such being 'Charlie's Bar', off Ledra Street. The odd weekend saw us transported to Kyrenia some 30 miles away and to a delightful harbour where the favourite was 'The Castle Inn', for the best Brandy Sour on the island.

Having spent an evening in Nicosia there was one drawback! All soldiers had to go through the prophylactic tent, be seen to get his wedding tackle out and to scrub it with water over an open trough, this was watched by the duty medic and provost staff! As far as the Medical Officer was concerned all soldiers were brothel visitors and so cleanliness was Godliness.

How come the officers and sergeants did not have to go through the ritual?

A Most Marvellous Padre Called Horace

During the Cyprus Tour of 1956–57 the Battalion enjoyed a most colourful man of the cloth in Padre Horace Maclellan, a Blackthorn wielding no nonsense fellow who on Sunday mornings, before his outdoor sermons, used to tour the tented lines belting the canvas sides with his stick shouting, 'Come on you heathens, who's for church?'

He persuaded four of us in C Company to take time off to take a trip to Jerusalem and the Holy Land from Nicosia Airport. Our personal contribution would be £15 to have an all-inclusive week in a Christian House in the heart of Jerusalem with coach trips to Bethlehem, the Sea of Galilee and the River Jordan. The trip was sponsored by the Council of Churches.

This tour of the Holy Land it is fair to say was one of the finest things that has ever happened in my life; it left a deep and lasting impression upon me. So much so that I have visited on two other occasions and with my charming wife Christine.

On arrival from Cyprus on this first occasion some 30 of us tri-service and civilian pilgrims were booked into a Methodist Christian House staffed by nuns. We had wine at the lunch and evening meals, and were able to go into Jerusalem during the evening although were expected to return indoors by 10pm.

During the days we visited most of the Holy sites, the interior of 'The Dome of the Rock,' the Coptic Church, the Wailing Wall, the Garden of Gethsemane. We walked 'The Stations of the Cross'. Horace, our Padre, was a most amusing and knowledgeable guide. We took in Bethlehem and the site where Christ was born. We swam in the Dead Sea and we were blessed on the banks of the River Jordan. What an experience. Though at the time Jerusalem was quite a divided city politically, we as tourists and pilgrims were not aware of it.

It was brought home to us one evening when we visited a small bar within Jerusalem's walls and not much of a stone's throw from the Christian House. Two of us had decided to go out for a beer, early evening found us sitting at a table within the bar but facing an open street. We hadn't been there long when we were joined at our table by an Arab in western dress who engaged us in conversation: 'What were we doing here? Where were we from?' We had the idea that the inquisitive fellow knew that we were from the Christian House. The conversation seemed to turn political very quickly and we were asked to express our views on Winston Churchill and the British Policy on the Middle East. He was joined by another Arab and the conversation became heated, so much so that we moved to leave and put our backs against the wall. Suddenly all hell seemed to break loose and others in the bar in western dress pounced on our two inquisitors, one produced a pistol! One stood in front of us and said, 'Police". We suggest that you leave now and go direct to your accommodation!' We were 'minded' by the Israeli Secret Police who were looking out for us and for our wellbeing!

Tragic Circumstances on Foreign Service

It is not often appreciated that soldiers' lives are lost and soldiers are often injured not through combat in engagements with an enemy, but through accidents and sometimes through just darned bad luck. The world is marked by the graves of soldiers who have been buried in foreign lands. Such a cemetery is sited just outside Nicosia at 'Wayne's Keep'. The graves are tended by the War Graves Commission. It is only in recent times that servicemen and women's bodies have been repatriated home to the UK. Really, only since the Falklands War 1982 have families been given a choice.

In Cyprus during 1956 a friend of mine from Bradford, Brian Kunkell, lost his life on the Kyrenia Mountain Range whilst climbing as a weekend sport. Alec Gurr went over the edge of a mountain road whilst travelling within the Rations 1 Tonner that had come to pick him up for his allocated leave period. Others that were in the vehicle stayed in on rollover, he was the only one thrown out!

A territorial lad, called up to join C Company Pte Gillette, collapsed and died on the early morning run. Sergeant Major Jimmy

56

Forster was killed in ambush and two other members of the patrol were badly injured when fired at by our own troops. It was a rule whilst on operations, 'No one moved out of area after 7pm'. No matter where you were you went to ground with sentries out till dawn. He broke the rule and it cost him his life. They were late back to their firm base in the mountains. All were buried at Wayne's Keep.

Sod's Law and the Locals

It also prevailed on the Greek Cypriot locals of a Kyrenia Mountain Range village during our cordon and search operations in1956. The village was Ayios Ambrosios.

Our company, 'C' Company, during the hours of darkness had thrown a cordon of soldiers completely around the village, the idea being that at first light the main village would be entered and all males would be told to make their way to the main school hall. Those males who hid within their houses would be ousted by trained military search parties and would also end up at the school hall. Once there, all would be looked over by Cypriot informers and those of EOKA persuasion or known terrorists on the wanted lists would be arrested into detention.·

It is most difficult at night to set an effective cordon, in particular in a mountain village of re-entrance, steep slopes and water courses. At first light some adjustment is always necessary to plug an obvious gap. It was during such a phase that, even though warned by loud hailer 'Bene scholia' (go to school), a male villager legged it and broke through the cordon to run down the mountain. All soldiers in sight of him yelled, 'Halt, Stanata, Dur', the three languages for him to STOP. He carried on and was shot through the head at 200 yards. At the subsequent enquiry it was found that the man who had legged it was a deaf-mute shepherd. He had a goatskin bag over his shoulder and was carrying a large, thick stick – Sod's law.

The Company Commander and a Brick

In North Cyprus mid-1956, west of Kyrenia there was a small offshore island usually fordable at even Cypriot low tides. This was known as 'Snake Island'. It was at that time a company group recreational base and up to 100 soldiers used to enjoy its tented recreational and wet canteen weekend facilities or 'Smokers'.

Swimming was the usual recreation during the day, beers at night under oil lamps, darts, board games and cards and just chewing the fat.

Now in 2013 and, as it has been for a number of years, the incumbent Cypriot President has it as a summer retreat.

'C' Company were there for a whole week of rest from operations when, mid-morning, the Company Commander together with his driver and Company Sergeant Major 'Cushy Mac' and escort, were seen to drive off in the OC's Rover, destination - Kyrenia! Fifteen minutes up the road. Out for a jolly into the harbour town.

The Company Commander at this time was Major Deane-Drummond, a WW2 and Arnhem Vet of some fame as he had hidden in a cupboard of a house occupied by the German Army for a number of days. He was never discovered! We, in C Company affectionately called him 'Cupboard' Joe. He was a dour man, not given much to conversation and during the War was a Royal Signals Officer with the actual rank of Lt Col. Like so many officers after the War to stay in Military Service, he had to drop a rank. Often a slot would arise and he would be promoted to his former rank in his turn.

As the story unfolded, as told by the Company Sergeant Major, the vehicle was being driven within Kyrenia town when half a house-brick from nowhere appeared and shattered the Landrover windscreen at the OC's side, hitting him fair and square on the head. Major Deane-Drummond received a fractured skull and we the Company thereafter never saw him for years. After recuperation and re-appointments he was promoted General; he had been the Director of the SAS during their epic battles up country in Aden when the SAS, 3 Para and the Royal Marines Commando did their stuff. That 'brick' certainly made a difference and a DSO in the making.

'Bernie the Bren'

As a Section Corporal in 7 Platoon 'C' Company 1Para, I was fortunate to have a superb Light Machine Gunner, 'Bernie'.

He was so skilful that he could fire single shots by the pressure that he applied to the trigger even when the weapons change lever was set to automatic. Bernie operated a Bren gun as the most skilled typist would operate a keyboard. Included within Bernie's armoury was the issue to him of an additional weapon, a 9mm Browning Pistol. This was a personal protection weapon as in a tight corner he would not be expected to swing his heavy weight machine gun around.

We were in the Troodos Hills in section order, lying on our newly issued sleeping bags, sentries out and about to settle down for a night's kip when I struck up a conversation with Bernie, who was on his sleeping bag next to mine. I asked him how he had come to do 14 days in detention having just been returned to me, for firing his pistol negligently in camp and through the tent walls. We were at the time sitting side by side and had been cleaning weapons. Bernie had his 9mm pistol in front of him on his bed and he had assembled it. I did not know at the time that he had placed the magazine on, but he had.

He was explaining to me how he had cocked the weapon to take it to bits for cleaning without first removing the magazine when he again did just that!! In explaining this to me, he then squeezed the trigger. BANG! The bullet that had been fed into the pistol chamber fired! The bullet head went through the palm of his free hand, between his legs and through his sleeping bag into the ground. When he had been rushed through the mountains to the military hospital and patched up and recovered, he spent another 14 days in detention with loss of pay.

The Commanding Officer when Bernie appeared in front of him ordered that he in future would never carry, nor be issued with a 9mm pistol! He was still a darned good gunner though.

Suez 1956. 'Operation Musketeer'

During September the 1st Battalion was withdrawn from operations in Cyprus and returned to UK for extensive parachute training. This was in preparation for an incursion into Egypt to sort Nasser and the Egyptian government's threats to the international waterway, the Suez canal.

Even within the Airborne Forces Museum there is little reference to the 1st Battalion ever taking part in the Suez Operation in November 1956. Our sister Battalion the 3rd Battalion mounted Operation Musketeer from Nicosia Airport and parachuted into Port Said to take over the airfield and town to provide the springboard for movement into Egypt. French and Israeli airborne forces also took a part.

The 1st and 2nd Battalions ignominiously went by SEA! Our government of the day hardly able to find the transport aircraft to parachute one battalion into action.

We sailed from Famagusta Port in an old Troopship, 'The Empire Parkistan', to dock a couple of days later in early November in Port Said. Recollections of coming into the harbour were of the statue of De Lesseps having been shot to pieces and of the entrance to the Canal waterway having been blocked with sunken ships, their superstructures sticking out of the water. The Port area was in the hands of the French Airborne and, as docking at the port's side was impossible, they covered our movement ashore down the ship's scramble nets. What a Mickey Mouse entrance.

Our Battalion spent the first day in and around the coastal area digging in a couple of miles out of town. My OC in the meanwhile was sportingly shooting at looters, some 400 hundred yards away, in and out of the expensive beach huts. We had a grandstand view of the Royal Airforce fighter jets one after the other rocketing Navy House.

The second day we were to move through the town and out to the road leading to Cairo. We commandeered a large bus as company transport and the driver, Pte Drain, even had the destination Cairo put on the roll up screen. We were in and around the abandoned Egyptian Army Barracks, the occupants having fled.

7 Platoon were ordered to form a strong fighting patrol and go and link up with 3 Para who, having gone firm on the ground, were now in all round defence. This would be the first sighting of 3 Para since their parachute assault. We met up and found them in very good heart. Rations and a few souvenirs were exchanged.

On the return to our Unit positions and whilst crossing open grounds near to a block of flats we heard our Bren Gunner Benny Thompson shout, 'Take Cover!' Looking in his direction we saw an Arab in civilian clothes bobbing and weaving within a walled garden area. He must have thought better of taking us on and, knowing that he had been spotted, pushed his hands above his head showing his rifle. The Platoon Sergeant Alfie Goodchild and I being the nearest to the gunman went to search him and relieved him of a couple of grenades and spare rifle magazines. Having searched the area and then closed ranks we took the prisoner back with us to Battalion Headquarters. There he was placed in the tender loving care of the provost, Sergeant 'Nobby Arnold' and the Regimental Sergeant Major, Bucket Lawrence.

We heard later that the prisoner chose to do a runner four hours before ceasefire and found that he could not outrun a bullet.

The third night saw the Company dug in around the perimeter of a large oil installation and as this was in part on fire we were silhouetted against some buildings. This led to the French Airborne opening fire as I moved to check on our sentries. Their machine gun took the slates off a nearby roof and caused me to take cover rather sharply. Nearest thing to a snake. In the meanwhile whilst 2 Para went firm and took up positions way out of town, they were to dig in to remain for a few weeks whilst the politicians decided on our move toward Cairo.

The Complete 1st Battalion of which I was still a part was ordered at some haste to return to the harbour at Port Said. There we boarded the naval aircraft training carrier HMS Ocean. We sailed back to Cyprus at best speed to the rumour that we had been recalled to mount the next airborne assault into the Egyptian interior. Once in Cyprus the American government intervened and the entire operation was called off. Anthony Eden our PM caught a cold over it all.

An American in Aldershot

Late 1957, I as a Corporal still in C Company 1 Para witnessed an event, even took part in a set of circumstances that is talked about to this day. I was about two months away from the end of three years of service with the Para and would leave on 'Demob' to join the police force, the West Riding Constabulary of Yorkshire.

At this time whilst in Aldershot and at Albuhera Barracks, the Company had posted into it a new company commander, an American on some kind of an exchange scheme. To whit, a Major

Garten – 'Gung Ho Garten' as the Toms would call him. The likes of whom we had never seen, nor in hindsight would ever see again!

He appeared on muster parade one morning for the first time, complete with swagger cane! Officers never had 'em. On the right side of his uniform was his American Insignia, on his left side Parachute Regiment Title and Pegasus Airborne Patch. He wore both USA and British Wings. He had high jump boots and a short, off the arse jacket. He was starched and pressed, and to the Toms looked like a bloody Christmas tree.

Within a week he had interviewed each officer and non-commissioned officer under his command. We were all photographed and were swinging on his office wall on disks, in platoon and section order. He had a large sign made in wood relief and placed above the company office entrance: 'SHAPE UP OR SHIP OUT'.

At that time we were in the throes of the annual in-barracks South East District Unit Inspection whereby a gaggle of fat, balding, unfit and non- staff officer types would descend upon the battalion to see 'the Chaps' parade in various forms of dress, from PT kit to full service fighting order. Within the barrack blocks it was worse, kit in lockers squared off, dustbins painted, stones whitewashed. The whole day came to a close with a Battalion Drill Parade and March Past.

We usually had a few days to prepare for this annual test; Monday to Thursdays dress rehearsal, parade and inspection on the Friday.

This inspection was manna from Heaven for this American Commander: on this he was going to make his name. We were unfortunate in that the Company had a newly promoted Company Sergeant Major who never stepped in on the unfortunate idiocy about to unfold. The old CSM would never have stood for it.

The Company was paraded Tuesday to Wednesday inclusive at 1000, 1400 and 1800 hours all in various forms of dress, or soldiers standing by their beds ready for open locker inspection. The American OC was even seen to scrape dust from the old Victorian nail holes in the barrack walls and put his hands around toilet bowl rims. Where one soldier failed on his boots not being polished highly enough or dust under the bed, the whole room failed. This led us onto the Thursday, the penultimate.

We had an in-barracks inspection at 1000 hrs. Then a drill parade on the square at 1400 hrs and, in the expectation that this was it, the Battalion was ready. The other companies were stood down, not so for us 'C' Company. The Company Commander ordered yet a further parade at 1800 hrs that evening.

Now by tradition Thursday was 'Pay Day' to single soldiers living within barracks. All would have been paid in cash at a parade during the day and most expected to leave barracks early evening for a night out. Whether or not the American OC expected to curtail this tradition or whether he was just being officious or bloody minded, no one was to know. Anyway the Company was ordered to parade within barrack blocks, married SNCO's and corporals in attendance. Whispers were about between 1500 – 1700 hrs and at the evening meal that all was not well.

At 1800 hrs the officer commanding and the Company Sergeant Major entered the first ground floor barrack room to find only the Platoon Sergeant standing there flanked by the Sections Corporal. All the single soldiers had scarpered. The same was found throughout the whole Company lines. There was not a soldier 'Tom' to be seen.

All the soldiers *en masse* had gone on their night out! Not in Aldershot where they could be found but in Guildford, Farnborough and even Kingston. As a result the Royal Military Police were informed to find the miscreant absentees...to no avail. The Regimental Sergeant Major was sent for and even the Battalion Commander was informed of the 'mutiny' at home.

The next morning, and by 0815 hrs all the soldiers had returned to barracks and to parade, not a man was missing. The South East Administrative Inspection went off without a hitch and the Company was stood down as was usual after all major inspections. 'Well done' was in order. Retribution was to follow!

On the following Monday, all the non-commissioned officers were interviewed by the American OC and the Company Sergeant Major, as were the older Toms. The Company Junior Sergeant lost his rank and all of the corporals (I being one), were put in front of the Battalion Commander. All of the corporals received a severe reprimand for failing to parade their sections. This verdict stopped me being awarded the 'Long Service and Good Conduct Medal' for many a year.

The Wednesday of the week saw the whole Company being paraded in Full Service Fighting Order, weapons carried, Para helmets worn. The American OC in fatigue dress, I hasten to add, complete with swagger cane and jump boots, informed the Company that he was about to take us on a 20 mile punishment march.

Well nothing could have bound the soldiers together more. They sang their way through Aldershot, Fleet, Farnborough and North Camp to return along the canal bank and up into Albuhera Barracks. Not one man fell out, all paraded outside the C Company office to be dismissed. The American OC limped off in his American jump boots. We did not see him until the Friday.

'This, Sir, was C Company. The proven Champion Company of 1957 – "Excelling in Shooting, Sport and Drill".'

On the Friday of the week we were shipped down to Devon, not to Dartmoor Prison, but to the famous 'Tors'. We were there for one week, dug in, and the weather was appalling. We were on hard rations, 24 hr packs. Except for normal dress, smocks etc. we had a poncho cape each, no sleeping bags. We patrolled at night and huddled up together in our trenches to keep warm. Unknown to the OC, patrols went far and wide at night. As much as seven miles out to secure fresh milk, eggs, ham, even bread from isolated farms. No one starved! We only saw the OC and the 2 i/c during the day, and after seven days Phase II of the company collective punishment was called off.

Back in Aldershot all NCO's were once again interviewed by the OC but no evidence was ever forthcoming on who set the 'walkout' off. No one was ever the wiser. The Company Captain 2 i/c was moved on. The Sergeant Major survived by the skin of his teeth and the American OC was found a job within his capabilities at Brigade HQ. His fancy sign, 'Shape Up or Ship Out' came down.

Many years later when I had been appointed as Regimental Sergeant Major of the 4th Battalion, The Parachute Battalion in 1974, my CO at the time, Lt Colonel John Rymer-Jones, asked me one day why I had never been awarded the Long Service and Good Conduct Medal. I was not wearing the ribbon with other medals.

I told him of the walk out of C Company and the experience of this American exchange major. The colonel said that at that time he was a staff officer also at 16 Para Headquarters and the American guy was 'a bum' and was moved on.

I asked the CO, as he had knowledge of that, would he consider putting his thoughts in writing to Regimental Records and as a plea of mitigation I might get my LS and GC 'Rooty Gong'. He did just that and some months later I received the Medal from the Chief of the General Staff on his visit to the North of England and to the Battalion.

There was a presentation within the mess. The CO kindly provided a case of champagne, I a case of Guinness. Now, that was a 'Bucks Fizz'.

As a footnote I was able to do a fellow RSM a favour. Years ago he received a 'Severe Reprimand' also in the same company and in the same circumstance. As he was now serving as RSM 15 Para my CO contacted his CO, the plea of mitigation was also written and accepted, and he was awarded his LS and GC. Well done! RSM George Brown.

YORKSHIRE WEST RIDING POLICE FORCE

November 1957 saw me leave 1Para after almost three years' service, with the Company Sergeant Major's farewell ringing in my ears, 'Corporal Godwin, you will be back!'

I left after a memorable party at 'The Foresters' and drove out of Albuhera Barracks on my newly acquired motorcycle BSA 350 cc B31 model tourer, Reg No SJ0 249. This bike, purchased from an MT Rene Craftsman for the princely sum of £75, was to serve me well for almost two years.

I spent time at home with the family at Queen's Drive, Ossett. Mum and Dad (Alice and Thomas) sister June aged 19, brother Christopher aged 13 and sister Melanie aged three. Christmas was at home with Grandparents.

Interviewed at Wood Street Police Station, Wakefield, the Headquarters of the West Riding of Yorkshire Constabulary, I was accepted as Probationary Police Constable PC 447 in late November 1957. Until an intake formed up in the New Year I was to work at

Wood Street, proofreading and filing police reports. The intake of probationer constables at Pannal Ash formed up in January 1958 to include during the 16 week course: Law, powers of arrest, traffic accident procedure, arrest and report writing, first aid, drill and swimming/lifesaving tests.

The Police Training College was at Pannal Ash, a few miles west of Harrogate. A walled school type institution with barracks type accommodation and messing not unlike military service. We had our own classroom and this initially took just over 40 students. Our main instructor was Police Sergeant Potter. Respectable, balding and very knowledgeable, he had a Law degree and LLB.

Two students, although in different classes, I was very familiar with. One was Peter Shepley my old Gomersal buddy, the other a Barry Hestletine from Leeds who I had met whilst serving in Cyprus, he being in the RMP. We met whilst on duty at Nicosia Prison. Peter was to join Dewsbury Borough Police in the days when towns and cities had and controlled their own force. Barry was to join the WRC and in actual fact served under my Father's guidance at Ossett, our home town. Father had a long serving pal in Wakefield Headquarters who decided all postings, some of great influence, hence Barry going to Ossett at my request.

Chief Inspector Mogg was the man! Where this friendship with myself became a bad thing was the speed with which my Father was able to change *my* posting. After the final examinations at Pannal, practical and a two-hour written test on law definitions and procedures, I was deemed to have come 3rd of a class of 43. I was rewarded as I thought with a plumb posting to Ilkley in the Harrogate Division. On arriving home during the Friday afternoon of course dispersal day, Father, at home asked me to where I had been posted one week hence? I told him 'Ilkley'. He said, 'We will see about that, there is no bobbying there, only bloody sheep dipping.' He then picked up the phone and telephoned the postings inspector, his pal Moggie!

As a result, one week later found me at Cudworth Police Station in the Barnsley Division. My posting had been changed to the high crime divisional area encompassing Cudworth, Grimethorpe, Barnsley and outlying areas, notorious in the highest crime league table.

I think with Father, a little jealousy of posting had crept in. He had always been known as a 'rough' copper and had never ever achieved a posting to the delights of the Harrogate Division. It was true to say, 'Once a South Yorkshire Copper, always a South Yorkshire Copper.'

Well, there I was, reported to Sgt Mark Andrews the Station Sergeant, interviewed by Inspector Raphael of Royston, the Area HQ, and found lodgings at the home of a widow Mrs Lily Tindall and her son Terry, half a mile away from the police station. Mrs Tindall's elder daughter was in a full time career with the military and I was to meet her daughter when she came home on leave. She was an instructor at the Women's Royal Army Corps Barracks at Guildford in Surrey. She knew all about Paras in nearby Aldershot and used to warn her girls of the perils of meeting the randy creatures.

The first weeks of duty as a young constable saw me under the wing of PC Dickinson, an old worldly-wise copper who in times gone by had actually served with my father at **Cudworth**, the place we were now at! Other coppers as I recall were Neil Armstrong, Paddy Gahan, Jack Brabham and Police Sergeant Phillips and there were others. I was kept busy serving summonses, patrolling, attending traffic accidents, making the odd early morning arrest, keeping the peace and being in the mix on a weekend to bang a few heads together when the pubs closed.

I was fortunate in that I had my own transport, a KR200 Messerschmitt three-wheeled bubble car, having changed from the two-wheeled BSA I had owned. This allowed me to return to home in Ossett on my one day off per week and a weekend off every sixth week. All the policemen worked shifts: 6-2, 2–10, 10–6. Sometimes split shifts when one was called to court to give evidence during the day. We were allowed 15 minutes only in the police station then it was out on the streets on patrol. Everything was recorded within the police pocket book. Rough notes to be written up later. Summonses were typed up in one's lodgings IN ONE'S OWN TIME.

We had no radios but were in communication at and being called at from various call boxes throughout the town. Movement was on foot or if urgent, by cycle. We had a boot and cycle lamp/battery allowance. When in a hurry for some reason we would hop on public transport.

I was fortunate to be able to squeeze a few days off to play for the Division at cricket and at times, even for days, made up the West Riding Constabulary Life Saving, Swimming and Diving Team, even travelling to London White City and Blackpool. My claim to fame at the famous Derby Baths at Blackpool was a running Swallow Dive off the 10 metre board.

We had our lighter moments and between the two hour telephone box reporting times, on the odd summer night, would leg up over the wall of Cudworth Park open air pool and cop a half hour swim. Visit the bakery and sample the odd hot offering, resisting the staff of course.

I once had occasion to visit an address on Barnsley Road at 5 am with 'Black Maria' to serve a distress warrant, or arrest one 'Cocky' Taylor.

'Good morning, Mr Taylor, I have here a warrant for your arrest unless you can furnish me with £400.'

Mr Taylor replied, 'Lad, I havn't got 400 half pennies. I'll get mi coat.'

Off we went via Wakefield to Armley Jail, Leeds, where I handed over Mr Taylor against a body receipt.

There was a sequel to the nocturnal swimming sessions at the Cudworth Park Pool. One late evening – 10 pm, a heavy gang turned up from Royston, in a Black Maria, large police van. There were six coppers and Inspector Raphael on board. We who had just come on duty at Cudworth Police Station were also to be involved. We were briefed by the Inspector that together with the park superintendent who would open the gate, we were to raid the swimming pool to catch night bathers who were making illegal entry and use of the pool and changing rooms. He would blow the whistle, we who lined the walls would shine our torches. Inspector, Sgt and Parky would enter the pool area and make arrests. At the signal we did as ordered and up to a dozen boys and girls naked as jaybirds were found squealing. All were taken home, appeared in court weeks later and were fined 10/-. It did not endear us to the Public and it certainly curtailed our night activities at the pool.

Pussy Patrol, Cudworth

Patrolling along Snydale Road one evening I was in the company of PC 'Jack', a much larger copper than I and well into his late thirties. He never had much of a sense of humour, was quite dour and never had much to say. We were passing a long, low wall that ran for a considerable length, Jack on the wall, me on the roadside. Out of nowhere appeared this cat walking along the wall, purring and trying to rub itself as cats do, but against Jack.

We suddenly stopped, Jack looked around, which caused me to look around too, whereupon Jack, quick as a flash, whipped out his police truncheon from within its slim line trouser pouch and belted the moggie on the head. In one movement he scooped the cat up from the wall and stuffed it under his folded shoulder cape. We carried on to the end of the wall where I had barely got my breath back in amazement. Seeing a dustbin with a lid he lifted the lid, dropped in the lifeless cat and replaced the lid.

I can remember saying to him, 'What the hell did you do that for?'

He said, 'I just hate fucking cats!'

Market Street – Mid morning

Having met Police Sergeant Andrews by appointment through the telephone box, me standing near the box at 11 am and the bell ringing, then he telling me to wait and meet him, he then initialled my pocket book to agree that I had been on time and where expected. We stood and chatted outside the Rock Cinema and small market square. No high viz jackets in those days. We were in sober uniform, blacked out at night and everyone in the town knew us and what is more, would approach us.

We heard a scream, a woman's scream and we rushed into the nearby Market Street. A woman was outside her terraced house, light smoke billowing from the open door. The woman was screaming, 'My Mother, my Mother.'

We dashed into the kitchen and there in a heap were smouldering newspapers. Up the staircase we went and all I can recall was skin that had been left on the steps. We found the old lady in bed under smouldering blankets. We opened the sash windows and threw the blankets out into the street. The daughter found sheets to place over her mum and Sgt Andrews hurriedly left to dial 999 for the ambulance.

He said to me, 'Keep her head to one side and pull her tongue out.' Quite quickly the Fire Brigade and ambulance turned up. I accompanied the old lady to the hospital, as naturally I knew her identity. At the hospital I was given the bad news that she was beyond recovery and she died within two hours. At home and in front of the fire her nightdress and a newspaper had caught alight.

Would todays coppers have waited for an 'ealth and safety' ruling – I wonder. The memory of burnt flesh is still with me.

The Town Clerk and the Bread Van

Whilst on the day shift and patrolling the town I met the Lollipop Lady shepherding the Snydale Road School children across the main Hemsworth to Barnsley Road and just down from the Snydale Road junction.

She complained that most mornings a driver of a car would ignore the HALT sign at the Syndale Road end and if he could see the road clear would, without stopping, shoot across the road ignoring her and park in the opposite Council Car Park. Her other *'bête noir'* was the delivery bread man who always came at a hell of a lick down the main road, usually ignoring her to pull up at a local shop 50 yards away on delivery. He came about 9am every day.

So, I waited! Helmet off, behind the wall: just before 9 each day for the car, 9–9.30 for the van. Normally I didn't bother much with Vehicles Tax. As far as I was concerned it was not my remit. However lollipop ladies were.

I bagged the two in one day. The driver of the car did ignore the halt sign and did make the Lollipop Lady skip. I followed the driver from his car into the council car park, told him what I had seen and having cautioned him, informed him that he would be summoned. I issued him with form HORT 1 to produce his driving license and insurance documents at the local police station within seven days.

The van driver was seen by me to come around the Rock Cinema corner and down the High Street at what I guessed was an excessive

70

speed. I waited alongside the van, watched him unload and take up the empties. I then moved in for A WORD.

This event of course was before the advent of speed cameras, speed bumps, surveillance street cameras and was down to the Mark 1 eyeball and common sense.

I told the bread man of our concern over speed and over the junction that he went through each day and of the proximity of the school. It didn't seem to wash. He wanted to be on his way. We then had one bolshie bread man and one annoyed copper.

As a part of my warrant to be a police constable I held a licence and was deemed to be a vehicle inspector. I held a certificate to prove it and had great delight in showing it to the van driver. Under the Construction and Use Regulations I examined his vehicle's trailing edges, his tyres, his vehicle documents, his insurance certificate, his loads, lashings, door locks. His weigh bills. I even had him drive over to the Public Weighbridge at the council area and offices across the road. In all, the whole affair took one hour and a quarter.

I told him that I was on days for the remainder of the week and on other weeks, and if in my opinion he was not driving with due consideration, I would carry out the same exercise no matter where, within Cudworth town. He was suitably impressed! Thereafter we had no more problems.

When the car driver eventually produced his driving licence and insurance documents to the duty Sergeant Andrews, he saw me when I next came on duty and said, 'Hey lad! Tha did the Town Clerk! He was fined ten shillings!'

Mrs Browns Betting Shop

What a farce this was before legal betting was introduced through betting shops on the High Street. Betting on the horses was illegal in the 50s unless carried out at the race track, so illegal 'Books' were made up in pubs, clubs and small illegal buildings where bets were taken.

There was such a brick built shop on spare land in Cudworth, where punters used to go in and out of to place their bets. All knew that it was owned by Mrs Brown the local bookmaker. Twice a year a police constable was ordered into civilian clothes, on duty, to go sit outside this den of iniquity to record within a couple of hours, 11–1 pm, who went in and who went out: 'Man in sports jacket, brown trousers, aged 40s seen in at 11.10, out at 11.20', 'Woman - pinafore dress, light blue in 60s in 11.15 out 11.20', etc...etc. Such a record this day kept by me.

Of course, the punters knew me and I was familiar with most of them. We even had a couple of hours friendly banter.

At about 1pm the Police Sergeant would turn up with a large police bus and driver. He and I would enter the illegal betting shop where Sergeant Andrews would inform all that they were under arrest, together with the counter staff. Betting slips that were to hand would be seized, as would be cash. Sgt Andrews would then sort the punters out, 'Mrs so and so, beggar off and make your hubby's dinner!', 'Mrs G, beggar off, you are too old to be in here', 'Albert, did you go last time? If so, sod off.' We would be left with half a dozen punters who would all troop into the bus together with Mrs Brown and her counter staff. Sgt Andrews and myself as witness plus the takings as found.

The whole party would then be transported to Barnsley Magistrate's Court where a special hearing would be set up for gambling parties from all over the Division. Mrs Brown, through her solicitor, would plead 'Guilty' to running an illegal betting shop and would be fined an adequate sum; the punters would be fined a small amount which Mrs Brown would pay. The Court satisfied and fines settled we would all troop back to the bus to be taken home to Cudworth. Mrs Brown would in the course of the journey give each punter £5 for their couple of hour's inconvenience. The Sergeant and I were invited to Mrs Brown's substantial house off the main Barnsley Road for a sherry! What a farce!

The Life Saving Team at Blackpool

At Police Training College at Pannal Ash during the 16 weeks course, all probationer constables were required and tested on the basic Bronze Medallion Lifesaving course. There was an in house 25m swimming pool. Students attended twice a week until

72

completion. I, as an already accomplished swimmer, was entered for the Award of Merit test, two up from the Bronze Medallion Test. I passed and as a result some months later, and whilst serving as a police constable at Cudworth, was called to Wakefield Headquarters to join the Force Lifesaving Team. As a member of the team we had formal lifesaving, pool and bathside drills, and on the odd occasion were called upon to take part in pool lifesaving competitions.

Each team had a captain and two pairs of swimmers and we were called upon to enact rescues in water of supposed canoeists in difficulties: swimmers in difficulty, non-swimmers in the water, and exhausted swimmers requiring help. I can remember taking part in competitions in Leeds, London and Blackpool.

The West Riding team had an A and B team. Overall we had an inspector in charge, Sgt Martin, who was the overall trainer, and A and B team captains and four swimmers in each team. My immediate team partner was Brian McCarthy and in the water we acted as stooges for each other. In 1958 our 'B' team actually won the British Police Life Saving Championships at The White City. The West Riding 'A' team came in second.

Most of the major police forces had swimming teams apart from life saving, and the Police Swimming National Championships were held at the Derby Baths, Blackpool, over a whole summer week. Our force team was booked into a guest house and we travelled from Wakefield Headquarters to Blackpool and return by bus.

I took part as a breast stroke competitor and as a 10 metre hard board diver. In diving at the end of round two I was laying 3rd. My inward, 'pike' dive in the last round did me no favours and I was out of the medals. Breast stroke saw me out of the semi-final, so after four days we were really done and had a couple of day's relaxation in the town in the evening.

On the penultimate evening I palled up with a Scottish police constable who was a bit of a live wire and far more 'Bird' aware than I was and we went out together on a night out. We ended up at a pub on the Blackpool Golden Mile called 'The Palatine'. Well known for 'Pussy on the Prowl'. Into the swing of dancing and a fair amount of booze and expense of many gin and tonics for a couple of 'Birds', procured by 'Jock'. We ended up at kicking out time walking the ladies home to their lodgings. *En route*, Jock ended up in a garage, I ended up within an outhouse and large open-air toilet. Sometime later with dark suit covered in whitewash where I seemed to have bounced off the walls, we met up and all had a good giggle. Farewell, a good night had been had by all. On the morrow, we were off to Wakefield and Scotland, the girls back to London.

There was to be a sequel though, who had blabbed I never knew. On the return journey by coach from Blackpool to Wakefield during a break at Todmorden, Sgt Martin asked for silence as the Inspector had a few words to say.

He thanked the Life Saving team for getting through to the semi-finals to be held in London, he thanked us individual swimmers for our best efforts and then he announced a special award for PC Godwin!

A large, circular brown paper parcel was handed over to me and to the raucous cheers of my fellow swimmers, I unwrapped A TOILET SEAT.

The Snydale Club Raid

In Cudworth town there were four Working Men's Clubs of different persuasions. Strictly speaking we, the police, could not go into a club unless invited, whereas we could enter a public house at any time during licensing hours. In fact three of the clubs did make us welcome at any time and we were usually offered a swift 'half'. It was of course in their interest as we were the guardians of their premises during the hours of darkness.

The odd club out, the Catholic Club, would allow us nothing, not even at Christmas. It was well known that there was a fair amount of drinking after time and often up to midnight! Closing time then was nationally 10.30pm. Friendly warnings from our Police Sergeant went unheeded and the local residents either side of the Club and along Snydale Road were forever making formal complaints on noise after midnight.

After much deliberation on one Friday evening a Black Maria from Divisional Headquarters with a heavy gang on board with warrant was sent to raid the Club. We policemen at Cudworth on duty that night were also picked up after 11pm to take a part in the raid. All I might add, without prior knowledge.

74

Fifteen minutes after leaving the police station we surrounded then burst into the Club. There, to our great surprise, were only three persons, a barman, a committee man and a chap moving glasses and sweeping up. There was 'Fugg' in the air and many glasses on tables but no customers!

In the aftermath and de-brief it was found that the only police constable that was left on duty at our police station to man the desk and telephones was an Irish Catholic police constable. He, unknown to our police sergeant, had found himself lodgings at a Catholic club member's house when first being posted! Interviewed at some length nothing was ever proven but who gave the tip-off?

We were all left to wonder. The Club members however never risked another raid.

The Sherriff of Ryhill

After a few months service at Cudworth I was posted, still within the Barnsley Division, to the village of Ryhill. The area bordered by Wakefield Division, Royston as the area Headquarters, Cold Hiendley Village, Shafton. In effect this was a detached beat. I was the only village copper, 'The Sheriff of Ryhill'.

Work, eight hours a day, six days a week but in effect, on call anytime.

Arranged by the area Sgt, a Sergeant Phillips of Royston, I was found lodgings at 'Laurel House', Station Road, Ryhill, the large home of Harry and Ivy Chard. They owned a local mini supermarket and taxi business. Ivy drove the taxis and had the area schools franchise. Harry serviced and repaired the taxis. They had a large Chow dog. They had never had a policeman lodger before but Harry thought it a good idea as I could look after the house and the contents of the safe under their bedroom floorboards whilst they took their odd holiday. They were a lovely middle-aged couple with a sense of humour and during my time there we got on really well. Ivy was a fountain of knowledge and tipped me off about 'the good, the bad and the uglies' within the village. They were childless as they had suffered a loss in their early married life. They had close relatives who often turned up at weekends for an afternoon tea delight.

It seems as though my predecessor, a married police constable

75

nearing retirement, had been one for the quiet life. He used to whistle on duty, walk the main streets and flash his torch around. Mine was an entirely different approach. I was covert, had rubber soled boots, never shone anything and popped up here and there when least expected.

During the day I visited shops, businesses, bakeries, the cinema and the pubs, outlying farms and the junior school. I made sure that most inhabitants knew me and that I was approachable. The same telephone box system prevailed on communication with Royston HQ but it was me ringing in every two hours. Unless I was wanted urgently at my lodgings, I travelled the mile or so to the rural farms and around the Ryhill reservoir by cycle.

I gave up my three-wheeled bubble car transport after a short while and was usually transported by my landlady's taxi or by the excellent bus service to Barnsley, Pontefract or Wakefield, or even by rail from Ryhill Station, to be axed of course in the 'Beeching' cutbacks of the 60s, when most rural lines were axed as being unprofitable.

My one day off per week saw me go home to Ossett to stay with my parents and to have an evening out with PC Heseltine, my police training college pal who was stationed with my Father. I continued to be a part of the Police Life Saving team and the beat policemen in the adjoining villages of Crofton and Cold Hiendley would cover for me as I often patrolled their 'Patch' for them.

I soon struck lucky as a copper and the local hoods had reason to be looking over their shoulders.

The Blue Van and the Carpets

It was midnight and as was usual if I was on nights, 10pm-6am, I would be adjacent to the public telephone box at the village main crossroads, five minutes before to five minutes after the hour to hear the 'ring, ring' if there was a message from the duty sergeant at Royston Police Headquarters.

'Be on the lookout for a large dark blue box van', was the message! 'Holding carpets stolen from Royston Co-operative this evening.'

As I was gazing out of the telephone box into the midnight air, a blue box van passed me and turned left to go down the main High Street. What was more, I knew the van and knew the driver and knew where it was normally parked. I didn't say anything at the time to Sergeant Phillips except to acknowledge the call. I replaced the receiver then I was on my way. Through the back alleyways of the terraced houses I was soon staring at the blue box van. It was parked in a cul-de-sac and to the rear of Mr 'D's house. The roll-top rear was locked but what was more important to me, the radiator cover was HOT. There was a light on in the house and so I knocked on the door. There stood Mr 'D' in his pants, shirt and braces. He looked surprised to see me in uniform.

'Good morning, Mr D,' I said, 'have you been out in the van this evening?'

'No, Sir,' he said.

I said, 'Well, that's funny because the van radiator is hot. I suggest that you get the keys.'

So together, at the rear of the van when I told him to unlock the back and roll it up, he was quite speechless. I telephoned Royston Police Station from Mr 'D's house, with his kind co-operation of course; sat on the keys until Sergeant Phillips and a detective constable made an appearance, then left them with the van keys and a box van holding a pile of carpets. All from Royston Co-operative.

The Motorcycle Ring

In the High Street one Friday late afternoon I was approached by a local twelve year old lad who pulled my arm and said, 'Mr, I know where that motorbike is that the Polish man had pinched from outside the cinema.'

There had been a 350cc m/cy taken early evening a week or so ago from the cinema car park. It was reported to me, but enquiries had failed to trace it.

I took the lad home and he told his story again to his mother whilst I listened. He said that the evening before he had been on the local bus to go to his mate's house in Fitzwilliam, a village some three miles away. On the way there and from the top deck of the bus, he had seen the motorcycle being wheeled through the front door of a terraced house, as the bus was stopped at the nearby bus stop. He said that he knew the colour of the house door. He said that there was no mistake with the bike because the Polish man, a neighbour, took him on the pillion now and again for a ride.

I asked his mother if she would agree to the lad and me taking the bus on the Saturday morning, he would point out the house I would get off, he would carry on to Fitzwilliam to the terminus then return home on the same bus. We would both be in civilian clothes of course. He in a school blazer. His mum agreed and on the Saturday we did just that.

From the upper deck of the bus the lad was in no doubt. He pointed out the house door, and I rang the bell to stop the bus and alighted at the nearby bus stop. It was just after 10 in the morning.

I went to the door, knocked, and when a young woman answered the door I announced, 'PC Godwin, Ryhill,' and showed my Police Warrant Card. With a foot in the door I then said, 'Where's the motorcycle?'

She at once started to cry and didn't stop me from entering the room. She pointed to what I eventually found was the kitchen. As she was sobbing hubby came from upstairs and shouted at her to keep her 'f...g mouth' shut. I cautioned him, told him that he was too late and that an independent witness had seen the bike being wheeled into the house on the previous Thursday evening.

His wife said, 'It's not ours, it's his brother's and we are storing it.'

I found it in the kitchen but without an engine.

I informed Royston Police Station and Headquarters and the heavy gang came up with detective officers and as a result, over a period of a week or so, the brother was arrested and interviewed at Crofton, a village within the Wakefield Division. Local youths were arrested as a spin off and it turned out that this was a gang who had been stealing motorcycles in the Barnsley and Wakefield areas; breaking them up for parts and disposing of the motorcycle frames in the Ryhill reservoir. In all 15 frames were recovered.

I was never called to court to give evidence as the case snowballed, encompassing two police divisions, many man hours by the detectives and many witness statements. I did however receive thanks from my area Police Inspector Rafael and the twelve year old lad received a present and my thanks to his mum.

78

Would it happen these days? Would a local schoolboy approach a policeman on the street? Would he find one? I doubt it!

The Hole in the Ice

From my lodgings on Station Road and on coming on duty early morning 6am, I usually made my way to an outlying crossroads/farm area where there was an isolated telephone box. There I would ring in to Royston HQ to get the news of the day.

On the trusty BSA cycle I would then return to Ryhill by skirting the Ryhill Reservoir. A 'B' road ran around a good half of the reservoir; the haunt of fishermen, courting couples and much wild life. Not at 6.30 in the morning!

As I skirted along the low metal pole fence making a natural barrier between water and road I was looking onto an icy surface. It was late November and we had suffered a hard frost. Not enough to make an ice skating surface but enough to make ice at the perimeter an inch or so thick. A gentle bank sloped down to the water. Whilst pedalling along I saw two holes in the ice, each about three feet square and a metal box thing seemed to be sticking out of one. Leaving my trusty chariot, I hopped over the fence to see, just under the surface, what I recognised as two safes.

So back on the bike home to find the telephone and a quick call to Royston HQ. I then arranged with the local farmer for a tractor and flatbed trailer, chains and wire ropes to enable the safes to be retrieved for display to Sgt Phillips and the area detectives.

Both safes, quite small and of manageable size to four adults were of course found to have been opened and dumped. The thieves no doubt thinking at night the safes would have rolled down the bank into the water never to be seen again!

The safes were found to be owned by a laundry and by a dairy in Barnsley, and by slick detective work and the modus operandi (the way the safes had been opened) the thieves were arrested within four days.

Yours truly was sent for by the Divisional Commander, Chief Superintendent Winstanley, and given a pat on the back.

'Been to my Mates'

79

Lurking in the shadows after midnight at the Ryhill Crossroads Shopping Gables, I was about to put a half a crown into the walled cigarette machine when, from the Cold Hiendley Road, something caught my eye. Forgetting the cigarettes, I put the coin back into my pocket and flattened myself into the gloom. From there I saw two youths with a suitcase each!

Opposite to where I was standing there was a bus shelter, which they soon reached. As they were about to pass I sprang out and shouted, 'Hold it right there and get into that shelter.'

I knew them both, as William and Charles Hunter. The elder 18, the younger 16 years of age. Both had previous 'form' for petty theft. They both in actual fact only lived about 50 yards from my lodgings at Laurel House in Station Road. I had them go into the bus shelter, open up the suitcases and asked them for an explanation as to the suitcase contents. They had books, pens, microscopes, cash, drawing instruments and other school items. I asked the elder where they had been and where the stuff had come from. He said, 'From my mates at Cold Hiendley, we went for the Railway Books!'

Escorting them home and informing their parents (locking the suitcases away meanwhile) and having the two interviewed by the on duty area detectives, brought out the fact that they had turned over the adjacent village junior school classrooms, 13 in all, broken locks, broken windows. At the quarter sessions the younger received probation, the elder 18 months. As I had said 'both had previous form'.

I was thanked by the Chief Superintendent, 'Well done.'

The Body in The Lake

Early one morning I had a visitor to my lodgings to report the body of a male person floating in the Ryhill Reservoir. The Reservoir was both in the Wakefield and Barnsley Division areas. So as an appointed coroner's officer, as all county policemen were at that time, the incident was mine to deal with. Having informed Divisional Headquarters, helped the local undertaker to carefully retrieve the body to the local mortuary for an immediate post mortem, I was in attendance to the coroner as he did his stuff. Shortly afterwards the body was released to the family but I was not privy to the coroner's findings.

I was summoned to the inquest a short time later at Barnsley Coroner's Court and I was to give evidence in what circumstance the body had been found. Whilst waiting to be called and for the court to convene I met an elderly policeman from the Wakefield Division who was also to give evidence having known the subject of the inquest; the body was that of a man from the Wakefield area. There was some talk of suicide.

He looked at me and said, 'Tha got body then?'

I replied that it had been found floating near to Ryhill.

He said, 'Well, I saw it first but I poled it round to thee. I didn't want bloody job.'

I was gobsmacked. It was true though. He hadn't wanted to deal with it so he gave it a shove into Barnsley Division's water.

My Landlady

One in a million, there will never be another like Mrs Ivy Chard. Middle aged, money driven and as sharp as a tack. She had endearing ways like being at breakfast before the school run dressed in a pink flannel set with long drawers, before she wrapped up in an overcoat and slippers to drive the school's taxi. She used to warm her backside against the open grate coal fire whilst puffs of smoke escaped upwards to add smudges to hubby's white shirts hanging up in the air on a pullied rack near to the ceiling.

Everything she cooked seemed to come out of a tin from her mini-supermarket, to be warmed up. She owned a Chow dog, a smelly thing with matted hair. It lived under the large square pine kitchen table. This had a hole in the centre through which Ivy used to drop the odd tit-bit for the dog.

The only time that the dog ever had a bath was when I tubbed it when Harry and Ivy took off on a week's holiday. She found out:
a) Because it had changed colour
b) She found hairs in the upstairs bath plug-hole.

She went ballistic! However the dog was forever grateful.

At my eventual wedding, dear Ivy picked me up from home in Ossett. I would not allow her into church as she still drove her taxi on my Wedding Day in the overcoat and slippers.

What a character! She matched my Father and what a co-incidence there was to follow. They both died at the same age, on the same day in February 1974.

A Little Nocturnal Fun

Being on the night shift 6-2 or 10-6 as one often was, one became very familiar with the local colliery shift workers and who was seeing whom, in some cases when the old man was on the night shift down the Pit. The 'clip-clop' of high heels back to home at 4am in the morning!

I was patrolling through the council estate one very early morning when parked up in a ginnell (lay-by) at the gable end of a house was a Ford Thomas van that I was not familiar with. It would be about 2am and there seemed to be people within the van making suggestive noises! The van was rocking to and fro, so I sneaked a peep through the two rear glass doors. Inside in the half-light from a street lamp were a couple, on a mattress performing gymnastics! I didn't put on the police torch as there was light enough for me to recognize a local lady as one being married to a local Pit Deputy (on the night shift I might add).

I stepped to one side, in shadow and hit the van roof as hard as I could with my gloved fist. I then melted away into the shadows. Within seconds there was commotion, the clip-clop of high heels, the revving of an engine and the squeal of tyres. The crashing of a gear-box.

On my way out of the estate I came across a man remonstrating with the driver of a Ford van who had driven through his wood fence and onto his sunken lawn. He had failed to take a corner. The driver was quite sober and after they had exchanged names and addresses (a civil matter) I helped to push the vehicle out! Now where had I seen it before??

82

The Policeman and the Hairdresser
'When Harry met Sally'

Not likely to be seen these days, a policeman on his feet and certainly never directing traffic. Whilst Doncaster Races were on in the 50s all available police constables were assigned to crossroads for miles around, to stand within and wave one's arms around on 'Point Duty', to help the flow of traffic toward Doncaster and afterwards to return to the outlying towns.

I was on such a duty at Shafton Crossroads, an intersection of Barnsley, Shafton, Grimethorpe and Hemsworth Roads. On the sides of the crossroads was a pub, 'The Fox and Hounds', a fish and chip shop, a garage and a ladies hairdressers. I was to work 2 x 2 hr shifts: 10 - 12 noon, 4 - 6 pm.

The afternoon was a hot one even in October and in uniform and with the constant arm waving, I was parched. In a break in the traffic I saw in the hairdresser's shop doorway an absolutely stunning girl with lovely hair, pouting full lips and an elfin face and the most gorgeous legs. I caught her eye and gave her the international sign, as I thought, for a cup of tea. She gave me the international sign for 'No' – a shake of the head!

Late afternoon early evening saw me finish the shift for the day and before pick up at 6.30 I took my uniform jacket off, slipped on a pullover and shot across the road into 'The Fox and Hounds' for a swift pint.

The Landlord behind the bar in the lounge was Mr David Smith and in conversation I mentioned to him that there was a stuck up bird in the hairdressers across the road, who would not even give a parched copper a cup of tea on a hot day!

He burst out laughing and then said that the bird across the road was his daughter and that she owned the hairdressing shop, 'Chez Nous', and employed one other girl.

As we were speaking in came Christine, his daughter, and we were introduced. 'The Fox and Hounds' was her home and there were her mum Lois, brothers Keith, Ian when at home from the Merchant Navy, much younger brother Philip and sister Susan. The pub (still standing and active in 2013) had a Tap Room, Concert and Lounge Bar. A Function Room upstairs where the 'Buffs' used to meet and a good sized kitchen, living/sitting room and adequate bedrooms for the whole family.

At that time Christine was going out with and in an engaged relationship with a draftsman. I was in an engaged relationship with a school-teacher who as a girl I had known since Ossett Grammar School days. Within a short time Chris and I had fallen in love, could not see enough of each other and as a result we both terminated our present engagements to our betrothed.

Chris was introduced to my parents and family and friends and I to hers. We often made up a party of Josie Telling, Fay Fisher, Barry Hestletine the Ossett PC, when time allowed.

Ours was a whirlwind romance. Ryhill and Shafton in distance was a half hour cycle ride. I had given up the three-wheeler by then and had no other transport. In fact by borrowing Christine's cycle I was often able to make it back on duty to Ryhill from Shafton, often by the skin of my teeth. Barry Hestletine my police mate had the occasional use of a car so we were able to get out from time to time to the Yorkshire Dales. We travelled to Wakefield, Ossett and Barnsley by bus. We went to local parties, one memorable one at Angus Norton's in Ryhill, an accountant. Christine's mum was a friend of the Norton's for many years, she was present at the party where I remember being given a bottle of whiskey at the table with the eats. The aftermath was falling down to land in a large pool in the large house car park and proceeding to give all a swimming lesson, laughing my pickled head off.

Three months after our first meeting and when I had been invited to Christine's home and 'The Fox and Hounds' for Christmas dinner, I asked her father David, on the 25th December 1958 for his daughter's hand in marriage.

He asked 'When?'

I said, 'In two weeks if possible, we could marry by special licence with your permission!'

He said, 'Is anything wrong, lad? And what about the hairdressing business?'

I said, 'I love your daughter, Mr Smith, and wish to marry her.'

He looked at me and solemnly said, 'It is now the 25th December. If you are still together in six months' time you can be married on the 25th of June next year.'

A Change of Direction
Return to The Parachute Regiment

Having found the true love of my life, although previously engaged to a school chum who I had been out with for the preceeding five years, it was time to map out a lifetime career. Happy though I was in the Police Force and seemingly appreciated, there was something missing when I compared the life that I had to my previous three years of Service in the Parachute Regiment.

Quite frankly I wanted more than South Yorkshire and working six days a week in that environment could offer.

Christine and I had many a conversation about my returning to the military, and although she had no knowledge of army life and no military background except for Keith, her elder brother, who was currently serving in the Royal Signals, Chris was willing to give life up in Shafton and back my request, after our marriage on the 25th June 1959.

As you can guess, both sets of our parents were horrified that I could think of such a proposal. I did, however, make one proviso. I was not going to return to the Regiment as a Private Soldier, I would only return in the rank that I left; that of full rank substantive paid Corporal.

In March 1959 I wrote to Regimental and Army Records and found that my application to re-enlist would be granted. I then tendered my resignation to the Chief Superintendent of the Division, Mr Rufus Winstanley, and went on interview.

He did tell me of a job well done, and in particular during my service at Ryhill. He asked me to reconsider but I politely declined. He had telephoned Father, he said, 'Who was most upset'. He wished me well and escorted me from his office. A lovely old fashioned police super was he, not far from retirement doing a hell of a difficult job in Barnsley (West Riding). Barnsley Borough had its own police force at that time.

I re-enlisted into the Regiment during April 1959 and reported to the Regimental Depot now within the new Montgomery Lines, especially built to house the Parachute Brigade. The Depot bordered the Fleet to Basingstoke Canal but not that far from the old Maida Barracks (about half a mile).

In the meanwhile as the time was but two months from our wedding, Christine stayed at home in Shafton to plan and make our wedding arrangements for the 25th June. I took off for Bournemouth by train one weekend and made plans for our Honeymoon at an hotel on the Westcliffe.

I had to visit the vicarage in the May to be interviewed by the incumbent Vicar of Felkirk Parish Church, the 12th century church in which we were to be married. Thomas Boyard Webster MA was the vicar, a bit of a stickler for tradition, lectures on 'The Sanctity of Marriage', banns to be read. Felkirk Church had been the Diocese Church since 1253, out in the County between Shafton and Ryhill, such a beautiful old church and grounds with the names of all of the past clerics inscribed on an illuminated board within the chancel. A lottery grant in 2012 saw the church restored to its former glory (new stone tiled roof etc.).

The Parachute Regimental Depot 1959

Since my previous service 1955-57 things had moved rather with regards to equipment. There was a new machine gun, rifle, a different diameter parachute and leg equipment bag.

I reported into the Depot and to the Headquarters' Company Sergeant Major 'Busty Bentley' MM. He made me welcome. I soon drew uniform and equipment, was tailored and settled into accommodation and awaited his orders as to which parachute battalion I was to be posted into. It was expected that I would have to attend a new course and probably a weapons course at Lydd and Hythe. In the meanwhile I was used within the Depot for various duties.

The second week of service saw me being ordered back to the North of England to collect an absentee prisoner who had been arrested and was in custody at the Royal Signals Barracks at Catterick. I went there from Aldershot by rail (complete with handcuffs!).

Being picked up from Catterick Rail Station by Signals Unit transport about 1400 hours I was taken to their Unit Guardroom. There was hell going on. The duty officer informed me that the prisoner had taken a metal spoon from the kitchen when having his

86

lunch, had secreted it on his person and had since removed two breeze blocks from his cell wall by use of the spoon, and had barricaded himself within his cell. The Royal Signals Staff was loath to force an entry and a guard had been placed outside the guardroom where a hole had appeared. Through the cell door spy-hole the prisoner was seen to have this spoon. I went along the corridor to the cell, kicked the door and shouted, 'Corporal Godwin, Depot.'

I then said, 'Get back, I'm coming in!'

The duty officer did ask if I wanted an escort when going in. I declined but said that I would knock when I wanted to come out.

On entering, the prisoner said, 'Hello, Corp, thank God for that. These craphats are driving me mad. I got bored.'

Having signed for the body, 'the prisoner', we were escorted and driven to the rail station to board the next train to Doncaster and then to London, Waterloo and Aldershot. In conversation I found out that the absentee's mum had been instrumental in him handing himself into the Royal Military Police in Leeds. They had him held at Catterick Garrison Jail.

As we were to pass through Doncaster where the mum lived he asked if we could break the journey, board a later train and 'pop to see his mum?' We did just that and still managed to arrive at Depot long before midnight. Mum fixed us up with a nice meal and was pleased to see her son, he was over the moon about it all and I never had to use the hand-cuffs! Job done!

Visit to 1 Para at Albuhera Barracks

After the prisoner and escort duty, and on the Thursday of my second week of re-enlistment with no parachute or weapons course on the horizon, I decided after muster parade at 0815 to take a walk, on a whim, to my old Battalion lines. 1 Para at Albuhera Barracks.

In corporal's uniform I found my way into the unit orderly room and ran into ORQMS Bob Bryant MM, the Chief Clerk, Cricket Umpire and all round good egg!

'Godwin,' he said, 'you are back. I didn't know that! Where are you?'

I told him that I was kicking my heels at Depot Para, awaiting a posting and courses to attend. He looked at me for a while then said,

'No you're not, you are playing cricket for the Battalion this afternoon at 2 o'clock. Go back to Depot Para and sit on your bed, Sergeant Major Bentley will send for you with a Posting Order. Get some cricket whites from the sports store and be on the bus here at Battalion Headquarters for 2 o'clock.'

That is how I returned to 1 Para. Same Platoon, same Company: 7 Platoon, 'C' Company.

I was never sent on a Para re-course and jumped with the Battalion a week later on exercise. I did however in the year attend a Weapons Instructors Course at Hythe.

As for the cricket, we beat the Royal Army Pay Corps that afternoon I was posted in and I took two wickets.

Marriage at Felkirk, Reception at Wombwell
Honeymoon: Bournemouth, Poole and the New Forest

Christine and I were married at Felkirk Parish Church on Thursday 25th June 1959, six months to the day after her Father gave permission. 10.30 in the morning saw a beautiful bright and sunny day. Our best man was Milton Scott, my sister's husband. Christine's sister Susan was bridesmaid. Most of our families were there, but as Christine's father David had to look after their pub, 'The Fox and Hounds', Christine was given away by a family friend, her 'Uncle' Mr Byron Telling. Josie, his daughter, was a close friend of Christine's and had been for many years.

All brides are lovely on their day but Chris was a knock-out in a tight waisted bridal gown, flowery tiara, white gloves, carrying a white, leather Bible.

We all went to a reception at Wombwell some miles away to 'The Three Horseshoes', a large roadside, well-appointed pub owned by Christine's Uncle Billy and Aunty Elsie, Uncle Billy being Christine's mum's brother.

After the luncheon reception and a jorney by Bentley to Cudworth Rail Station we were to arrive at London's Kings Cross Station early evening.

We then went by taxi to The Tavistock Hotel in Tavistock Square, for the princely sum of 4 guineas, 'Bed and Breakfast'. Afterwards we had a most lovely evening. We dined at The Café Royale where we had mixed grill, bought sweet violets in Leicester Square and walked Trafalgar Square and took in the sights, then walked along Oxford Street taking in the sounds of London. Then back to the Tavistock in lovely weather at the end of a most stress free day. Everything had gone well.

The next morning saw me escort Mrs Godwin onto the Bournemouth train to arrive at our Honeymoon Hotel, 'Jennifer's', on the Westcliffe just above the town centre and overlooking Bournemouth Bay.

The hotel, private and well-appointed, was owned by a retired major of the Royal Army Ordnance Corps. The room, pre-booked by me during a flying visit from Aldershot, was charged, full board at £47 per week. Major and Mrs Grinham made our stay a delightful one.

We hired a Vespa scooter as I had a motorcycle license and in lucky sunny weather during the week we took in The New Forest, 'The Cat and Fiddle' pub, on more than one occasion, over the ferry to Corfe Castle via Sandbanks, to Poole harbour and the Potteries, Fossil hunting at Kimmeridge, and East and West Bournemouth Beaches and the Town. I cannot ever remember it raining once, we were so blessed. We had a particular liking for the Old Harry Rocks, a famous peninsular of rocks jutting out in Studland Bay with a cliff top walk to go and see them.

The week passed all too quickly and on the following Friday we had to travel to Aldershot to an accommodation flat booked by me in the centre of Aldershot town and for me to report into work in 1 Para and for Chris to take up life as a new Army Wife.

Married Quarters in Aldershot

Military Quarters were extremely difficult to come by and one was allocated a quarter against a points system based on rank and length of service and need with regards to children.

I had applied, and from my wedding date, but the chance of an allocated quarter within two years was remote. To stay together in Aldershot or nearby we were forced into the private sector. Then, as now, rental less bills took over a quarter of our income! Then £15.70 a week! (Total salary after tax).

89

I had booked a flat in Aldershot previously rented by a corporal in the same company as me who had left the service for civilian life, having paid a month's rent in advance, but never seen it! I held the key.

From honeymoon and with our couple of suitcases we took in the flat. Upper storey overlooking the main Victoria Road – it was awful. Flies buzzing everywhere. Chris sat down on something and said, 'Tom, I can't stay here.'

My world was shattered but with 'Plan B' plucked out of thin air I said, 'Come on, we will go see Uncle Stan and Aunty Hilda in Wimbledon,' a half hour rail journey from Aldershot. Uncle Stanley had been aircrew during the Second World War. Pilot, navigator and rear gunner. He had survived with only one admittance to hospital. Aunty Hilda was in the WRAF and that is how they met. They lived at no 18 Kohat Road, South Wimbledon.

They came to our rescue in a big way and Christine was able to stay with them and in their care for the next six weeks or so until I found a suitable flat in Farnham Town at no 15 Thorold Road, in a street just below Farnham Park, and for me a 20 minute bus ride into Aldershot. We were there for a few months and we rather fell in love with Farnham: 'The Seven Stars' pub, the local bakery and many of the neighbours who were very hospitable.

The Regiment, realising the difficulties that young married couples were in, then came up with an absolute master plan to ease the problem. 'Pegasus Village' was born.

Before we moved from Farnham into the regimental arrangements set up within Pegasus Village, we were granted summer leave. This was during the period of the August Bank Holiday weekend. We had not seen our parents and friends since our wedding day, in late June, and from Farnham we were hoping to try to make independent travel arrangements to have our own transport.

In Praise of the 125cc Vespa Scooter

In 1959, and a couple of months after our marriage, I was granted summer leave. We were living at the flat in Farnham and at the time were without transport but wanted to travel north to see our parents and friends. A hundred yards or so away from our flat there was a garage and there were scooters for sale as I well remember. A 125 Vespa for £125. Well beyond our financial reach. I visited the garage and asked to hire one for ten days. Although they did hire at branches at Guildford and Wimbledon, with it being the Bank Holiday weekend, all scooters had been booked.

I then, as I thought at the time, came up with a brainwave. In hindsight, the most cuckoo idea of all time. I would take the train, Farnham to Bournemouth, and hire a holiday scooter, as we had done on honeymoon. I made a telephone call, booked a 125cc Vespa for ten days, took the train the next morning, picked up the scooter paying a £5 deposit then returned to Farnham driving the 75 miles.

The next day I persuaded Christine to hop on board with squashy bag and we were off on our journey to Yorkshire.

Thank God it was a lovely sunny day as we went via Windsor, Watford, Hatfield, onto the A1. Through Stamford, Newark, Ollerton and Doncaster. The traffic was so dense that we actually kept pace with an MG sports, Stamford to Ollerton! We kept passing him on the inside! We arrived at 'The Fox and Hounds' at Shafton some 200 miles and in journey time, with stops, 12 hours after our start time! On occasions the engine overheated, cut out and we sat on the odd wall until it cooled down.

All of our journeys during the following week were short ones as we popped around to see my parents at Ossett, Grandparents at Brighouse, Christine's friends and relatives and we made a journey to Felkirk Church and met 'our' Vicar.

At the end of the week we decided to return to Aldershot and Farnham, not by the A1 but by the route Ollerton – Oxford – Reading. It rained most of the way, Chris wore a large army waterproof cape and I remember her being strapped to me with a long leather belt. She slept most of the way and remembered little of the journey.

The day after arriving home in Farnham I drove the 125cc Vespa back to its hire home in Bournemouth. A little outside Bournemouth I pulled in at a garage and cleaned and polished the scooter.

When I handed the Vespa over to the garage rep he seemed pleased, gave me my £5 deposit back then as I was leaving he must have noticed the speedo! He shouted, 'Hey! You have done 996 miles.'

I said, 'Don't be daft!' – '96.' Then scarpered, back on the train to Farnham.

Chris and I have often wondered. What a machine. 996 miles, top speed 35mph, two up and a squashy bag.

Oh to be in love.

Pegasus Village Aldershot 1959

As was a fact in the 50s and 60s, military quarters were extremely difficult to come by for young married couples. The Regiment came up with a brilliant idea to give some respite to the Regiment's own. Driven by the Depot The Parachute Regiment Paymaster, Major Briodie who did a deal with the Redskin Caravan Company of Chichester, 42 caravans were provided on hire purchase to individuals.

The information was passed on Unit orders and applicants were requested to rent one of two 30 foot caravans or one of the rest of 22 feet. All were to have piped water and electricity and a bottled gas supply to run lights and a small fitted cooker. A wood burning stove was also provided.

The caravans were arranged on hard standings, off pathways of an old isolation hospital formerly sited within woods on military land about a mile from the centre of Aldershot. An easy walk through pathways and along the 'B' roads connecting the site. The old hospital Nissan Huts having been cleared, the site was left with communal buildings and even a bathhouse that was soon converted by the Royal Engineers for use by its new residents. In a short time there was on site a NAAFI shop, a clubroom/bar, a playroom for children and a laundrette and bathroom/toilet facilities.

The hire purchase or 'rent' was payable monthly through one's pay account, to the caravan company. Utility bills paid in through the Depot Pay Master. These arrangements were a Godsend to those of us who had been renting through the private sector. Attendance at work for all was a 15 minute run thro' the woods.

The site was formally opened by General Sir Richard Gale in October 1959, a tree planted, a plaque displayed and a maroon and blue sign erected naming 'Pegasus Village' at the entrance to the site. The area was secured by metalled high fencing all around the two acre site, except for the gated entrance.

Christine and I moved into a 22 ft. caravan having vacated our flat in Farnham in late October. We were in an ideal spot, at the far corner from the entrance with woods on two sides. We had one neighbour to our kitchen side, the other on a raised hard standing some ten yards in front and their rear facing our front.

All of the occupants were of an age 20 to 30 with just a couple of exceptions i.e. married sergeants and a super old retired married sergeant caretaker – Buddy Lannery and his wife Elsie.

Many of us knew of and were friends before we came on site, through the medium of the Corporals Clubs in the Battalions. Those who come to mind now are Cpl Bill and wife Beryl Millington, Victor and Kate Beale, Peter and Pam Kirby. Cpl Derek Crow. Cpl Kenneth Dawes. Bob Hull. Sgt Pat and Ray Sheehan. Sgt Aspby. Cpl Champness.

For recreation the Aldershot cinemas were but a half hour walk away. Our caravan site clubroom/bar ran by the caretaker was open Saturday evenings. We all had rental televisions within the caravans and the Fleet Canal was a walk through the woods and I even had a 22 foot canoe! Chris and I used to paddle to a pub for Sunday lunch.

We all soon built our own individual birch tree fences, gates, laid lawns, had small sheds and in our case had a sandpit and guinea-pig house sorted for when our first born daughter Tanya arrived in January 1960.

Tanya was born at the Military Louise Margaret Maternity Hospital that would put any civilian hospital to shame. The midwives were all serving Captain or Major 'Sisters', immaculate in their nursing uniforms and scarlet shoulder capes. The nurses were all qualified and from The Queen Alexandra Royal Nursing Corps, their Depot being in Aldershot. The whole place was immaculate, run by matrons not administrators. MRSA was unheard of, nurses inspected when arriving for work and men absolutely banned from delivery wards.

I celebrated my daughter's arrival at The Military Arms, in Aldershot, half a mile down the hill from the hospital! A telephone call saw me leg it up the hill with the flowers to see mother and my new daughter.

Christine did have rather a rough time of it. The baby arrived much earlier than expected and Chris had a very rare blood group that caused some complications. In fact when it all was about to happen I shot to my Company Commander's house off Knollys Road, Aldershot, informed him that things were moving fast, so fast that my wife had been taken in and that we didn't even have a nappy; when Mrs Callaghan intervened and said to her hubby, 'Cpl Godwin MUST have a week off, darling!'

So off I went – nappy hunting!

The Millington's at Pegasus Village

Bill Millington was a fellow Yorkshireman in C Company, very good shot and inveterate smoker. Bill spent days in his time off, digging out the soil in his caravan garden patch for a large, at least three feet deep ornate garden pond. He lined it, paved the surrounds and stocked it with water plants and fish.

I passed his caravan one day having been to the Naafi, and looking over his birch and wire fence at his ornamental pond saw his toddler face down in it, nappy upmost! I vaulted the fence, grabbed his lad out and by inverting him was able to get some air into his lungs. Hearing the commotion, Bill's wife came out of the caravan and was out in a rush to comfort him. The next day, Bill filled the pond in.

We all took to the surrounding woods now and again to collect old timber. Usually fallen branches. Each caravan had an in built insulated timber burning stove. We would go out, forage, come back, cut up the timbers into sizable proportions then store the logs under the caravans.

On such a forage and a good few hundred yards off site, Bill and I came across this broken branch, one that we could hardly lift. I said 'too heavy,' but Bill insisted and called me a wimp. We heaved it onto our shoulders and set off in the struggle back to the caravans. The bloody branch even had a bend in it. Well, we got the damned thing back to Bill's caravan hard standing, now the problem was to put the branch down. It was much too heavy to lower so my idea conveyed to Bill was to shrug it off our shoulders and to stand back on my count of 1, 2, 3. We did just that and jumped away. With a bend being in the log, Bill's end of the log seemed to follow him, rotated and the very end smacked down on his plimsolled big toe. It burst it like an over ripe plum. He then rolled around making wolf like noises. I rolled around and could not stop laughing. Out came dear Beryl. Cold water, cold compress – hospital! Dear Bill.

Years later we had one more episode in Dhala, South Arabia involving a grenade!

But that is another story.

Pegasus Village: Ken and Shirley Dawes

Another of our 1 Para friends, Ken, was a L/Cpl Medic whilst in the village and later to be the Medical Sergeant for 1 Para for many years.

Ken was a Woodsman and had been a gamekeeper in civilian life. He was an ace shot with a 0.22 air rifle and also with a 0.410 shotgun, both of which he owned.

There was a bounty payable by the Aldershot Council at that time, 50s – 60s, on grey squirrel tails. The little blighters in woodland used to do untold damage and of course to birds' nests and eggs. The bounty was 6d a tail, in modern money 5 pence. Ken made quite a supplement to his army salary, once a month paying a visit to the Town Council office.

I used to go with him on the squirrel shoots around Pegasus Village and it was fair to say that he could often glimpse what I could not see.

On the odd occasions, usually on a Saturday morning, we used to take a cycle ride over the Hogs Back Guildford to Farnham road, pop down into Seale and Puttenham and lift the odd pheasant from the recreation grounds with the assistance of Ken's 'fold away' 0.410 shotgun.

On one occasion we were out when he wandered into the Hampton Estate and bagged a pair. He was chased on the road by a Landrover, which he could not outrun. Having appeared in Farnham Court sometime later with me as character witness to say that he offered no violence, the estate owner told him to knock on the door the next time he wanted a pheasant. He did not want the birds disturbed. Ken asked for the ones that he had SHOT.

The Devizes to Westminster Canoe Race 1961

This makes the Oxford/Cambridge Boat Race look like a 'punt in the park', yet it takes place finishing on the Thames over the Easter weekend and gets no publicity. The non-stop course for double canoes is 125 miles long portaging at 77 locks. The average time in 1961 was about 20 hours. Now with modern, lighter canoes and required lightweight survival kit, knock off five hours. It is still a formidable race, even to complete it. The Olympic rower, Sir Steve Redgrave, tried it in 2012 and failed to complete the course.

The race starts in Devizes in Wiltshire and runs along the Kennett and Avon Canal to join the River Thames at Reading and then onto Teddington where the Thames becomes tidal, onwards to Central London to finish at Westminster Bridge and what was then the steps of the LCC (London County Council) building.

In 1961 the Kennett and Avon Canal was disused in parts and canoeing pairs had no option but to carry and run with their canoes. Our canoe was so old fashioned and heavy being a 'Wessex Fibreglass' model – all up weight with obligatory safety kit about 108 lbs. Laughable by today's standards.

During the course of the race one had a choice, canal or river by day or by night, both equally hazardous. Risk the canal at night and the very low bridges to catch a paddle across the face and remember where the dry stretches were, or the River Thames at night remembering where the locks and weirs were?

My partner, Cpl Callum Mackenzie and I opted for the River Thames at night as the lesser evil. Callam had tried the race the year before but had withdrawn at Maidenhead with a sprained shoulder and a different partner.

1st Battalion The Parachute Regiment in 1961 entered six canoes and we, the doubles team, spent six weeks prior training throughout the winter months learning the canal and rivers by day and by night. The race takes place starting during Easter Friday and finishing by Easter Monday.

The trick was to work out slack water at Teddington and work a start time backwards from Devizes. It would be of little use arriving at Teddington with the river running from Westminster as the paddlers would not combat the 7 knot tide. One either wanted slack water as per the Oxford/Cambridge race OR the flow going down river to the sea.

On our race timing we did hit it right at slack water and finished the race, coming 14th in the process. In all 173 doubles teams worldwide were entered. Not all finished. The 1 Para teams finished as follows: the first team came 4th to win the collapsible 'Tyne' Class. The next team came 7th and 11th, our team 14th, the last team from the Battalion came 42nd. One team was disqualified, they had misread the tide at Teddington and ran out of time.

It is fair to say that afterwards I slept on and off for three days. I swore that I would never do the race again, nor have I.

Some memories of training were unforgettable! My first canoeing partner was Sgt Spike Delaney, an Ulsterman, fond of the Black Stuff (Guinness) and cheese sandwiches. We could hardly pass a pub during lunch hours. I soon moved on to try another partner then ended up with Callam Mackenzie. We were up for it! Westminster or bust.

The River Thames one day of training was in spate and really we should never have been on it. We were informed by the lockkeepers not to go near to the weir streams but to hug the banks of the river to make our way into the lock cuts. All six canoes were more or less together this particular March morning and with the weight of water we were going like the clappers downstream. We were approaching **Pentenhook** Lock, the biggest on the river with the most vicious weir stream. In plenty time all canoes but one ran from the right river bank to the left to glide into the lock cut. One of our teams took a chance, cut across too late and got whipped into the weir stream between earth banks then concrete walls.

Luckily there were canoeists from other Units on the banks; some shouted and ran for the lockkeeper. We saw him run the banks with boat hooks. By the time we followed and were able to see the rescue, both our canoeists, Ptes Repper and Carty had the presence of mind to broach the canoe against the piles in the river that held the gantry/walkway. The canoe was breaking up and disappeared. Thank God, our canoeists were pulled up by boathooks by the lockkeeper and helpers.

The steel drawbridges were raised around the corner and the main river and weight of water thundered over a 20 ft. drop, some hundred yards wide. We rang for Unit transport and whilst waiting the lockkeeper informed us that six persons had gone down the weir stream the previous year and all had drowned. In any event, we were to go no further, he banned the remaining canoeists from doing so. We did look downriver and against a Water Grill, (Thames Water, take off point), we found a fibreglass seat and half a paddle! Repper and Carty were lucky that day.

The canoeing team members as I recall were: Major Jack Thorpe, Capts Bob Keay, Rudge Penley. Sgt Delaney, Cpls Quinn, Godwin, Murray, Mackenzie and Ptes Algenia, Repper and Carty. Cpl Bob Myers was our regular 3 ton driver. The Co. Lt Col Geoffrey Pine-Coffin came to see us in training usually at The Richmond Canoe Club. Sgt Blick of the RAF, an Olympic Canoeist was our trainer.

Promotion and a Trout Pool to remember

In 1961 and at Aldershot Blenheim Barracks but still with the 1st Battalion I was posted from C to D Company. On promotion to Sergeant, my new CSM was W02 Malcolm Assenti and I was welcomed into the Sgts Mess by W01 John Bromley. One of the first notable memories was at the early annual shooting competition winning the Sub Machine Gun Cup. On the Thursday, S/Sgt 'Spanky' Roberts the Battalion Armourer and Sgt Tom Foster a veteran shot and I, had all tied with the same score. Come the Friday and with Foster's threat ringing in my ears that he came second the year before, we shot off. I won and was presented with a handsome glass bottomed pewter tankard.

At Blenheim Barracks for but a few weeks I was sent to the Depot, The Parachute Regiment to broaden my Military Education, to get me out of the Battalion for a while and to allow me to take recruit platoons on training to the Brecon Beacons and to live firing exercises at Sennybridge Ranges in Wales. Theirs was the final assessment exercise before leaving for parachute training.

One platoon I remember was at Sennybridge when the weather was awful. The insulated containers of hot food from the kitchen never appeared and I was left with recruits, wet, starving and thoroughly miserable. There were trout pools on the ranges, feeding into the River Usk and so I decided to feed the multitude – 30 or so, hungry soldiers.

I threw the pyrotechnic thunderflashes into a wadable pool and to my amazement up came over 30 trout of all sizes! I had expected maybe 12. We did have tinned margarine and hard tack biscuits, we now had a hell of a surplus of plump trout. Before dark and before breakfast the recruits made use of their hexamine cookers and the margarine, cooked all of the fish, then we carefully buried the bones and skin and returned the area to normal. Poaching on the ranges was a dastardly sin and still is.

Put the clock forward 14 years and this tale had a sequel. In 1975, I was then The Regimental Sergeant Major of the 4th Battalion, a TA battalion, headquarters in Pudsey, Yorkshire. I had about six weeks to go to be posted back to the Regular Brigade as the RSM of 2 Para. Into Pudsey and to Command 4 Para came a newly promoted Lt Colonel John Kent. I remembered him as a Captain when he ran the Para Battle School at Brecon in Wales and we had always hit it off when I took my recruits through for training. On being introduced, his memory had not failed him. He shook my hand and said, 'Godwin, you bugger! I have been waiting all these years to meet up with you again! You cleared that bloody trout pool at E-Craig? Didn't you?'

I declined to answer.

He smiled and said, 'No food, eh? I had a hell of a time with OC Sennybridge for months afterwards. In the end we blamed 3 Para mortars for poisoning the water. It was you though, wasn't it?'

THE PERSIAN GULF BAHRAIN 1962

Leaving Christine and Tanya behind at Pegasus Village, Aldershot and as a Sergeant in 1 Para I went off on a year's un-accompanied Tour to Bahrain, in the Persian Gulf. We took over from a sister Battalion as the whole Brigade was to rotate its three Infantry Battalions and supporting Arms throughout most of the 60s.

We acclimatised, exercised in the Gulf States, flew down to Manama and Salala, attended training camps and attachments to and with the Trucial Oman Scouts. We used Bahrain as a firm base to travel to Aden for six weeks or so in the Town and to protect the 'Up

Country Emirs', from increased Communist driven threats.

Our camp in Bahrain was set up on the highest part of the Island to help combat the intense heat and humidity. Initially in 4 men tents throughout the early months with the help of engineers we transformed the camp into Twynam Huts with air con., messes and kitchens, and by 1965 with following battalions, we had a parade ground, a swimming pool and various squash, tennis, quoits courts. For obvious reasons we were sited only three miles from The Ruler's Palaces and would be of help in times of unrest. The Ruler was Sheik Isa bin Sulman El Kalifa. Their family had ruled since the 18th century. The Sheik allowed off duty soldiers in organised parties to make use of his private 'Thompsons Beach'. If one was lucky, usually to the chosen few officers and warrant officers, one could be invited into the AWALI Gulf Oil Complex, a 20 minute drive away and use their pool.

The Battalion trained hard and I as a Platoon Sergeant of D Coy 1 Para was with the Company when as a part of the Battalion we parachuted onto the Jaweiser Airfield in one of the Gulf States and advanced to contact over 32 miles in 18 hrs to Manama. The lead company was 'A' Company, led by Major Jack Thorpe an ex-APTC instructor with the famous 'Nobby' Arnold as Sergeant Major. They were out to prove the fittest company in the Battalion! They were.

Our OC was 'Beanie' O'Kane, Major and bloody good soccer player. Later as a 44 Para Brigade Commander and Brigadier to be killed as the result of a parachuting accident. Tragic!

My tent mates back in camp were Sgts Reg Melladay, Bob Hunter and Geordie Tate.

The Company Sergeant Major was WO2 Charlie Altas, a fellow Yorkshireman.

I had only been in Bahrain about six months, even less than that, when the OC sent for me and said that the Yorkshire Battalion TA in Pudsey required a permanent Staff Instructor. He thought that I would fit the bill: 'A Yorkshireman for a Yorkshire/Lancashire Battalion'. God bless him, I was on my way. Not before however we did a Company Drop on to Yas Island in the Gulf, a Godforsaken place. I handed over my platoon to Sgt Eddie Magee who I knew well as he, in England, also lived in Pegasus Village. Eddie in later life having left the Paras on retirement became rather famous on a

Yorkshire TV outdoors survival series. He also tracked a murderer out of doors who had eluded the police for some weeks. 'Good lad was Eddie.'

One member of the Platoon was no doubt pleased to see me move on! The Platoon Commander. He was a lazy Lt. We didn't often get them but he was a short service, National Service Officer. He just could not keep awake in any situation. Even in Platoon Headquarters with only he, me, the signaller and a runner, whenever it was his turn to man the radio when we went to ground, for any length of time, the bugger fell asleep. When I left him one morning out in the flinty desert whilst on exercise it took him a couple of hours to find us. In Hamala Camp with a prepared compass/sketch exercise all planned for the following day I asked him to parade at 0815 to inspect the platoon before moving off to the south of the Island some 12 miles away. He never turned up. I did the inspection, waited until 9am then ordered the platoon onto the 3 tonners to transport us to the Ex area. We were to end up at Thompson's Beach to catch a swim, mid-afternoon, lunch being provided. Some hours later successful exercise over and at the water's edge on the Sheik's beach, this lone figure was seen running along the beach, light fighting order, with rifle and equipment. It was our Platoon Commander. He had run all the way from Hamala Camp to our RV as he dare not let the Commanding Officer or Sergeant Major catch him in Camp after 9am. I told him, 'Sir, every time you fuck up, I will leave you.'

At the time and throughout the 1962 tour in Bahrain the Battalion had a cracking Regimental Sergeant Major W01 Pete Kelly. Marvellous sense of humour, approachable but his word was law, once give. The Toms lapped him up, the Sgts Mess backed him up.

I was Battalion orderly sergeant one day, starched KD, red sash and about to walk into the Sgts Mess through the open side door. It was time for afternoon tea in Hamala; siesta over. Through the door as I approached, backwards at a fair rate of knots, to land on his back, bloodied nose and a mouse of an eye, came the Battalion Pioneer Sergeant. At the best, a mean nasty piece of work who had of course the powerful protection of his boss, the Quartermaster! This Sergeant gave everyone a belittling hard time, usually sarcastic. He was usually on to the attached Arms on Tour and in this case

101

within the Mess was taking to task the Pt Sgt, Army Physical Training Sergeant Glyn Morris, the current Army Pole Vault Champion. Glyn, a super Sergeant, super fit, liked by the soldiers, fit as a flea, usually dressed in the shortest of shorts and an APTC singlet certainly whilst on siesta. The Pioneer Sgt was always onto him, usually calling him a 'Craphat Puff', although Morris was trained. On this afternoon Morris had had enough! The Pioneer, as he would, complained to the RSM about being assaulted, 'Within the Mess' I was sent for by the RSM as a witness, 'Sgt Godwin, was Sergeant 'X' struck in the Mess?'

'No, Sir. In the doorway! To land on his back outside!'

RSM - 'Case dismissed!'

Posted to 12/13 Para

What a mix. of the 12th Yorkshire and 13th Battalion Lancashire Parachute Battalions. Now a joint Territorial Reserve Battalion, staffed with us regular army instructors who kept the pay and attendance records for these part-time, drill night and weekend soldiers. As a Sgt Instructor I also ran range weekends, ballooning programs, recruit training and drill.

The Battalion had companies in Liverpool, Oldham, Pudsey, Leeds, Goole, Norton and Gateshead. The Company Commanders (Majors), were all part-timers and held other responsible occupations i.e. bank manager, solicitor etc. Officers and SNCOs and Toms were all trained and were required to attend for training during as many drill nights and weekends during the year. Attendance at a two-week camp was also expected. Four jumps a year was mandatory as was attendance at a firing range. For this commitment all received Annual Bounty, usually paid at one drill night in cash. Many officers and soldiers had seen Regular Army Service.

I did enjoy serving with the TA. They were a great bunch of lads, game for anything, good shots and loved parachuting. Whilst with them on this tour as a Sergeant I was sent on a Parachute Instructors Course to Abingdon. Qualified as an APJI, I thereafter took ground training back at the drill hall and was qualified to dispatch parachutists from 'Big Bertha', the Balloon. Usually at DZs at Church Fenton, York; Temple Newson, Leeds; Town Moor,

Newcastle. My tour with the TA in 1962 was for two years. Initially I served at Brighouse near Leeds (C Company) then at Leeds, with a splinter platoon at Goole. The armouries and ammunition stocks were of course in my safe keeping, although issue of weapons was logged by the TA Company Sergeant Majors.

I was very lucky to return to the Battalion which in 1973 had been renamed 4 Para. I did a tour then as The WO1 Regimental Sergeant Major and during The Presentation of New Colours by HM the Queen in 1974.

So two tours 62 – 64 PSI (Sgt). 73 – 75 RSM. WO1. On the first tour, Christine, Tanya and I left Pegasus Village where Christine had set up home whilst I was serving in the Persian Gulf. We all moved into a married quarter in Dewsbury Road, Leeds. The worst military accommodation that we ever occupied. Coal fires, a Foundry nearby with a coal distribution yard and a Remploy Factory outside our perimeter. The only bonus was a nearby bus stop for transport into Leeds 3 miles away. I passed my Driving Test early on in the tour and for duty was issued with an Army Landrover. Even the RSM of the Battalion was housed within these terraced houses. Accommodation for marrieds was as usual so difficult to come by. Chris deep cleaned all issued furniture in the quarter to find a biro-marked suite, stained mats, stained mattresses. We had this lot withdrawn and purchased our own furniture. We were not prepared to live like tramps.

We fulfilled the character role one evening when we attended the 'Tramps Ball' in the Sergeants Mess at Pudsey Headquarters. The RSM Andy Morrison, ex-RSM and WO1 of 2 Para, who was on his final posting and eventual retirement, gave Chris and me a lift to the Ball. On the way and in his Wolsley 2200 large car we called at a garage for petrol. The garage owner didn't like the look of us in the dark and called the police. Our Tramps' costumes were so convincing that we had some explaining to do as to what we were at, before being allowed on our way.

During this tenure of appointment at Leeds, my Mother, Alice and Father Tom had taken over a public house in South Ossett. 'The Crown Hotel'. Father had completed over 25 years in the police force to retirement. We were lucky as Mum used to come over on the bus and babysit occasionally to allow us a night out.

103

Whilst at the TA I used to shepherd the new recruits at Battalion Headquarters, usually on a Thursday Drill night evening, in to see Doctor Gibbons for their first medical. 'Gibbo', was the Registrar at a Leeds Hospital and also held a military rank of Major. One evening as I escorted a recruit in to see him 'Gibbo' asked me why 'I' was limping? Within three days I was taken into Chapel Allerton Hospital where he as Registrar sorted my knee out and made me immobile for three weeks.

I was to meet Gibbo on many occasions during the years he held the rank, eventually of full Colonel and he was Chief Trauma Surgeon in Northern Ireland. When that evil woman Bernadette Devlin was shot in Northern Ireland, Col Gibbons actually saved her life. He told us afterwards that he had no option under the Medical Oath that he had taken. The only pleasure, he said, whilst operating, was that he wore his PARA TIE. We used to meet on the drop zones, usually on Salisbury Plain, to cover Unit parachuting. Me as a Captain or Major DZ Safety Officer, he as medical cover with his team.

I remember only being in a 'Flap' just once at the TA. I had in my second year drawn from the Battalion Paymaster in cash, the bounty for C Company to be paid by me at the Drill Hall in Brighouse, on one Thursday evening. I had arranged to meet the Company Sgt Major Laurie Marsden and the CQMS Ernie Southwell in 'The Stotts Arms' on Wakefield Road a half mile from the Drill Hall, to let them know that I had arrived, by Landrover and to sink a swift half pint before paying out the Bounty. Well we had the swift pint then left in our own transport. When I arrived at the Drill Hall I went into my office to find the pay sheets, then realized I had not brought the briefcase full of cash with me up the stairs. In effect I had left my briefcase in the PUB! I rang the Landlord immediately!

Sid said, 'You left a briefcase here, I have it behind the bar.' I drove there and back post haste, over £2000 the richer. No one knew but me!

Bahrain, Persian Gulf 1965/66. Accompanied Tour.
Travel to and settling in.

With a couple of months to go to the end of Tour at 12/13 Para in Leeds, I was fortunate to be telephoned by WO2 Reg Melladay D

Coy, 1 Para. He asked if I would like to be posted to return to 1 Para, and if so would Chris and I wish to be added to the marrieds list to go to Bahrain on the forthcoming accompanied Tour. The couples to go had been placed in a draw as only 94 couples were to travel owing to accommodation restrictions in Bahrain. There were no married quarters and accommodation would be taken up through private contractor already arranged. Reg said that he and his wife Margo had won a place in the 'raffle' draw but that Margo wished to stay in the UK. Reg kindly offered Christine and me their place. So back to 1 Para.

We left Aldershot in November '64,(leaving 12/13 Para had us take up a short tenure in the new Waterloo Park until the flight to Bahrain). The flight was memorable! By Britannia Aircraft from Gatwick we took off, flew into a flock of birds and had to land at the RAF Station Airfield at Lyneham in Wiltshire. There we stayed one night in transit accommodation. Off the following day we landed to refuel in Cyprus where all passengers including Christine, four year old daughter Tanya and I sat on our suitcases at the side of the run-way whilst another suspect engine was given an inspection then all clear. Finally we took off to land at RAF Murharrag near Manama in Bahrain. The Battalion advance Party administrators then saw the married families off into their rented accommodation.

Our flat was part of a small complex called ZEERA buildings on the outskirts of Manama, the capital town. We had an upper two-bedroom flat, spacious entrance hall, sitting room with external walk on balconies, private stairway entrance and an upper flat roof access to washing lines/sunbathing, also an adequate kitchen. The flats, of which there were 12, were built around a paved garden looked after by Ali, the gardener! The children loved him. Outside the walled complex there was a fair sized lake to one side, full of exotic water plants and terrapins. There was ample parking on hard earth roads around and nearby a small supermarket type shop. The flats were air-conditioned and although the humidity was very high being on the upper storey often allowed us open windows as we caught the breeze. Settling in, I was allowed a few days off before reporting into Camp some 15 miles away! (The old familiar Hamala Camp which I knew well familiar with, having done part of an earlier tour there in 1962).

I purchased my own transport to allow me to get there. An ancient Ford Consul for the princely sum of £75.

Drinking water by water cart was 3 rupees a gallon, the same price as a gallon of petrol. A pint of delicious king prawns was the equivalent of £1 Stirling.

Tanya, aged four, was enrolled into the local 'Sacred Heart' Kindergarten School and what an excellent school it proved to be. She had a friend, Alison Beale, mum Katie, father Sgt Beale, the family believe it or not were neighbours at Pegasus Village, Aldershot when we all lived there. Other near neighbours also here in ZEERA buildings were Violet and Jim Ferguson,a Cpl in 1 Para.

Down town Manama was and still is an eye opener. One could choose the very best of materials: silks, English cloth, linens, cottons and have a dress made up in two days, a suit made up in a week. Desert Boots made up to the shape of one's foot in a morning. The Souk (Market) really was something with fresh produce. The jewellers held Bahrain fresh pearls. Gold 18 carat was cheap as were gold rings and even dollar pieces. Supermarkets were to be found and most meats, lamb, pork, beef were sold in frozen blocks; of the highest quality.

Once settled in and with some time off for families, the Sheik of Bahrain, Sheik Isa, made his private beach available at Thompson's Beach. On a Saturday/Sunday, if one was lucky with a weekend off, his staff used to serve coffee and cakes at four person beach tables.

There was much to see on the Island. The Dulman or Graves Area was a vast acreage of Medieval Burial Grounds. There was a zoo to visit with an Old Portuguese Fort and exotic gardens, even a giraffe that accepted bananas from children. Manama had a Port where one could contract a party to take a Dhow trip or fishing. There was a 'Malcolm' social club at RAF Murharrag. Within the Battalion Camp at Hamala there were Officers, Sgts and Corporals Messes, and a tiled swimming pool, a Naafi bar and restaurant, a camp cinema and stone-fronted, all denominations, church. An open air cinema and open air theatre. There were also soccer, tennis, quoits and volleyball pitches. The camp was improved year by year with Royal Engineer help and all ranks labour.

By 1965 all ranks when in Camp and in Bahrain lived within and ate within air-conditioned Tynham Huts with concrete floors

106

laid, the huts were built in sections by Company groups, usually in the cooler evenings 5–7pm. Each construction exercise was called a 'Windmill Exercise'.

With families to consider, life took on a five day a week routine in Bahrain. Company groups were of course sent on Operations from Bahrain, in particular to Aden, the nasty flashpoint within the Persian Gulf and also on roulement tours, usually of six weeks duration, 'Up Country' to thwart communist and terrorist infiltrations to the Gulf States. In Bahrain with time off, the marrieds used to invite the singles to curry lunches and in particular at Christmas to Christmas Dinner. Our usual guests were Sgt Reg Melladay, Sgts Bobby Hainey and Ron Lewis. Skip Attree and Freddie Blake, all unaccompanied Sgts living in Hamala Mess. Sgts Aussie Fotheringham and Barry Andrews were same Company friends.

When Chris and I attended Mess Nights in Camp we were never short of baby sitters. My platoon soldiers used to love to come down to have supper, a couple of beers, music and somewhere private to write their letters. We had two regulars, John Carey, who eventually became a WO2 and is now, in 2013, the President of an association Past Members Club. The other, a small 5'6" Lancashire lad who Tanya thought was a gnome. He had a shaved head and was called 'Baz'.

The Commanding Officer, Lt Colonel John Graham, with a leaning towards the theatrical and a real concern toward families, his Battalion Group and the real welfare and wellbeing of his soldiers, was a most remarkable CO. He took over the Oil Group AWALI Theatre on the odd occasion and had officers and soldiers enact scenes from, 'The Battle of Waterloo', 'Life on the Somme' etc. At Christmas he persuaded all ranks to put on the Production, with lighting, costumes and many rehearsals leading up to the two-night spectacular, of 'Paraella!' Putting the UK 'Cinderella' to shame. The wives featured of course. Christine became a harem dancer, with yasmak, flimsies and pale blue knickers, flanked by Katy Beale and Valerie Cross, the Armourer S/Sgt's wife. The three did a Harem Dance. The Second-in-Command was the little Devil, all 5'6" of him (Major Benjamin). The OC Sp. Company all 6'4" was the Good Fairy, complete with Boots and Tutu. Sergeant Major Alec Covey featured as did the Doctor. The production ended with a chorus line of 12 of our wives in high heels, short shorts and white mess jackets doing a routine that could have graced the Palladium.

The off duty 'Toms' loved it. The whole hour show, with narrative from our Irish Pay Sergeant John Motherway, an interlude and music throughout by our Regimental Band, was a hit. When the girls came on of course 'Toms being Toms!' about 600 of them started yelling. The Provost Sergeant was going ballistic to the 'Toms' yelling 'GET 'EM ORF'.

Operations in Aden and Dhala 1965/66

The Battalion of course was an Operational one and 1Para were a part of MIDDLE EAST Command. My particular Company Group complete with 3" mortar sections from Support Company, Heavy Machine Guns, Anti-Tank Weapons and our normal Rifle Company Platoons were flown down to Aden to land at RAF Khormacksar then onward by 3 tonner or helicopter to the inland bases at Thumier or Dhala. There we took over platoon defended positions at 'Monks Field', 'Hotel 10' and Cap Badge.

D Company Group, my company, carried out 3 x 6 week Operational tours at these locations. One in Aden Town and two up Country at Dhala and Thumier where there was an airstrip. Beverley Aircraft could also get in and out on the shortest of runways 2 miles from Dhala Town.

We usually took over sanger fortified positions from previous Para companies or from Royal Marine Commando. We defended Aden Town and the Emir of Dhala and citizens from incursion from the North, from the Yemen which was Communist supported. Now of course, as then, Muslim Terrorists are still fighting the West.

Vehicles were drawn from Ordnance Parks in Aden and so the Company Group was mobile. From Aden Town up to Dhala was a 12 hour horror drive. Rising from zero to 7000 feet, on tracks bulldozed over years by Pioneers and Royal Engineers.

The first tour in Aden Town saw us cordon and search the vehicles and pedestrians on the main thoroughfare **Malla Straight**. Over one hundred vehicles were turned over and 600 pedestrians. As a result No2 and No5 of the Egyptian Intelligence Service were caught when a pistol was found on one of 'em on a shake down.

They were flown out from Aden. On one vehicle patrol in Malla, I had our driver chase a gunman into a laundry where, having hidden, he gave himself up and was securely tied to my escort Cpl Ghani to be taken under arrest back to Radfan Camp Headquarters our temporary base. Radfan Camp was a tented camp holding two Regular Infantry Battalions to the north of the Town. In there, Patrols in the area of 'Sheik Othman' stopped incursion from the North.

We as lodgers had tents, camp beds and sleeping bags and were fed when within their base. Our Company Commander Major Rick Oddie was a hard taskmaster, we patrolled and searched as no other and he was sent for by the C in C, Admiral Le Fanu, one day for a 'Pat on the Back'. The week after, we were sent up country as being too hot for Aden Town. The Civil Servants and Staff had received complaints! We were, however, the only Company up country where the C in C elected to stay overnight. I had to find sheets for his sleeping bag. His RMP Escort and Heli Pilot could not believe it when, on a morning visit to the Company and having been WALKED around the Company Positions of Monks Field, Hotel 10 and Cap Bridge, he said that he was to be picked up the following morning.

He and Major Oddie got on well, Oddie being a 'Soldier's Soldier'. He had as a Subaltern boxed for the Battalion. His answer once to a Platoon Commander who complained about his Platoon Sgt over training, was for the OC to say, 'Take him around the back of the hut and sort it out!'

Out of Aden to Operations up Country. '65

The Company Group having patrolled Aden Town for ten days and tipped the place over, the Powers that be decided that we would be better employed up country 70 miles to the north, and as a sister 1 Para Company were to be relieved, we were to occupy the defended areas at Monks Field, Hotel 10 and Cap Badge. We were to secure the Camel Train routes through the Danaba Base Area and show the Militant Hill Town villagers that the area was still a British Protectorate. Tribesmen were to be vetted making their way on these routes *en route* to Aden Town

109

In Radfan Camp in Aden and whilst the Company had been there I was acting as The Company Quartermaster Sergeant. Arranging all supplies, mail runs, vehicle re-fuelling etc. The Coy normal CQMS was on leave in UK when D Company was warned of the move up country, a seven hour drive to stage through Habilayn/Thumier, currently held by the Scots Guards. I was to remain in Radfan Camp on the Company move out at 5am and leave for Habilayn later by helicopter from Khormaksar RAF Airfield. Collecting any mail. Then I was to arrange for water supplies and hot food with the Scots Guards to be provided at an RV immediately outside their camp and *en route* to Monks Field.

All went to plan. The dusty convoy was met and fed. I then joined the Company HQ on their two hour remaining drive to Monks Field. The Company settled in, took over the other two defended locations at Cap Badge and Hotel 10 and the sister company left for Aden on the same transport. The next day saw the OC. Sgt Major and I tour the three positions on foot, a total distance of about seven miles. I then took off on the PM supply helicopter to Thumier/Habilyn and to live in the Scots Guards Camp under their protection for the next month.

From the Ordnance Park at the same location I was to arrange and have delivered all supplies for the Company HQ and platoons usually by helicopter once a day or by Beaver aircraft: ammunition, mortar rounds, foodstuffs, canned and fresh rations. Fuel and even, condoms for putting over weapons flash hiders, (keep the dust out). 'Not for camel shaggers'.

I shared a tent in Habilayn Camp with a Warrant Officer Knibbs. He had been sent up country for a break from his normal duties at the Military Prison in Aden, Fort Morpath, where the Aran dissidents normally ended up. Knibbs spoke perfect Arabic. So much so that one evening whilst we were sitting outside our tent we saw local Arab workers passing something under the barbed wire fence surrounding the Unit Naafi Tent where they worked, the Arabs having walked up and along the adjacent camp airstrip. Knibbs hearing their conversation in the still air said, 'They are passing cartons of cigarettes'. Out of the tent I went on the 'blind' side, to the Scots Guard Room to have 'em nicked. Meanwhile up at Hotel 10 things were hotting up!

110

Aussie and the Camel Piquet

'Hotel 10', a Platoon defended location, was on a rocky outcrop overlooking a heavily tracked crossing point where camel trains and the odd beat up truck would pass to and fro, usually on the way to Aden. The crossing point below was manned during the daylight hours by a section who used to search the odd animal train or vehicle. They were usually in position by 0600 to find groups of Arabs waiting.

One particular morning when the section and part Platoon HQ, Sgt and the Signaller, were on their way down the considerably steep slope, it was all too deserted. The Platoon Sergeant, a canny Australian and ex-Korea Vet who had joined the British Airborne for a career change, smelt a rat! Sgt Aussie Fotheringham clicked onto the fact that there were no waiting Arabs at the crossing point. He ordered the searching section to take cover. They did so and he held them for 20 minutes. Down below, as expected, the piquet area disappeared, the result of a large explosion! Aussie held them for another half hour and sure enough, up went a second explosion! An hour or so later the first Arab transport was seen and life returned to normal.

There was a sequel, as two days later through the piquet area came a couple of Arabs who were not local. We had a local Arab on strength so to speak and he bubbled them.They were taken to Company Headquarters at Monks Field and through the persuasive powers of the Company Sergeant Major the OC and an interpreter, and with a little help of a 33 electric detonator up the nose, they sang a merry tune. They were transported to Fort Morpeth Jail in Aden Town.

Normal life in Bahrain and an extraordinary experience

Returning to Bahrain from Aden, we had time off, before taking up normal training with the family; Chris and I and five year old Tanya, made the very best of the Sheik's Beach, small zoo and the beautiful flowered area of Thompson's Beach.

Being a powerful swimmer my best enjoyment was in the water.

111

Off from the Sheik's jetty I left the girls with friends for them to take up the offered coffee and cakes at the sandy Beachside. The Sheik even then must have had some kind of closed circuit TV, as one Saturday morning after more or less three visits during the week, I was approached by Mohammed, the Sheik's aide. He asked me to accompany him to the Sheik's beachside bungalow, and there to meet the Ruler in person. Sheik Isa asked me why I never took coffee and cakes served at the tables to families and why I was always in the sea. I answered that I came to the beach to swim, to snorkel, to see exotic fish and even the sea snakes. I cheekily remarked on his speedboat! No propellers but water impellers, and hinted that I would enjoy water skiing behind it. The result was Mohammed fixed it for me and weeks later we were invited with close friends to the Sheik's private pooled bungalow a few hundred yards up the coast. We in future visits met the Sheik's other friends from the Awali Oil Complex and were into an opulent world that we never knew existed.

A Private Visit to the Sheik's Palace

The Ruler of Bahrain, Sheikh Isa used to attend battalion parades, band concerts and the like, in his honour. He was, in our eyes, pro Brit, pro West, otherwise we would never have been allowed into his country. He had a son being educated at Cambridge and he himself spoke perfect English. Occasionally for all his wealth and power, he would surprise the odd officer or soldier out and about. One of our attached RAF parachute Jumping Instructors 'Jess', on his own during one Saturday morning, was seen by the Sheik admiring his horses in the Sheik's stable paddock. He questioned his interest then asked him in for lunch.

Christine and I, together with Tanya and friends Vic Beale and his wife Kate and Dick and wife Terry Thorne were all at Thompson's Beach one Saturday morning, and for once I was seated, drinking coffee and eating cakes! Mohammed came along to issue a surprise invitation to the six adults to visit the Sheik's Private Apartments in the Ruler's Palace on the following Friday evening at 7.30pm. I informed the Commanding Officer, Col John Graham. He said, 'Go along, you will love it! Rosemary and I have already been. He will

112

give you a guided tour of the State Apartments.'

In our battered cars we turned up on time at the Palace car park. We were met by Mohammed and staff, shepherded in, offered drinks, whatever requested, introduced to the Sheik, he in casual Arab dress, white and gold, we in light weight suits, the girls in cocktail dresses. We were escorted into the most fabulous Buffet Area where the Sheik's Cook grilled or barbied our individual steaks. The choice of eats was fantastic, from sea food to sticky cakes, the tables groaned.

The Sheik explained that what was displayed would feed his household throughout the weekend. We as Guests were to have first choice. We sat around as music played, the latest UK hits. The Sheik spoke of his son in Cambridge, photo albums came out and he told us of the recent visit of HM the Queen and Prince Philip. When he called her 'Liz' it put me off a little.

He then showed us around the opulent rooms of his private apartments. There were glass cases around exhibiting gifts from Rulers around the world. Christine seemed to make a particular remark when seeing an ornamental Ivory Powder Box. The Sheik motioned to his aide to give it to my wife. We were told by the aide that we could not refuse to take any gift offered as it would be an affront to the Sheik's hospitality. We left the Sheik's presence about 10.30pm astounded. What an Arabian Night to remember. The girls were given a gift of a necklace of real Bahrain fresh pearls with earrings to match, gold mounted and chained. Our elder daughter Tanya wore the set on her wedding day. I was presented with a gold Omega watch as were the other male guests. Our present to Sheik Isa? A 'Max Miller' long playing record! It creased him!

Aden/Dhala. A second visit of D Coy 1 Para

It was early December 1965 and the Company flew down the Gulf from Bahrain to take over from The Royal Marine Commando at Dhala Camp. A fortified *Beau Geste* defended area of about two acres with stone walls, sangers with overhead cover, gun pits and a Claymore mined exterior.

We were there to look after the wellbeing of the Emir of Dhala and to escort the Political Agents, contractors and the like when doling out the UK cash on the provision of new wells, agricultural projects and the like. The Aden Federal National Guard was in an adjacent Camp and they also sent out patrols to stop the ADOO, or dissidents from the Yemen, from infiltrating South. This was the second six-week tour that our Company had copped, the other rifle companies having only carried out one Operational Tour.

It was rumoured that our OC. Major Rick Oddie was not smooth enough to give presentations in the cinema in Awali of Famous British Battles. Rick talked through his nose being an ex-boxer.

Anyway, here we were and the Company soon made its mark. Assistance was requested from the RAF to site an anti-tank gun on a pimple some 300 feet above and just outside the camp perimeter. This proved too much for the boys in blue and the Wessex Chopper, so the OC had the Company heave it up using Toggle Ropes. We were well above 5000 ft.! Once up there the OC had it test fired as it covered the main hard earth road, Dhala to Aden. The anti-tank crew was delighted to be given the order to fire this weapon to zero in. It had a 0.5 spotter round with an incendiary tip. When this was ON target, then the main hollow charge shell could be released.

Most of the Company watching this spectacular show saw the spotter rounds blipping through the air across the valley some 800 metres to just below the Dhala Road. The OC decided that he wanted to see the effect that the main charge would make so he gave the order to 'FIRE'. Eight hundred yards away a part of the Dhala Road disappeared. The explosion was deafening in this silent valley. Percussion reverberations. Hot foot into camp the next morning came the British Political Agent. He forbade this weapon to ever be fired again. The expensive Lyncrusta ceiling within the Emir's Palace had detached itself and lay in heaps on the floor.

We had cause to have a second visit from the Political Agent at the end of our second week! The OC had decided to set up a strong fighting Patrol of half the Company, complete with general purpose machine guns and light mortars. We were to patrol the rocky villages to the north with visits into and around their stone dwellings. We were sure that no Brits had patrolled there before.

The OC., CSM., I as one of the Platoon Sergeants, one other and about 60 Toms made up the party. We were to be out for five days. On the fifth we were to be picked up at an RV in a Wadi, arranged with the 2 i/c. Keeping to the High Ground and well above 4000 ft. we found the villages. Crops and goats, sheep and donkeys on the man-made terraces. We made our presence known, visited dwellings, searched store areas and had coffee with some of the elders.

At night on the highest ground with sentries out and alongside stone sangers we waited for an attack. The OC insisted on the Union Flag being flown on a collapsible pole before last light and as he said, 'The buggers know we are here, if they think they can take us, well, come on.'

We were out of communication with Dhala base after two days, which caused the Political Agent to have ducky fit, not knowing where we were. Nevertheless, all would have been fine but for a cock up on the return journey back along the Wadi, pre-arranged. Three by 3 ton vehicles with escorts and a Landrover with an armed party had met us on time and at the right RV and off we drove back to Dhala. Twenty or so in each floor plated, sandbagged floored vehicle. Tail boards down and hanging. Soldiers alert, weapons facing outwards. When – BOOM.

The idiot RASC driver of the Headquarters vehicle that I was in had not followed the immediate tracks of the vehicle in front, had cut a corner and this vehicle had run over a planted Mark 7 mine with its rear wheel. Our 3 tonner was blown onto its side, we were all thrown out. The rear wheel and axle disappeared, as did the tailboard. Small arms fire to no effect came in from the hills some 800 yards away. No-one was badly injured, all were treated back in Dhala Camp except for the OC, who apart from wandering around immediately was taking snaps with his posh Agfa camera whilst the Toms dived for cover; he was found to be suffering from amnesia and was choppered to Steamer Point Hospital in Aden for treatment.

Two days later I caught the mail chopper to visit the OC to see to his needs to find that the bugger had discharged himself and he actually beat me back to Dhala. The Political Agent was more than a little peeved not to have known where we had been. Word did filter back though as it was impossible to visit these tribal lands and villages without being 'clocked' all the way. Word had it though that we had been where Brit Patrols had not been before.

115

Bill and the Leakers

The Company Quartermaster Sergeant this time being on the sick list and back in UK for treatment, I was given the Admin Appointment as the Senior Sergeant, the others being Sgts Hainey, Andrews and Fotheringham. Reg Mellady was still the CSM.

Inspecting the ammunition stocks one day in the Sanger store I found a box of leaking 36 grenades. No problem when found as the detonators were stored in a metal container separately. The grenades however could not be primed and thrown and should be disposed of. I told the OC who agreed the plan to take the grenade box and contents a good half mile from camp and explode the lot with the use of 1lb of gun cotton, a 1oz primer and a length of safety fuze.

Carrying the grenade box and explosives did not leave me much option for a personal weapon when out of our defended camp so I armed myself with a 9mm pistol. I took with me as escort Cpl Bill Millington, bloody good shot and a soldier that I had known for years. He took a 7.62 rifle and spare magazines.

Off we went warning the sentries and all, of the explosion to be within the hour and having found a reasonable area I set up the grenades, the explosives and cut off a length of safety fuze. Now this fuze burns within 27 to 33 seconds a foot, so giving us a couple of feet, I lit the fuze and we retired behind a set of rocks to shield us from the blast when the lot went up. Bill and I were looking at each other when I said to Bill, 'Where's your bloody rifle?'

He said, 'I left it near the grenades when I helped clear the ground!'

He made a move to go retrieve the rifle but I grabbed him, we waited! Probably the longest 20 seconds in his life. With our fingers in our ears, off went the explosion. 12 grenades, 12 primers, 1lb Guncotton, 1oz primer.

On viewing the site there was a large hole in the ground. The Rifle? All woodwork had disappeared as had the magazine and contents, but the metal of the stock was there as was a bent barrel. The flash hider was split and we found a return spring. We legged it back to camp! Escort? What bloody escort? Bill paid for the Rifle. Well 75%.

116

Dhala Prison Visit

Whilst at Dhala, the Emir invited us, the officers and senior NCOs to visit the local town prison, where as well as the usual dross, political prisoners were held.

This stone built fort with inner square keep was medieval to say the least. I would guess that the massive outer wooden door with wooden windlass lock would have been centuries old. The prisoners that we were allowed to see were held in communal rooms, there were no individual cells. The individual cells were built within the keep. Evidently where 'The hard men' were held. Prisoners within the communal rooms were chained to metal bars set in the walls. They were a good sleeping space apart and squatted or slept on the hard packed earth. No uniforms! They were dressed in we guessed what clothing they came in with. They must have been escorted for meals or ablutions as we saw no sign of buckets, bowls or eating utensils.

One prisoner stood up as we entered and made a move to speak. A guard battered him. Our OC 'Major Rick Oddie' said, 'No, let him speak.'

The man had the balls to say, 'One day, Major, you will be in here!' He told us that there would be a revolt against the Emir when the British eventually left (as there was two years later in 1967, on the withdrawal from The Aden Peninsular). He said that he, the prisoner, would be a part of the eventual new Local Government. The OC asked him where he had learned such a command of English? The prisoner said that he was Adenese by birth, had emigrated and lived in BIRMINGHAM, England and had now returned to Aden to take a part in the uprising!

Our tour did not last long as we were not allowed elsewhere but we did admire the fortification building works and security. The Company Commander was allowed to take photographs during our tour and these would have been a best seller to any geographical magazine. Unfortunately on arrival back in our camp he found that he had left his lens cover on throughout! – Damn.

117

Dhala Tour over, Vacation and Tragedy

On handing over our defended camp and area to the next roulemont company, our six weeks at an end, we were to move out from the Dhala airstrip by Beverley Aircraft. The staging post was to be at Al Dhimna before our onward move to Bahrain.

Our Company Commander Major Oddie, task-master as always, made the decision that the support element of the Company Group with 3" Mortar Section, Heavy Machine Guns and anti-tank guns and crews *would* travel by air together with remaining stores for our survival, weapons spares and ammunition and myself as OC the Party. The aircraft would appear at the airstrip late afternoon.

In the meanwhile, the bulk of the Company, the rifle sections would 'march' or patrol the route Dhala to Al Dhimna, an estimated journey of some six to eight hours, through 'Bandit Country'. This Company Patrol was to end in tragedy and the Company's Tour would not end unscathed.

En route, one shot from the hills, unseen, unspotted, caused the death of one of our private soldiers, Pte 'Bertie' Gray. A bullet through the head. This travelled on and as the troops were on a hillside at the time, struck another soldier Pte Glimstead, and lodged in his back. (Ever since, Glimstead wears the head on a chain around his neck).

Radio contact with HQ Aden caused a helicopter to be dispatched to the scene where the dead and wounded soldiers were casevac to Steamer Point Hospital in Aden. The Brigade Commander ordered the Company to return to Dhala Camp and to patrol no further. (A step too far).

I was fortunate to be in on the airwaves conversations, as I was in the Operations Room at Dhala having been monitoring the whole move during the morning and awaiting for air news of the aircraft. So the Company returned some hours later to a prepared scoff and water of course. The Company Commander spoke to the whole Company of the loss and circumstances. I took the Support Element etc. to the airstrip as planned, for the pm Beverley Aircraft and set up at Al Dhimna our transit accommodation. The very next day the remainder of the Company were to travel, but this time by AIR, as originally planned by Headquarters Aden Brigade!

118

Pte Gray was buried with full Military Honours in 'Silent Valley', in Aden, but has since been repatriated back to his home town in Scotland. Aden now of course being a part of the Yemen. Given up under a Labour Government in 1967.

"Out of the Blue" – return to Aden

After the six weeks or so in Aden and up country Dhala the Company returned home to Bahrain. I joined the Company at Hamala Camp, cleaned weapons and sorted the stores out and then late Friday afternoon saw myself free to travel home to Zeera Buildings and to Chris and Tanya, there to enjoy at least one long weekend at home, the beach and possibly to the Mess. The marrieds, of which there were but few, accompanied within the Company, had actually been given four clear days off.

On arriving home I was in for a surprise! Chris was busy with tea and biscuits for a male visitor, the Adjutant, Capt. 'Birdie' Martin. He didn't mince words, as the Captain of the Battalion Swimming Team and an excellent swimmer in his own right, he said:

'I have come to see Chris to ask you both to agree that you return to **ADEN**, Monday next for two weeks with the Battalion Swimming Team. We want to win the Middle East Swimming Championships. You are our best butterfly swimmer and we need you.' He realized that I had just spent six weeks away. The decision rested with Chris! (No pressure, honest). As a result Monday morning the Battalion bus picked me up for the Airport. I joined the Team. We won the Middle East Swimming Championships – I swam butterfly!

Journey Home from Bahrain 1966. Manama – UK

Even more eventful than the journey out a year previously from Gatwick, when on take-off we flew into a flock of birds and had to divert. What this time? Well, the Company was powerful enough. The Chalk Commander was a Senior Major, with his wife, the CO was also on board with his wife and the Paymaster (always a good sign) and a sprinkling of Sergeant Majors to keep the 'Toms' happy. I hate to add, all Royal Airforce Flights are dry! Baby food and pop excepted! Oh and tea, in plastic cups.

119

We had been flying for a couple of hours or so when we heard 'This is the Captain speaking. No cause for alarm but I am about to close an engine down.' On our intended route over the Alps we would have to divert. 'To save us inconvenience later on in the flight, I am now going to divert to Istanbul where the engine will be inspected. The flight will spend the night in hotels in Istanbul.'

We ended up with the singles in one hotel, the marrieds in another. The CO told the Paymaster to, 'Fix it', with regards to local currency and we all enjoyed two nights in Istanbul. Taxis by day to the Souk. A happy stopover was had by all. The Aircraft Britannia's duff engine was replaced.

The reason why the Captain had told us of the engine shut-down he knew, was because unlike modern aircraft, we the passengers would have seen that the PROPELLERS would have stopped on the one that he shut down. Better that we knew! And why.

Family Recollections Aldershot 1966-67

Christine, Tanya and I returned to Aldershot from Bahrain during early 1966 and took up residence in Oak Court, a newly built block of flats on military land but as near to the centre of Aldershot Town as one could possibly get.

Aldershot's two main cinemas were just across the road and M&S beyond that. Through C/Sgt John Motherway the Battalion Pay Sgt who had a weekend job at 'Days' Motors of Fleet, we were able to purchase a Morris 1100 car in British Racing Green. This allowed us to get out and about more and we went often, during weekends to Windsor and by the river, to Wimbledon to see Uncle Stan and Aunty Hilda, to 'The Donkey' at Elstead for Sunday lunch and when finance allowed to Yorkshire to see both our parents.

It was a fact that if we had £5 on a Friday evening we could journey north through Windsor, Slough, Uxbridge, Watford to Hatfield to join the A1 (£2.50 for petrol, £2.50 to spend over the weekend at either of our parents pubs!) The Fox and Hounds at Shafton orThe Crown Hotel at South Ossett, the pub my Father had taken over on retiring from the Police Force.

During a weekend visit to Aunt and Uncle at Wimbledon we made time to call in at the Battersea Dogs Home. There were the

120

number of dogs in the home the day of our visit as days of the year 364! Information from a kennel maid. We were taken up by a lovely brindle Cairn Terrier who had only come in that day. About two years of age it took an instant shine to our pigtailed daughter Tanya. It just had to be ours. This Saturday morning there was some kind of a photo-shoot going on at the Kennels and a lovely photograph thereafter appeared of Tanya with the dog in the 'Aldershot News'. We had to wait seven days before we could take possession of the dog, in the event of the real owner turning up and then on payment of a fee of £25. The dog we named 'Whisky' was ours. It was certainly a 'town' dog as on the first walk we ever took it on in Wellington Avenue, Aldershot, it went barking mad when it saw its first TREE. We had 'Whisky' for years where it even used to duck dive for pebbles in shallow streams.

So we had an addition to our family! Unknown to us at the time within 12 months we were to have another! A baby girl Trudy Amanda. We always said the product of a lovely holiday in Devon and Cornwall having borrowed a Bedford Motor Caravan in the summer of 1966 and taken with us plentiful supplies of Somerset cider.

During this year Father came down on the odd occasion to stay with us and to watch the Battalion Boxing Team on its prowess towards the Army Boxing Finals. He became a welcome visitor to the 1st Battalion Sergeants Mess. Sister June was an occasional visitor as was Christine's brother Keith, and we had a rare visit from brother Ian.

It is fair to say that when back in UK the Battalion often had extensive periods of leave, sometimes up to four weeks duration. Quite rightly so, as when off on four, six or annual Operational tours one would work seven days a week and often a 12 hour day.

However, in Aldershot with four weeks leave and having done the rounds of relatives, golf and gardening, coastal trips on weekends and the river, there was time to earn a little money. The place to go was SIMONDS BREWERY at Reading. Casual labour was taken on starting on the Monday at 7am – for the week. The 'Recruiting' office when one turned up at 7am preferred to take on Service Personnel on leave, this was well known. Payment in cash was made at the end of each day, a very handy arrangement. With friends, we used to make up a group of four: Reg Melladay, Vic Beale, George Brown, sometimes Ken Dawes. We went in all departments: Bottling Plant, Brewing Dept, Barrel Line, Dispatch. What a happy band were we. The longer the day, the merrier we got! Well there was free beer on tap. By 5pm no-one wanted to go home. Reg Melladay and I even volunteered for the odd Saturday morning to empty and clean out the Barley Wine Stainless Steel Pipes.

Other employment in vogue on this, 'Moonlighting' was to be taken on by the demolition contractors knocking down the old Victorian buildings in the Aldershot Military Town, as the New Montgomery Lines was taking shape. This was instantly curtailed though on Brigade orders as a result of the Brigade Commander seeing tiles being thrown from the roof of an old Officer's Mess, and the soldier chucking the tiles to be the RSM of the 3rd Battalion. This figure had stood up, between throws, and SALUTED!

As a young family we were lovingly looked after by our parents, remembering the time, during a week's leave, without notice, the journey was made to 'The Fox and Hounds' to find Christine's mother, Lois, about to take off for Blackpool on a week's break with two of her younger children, Philip and Susan. Mum had us go with them to an Aunt's Boarding House, that morning. At no notice Philip actually slept on a 'Put U up' in a broom cupboard. As well as the normal Blackpool delights, the Tower, the Piers, the Pleasure Beach; Mum treated us to a super sea-food extravaganza at 'The Blue Parrot' Restaurant.

Promotion and Progress, Change of Employment. 66/67

During 1966 word came through whilst at Albuhera Barracks that I had passed the 1st Class Certificate of Education. This I had sat whilst in Bahrain. It was required for advancement to the rank of Warrant Officer. In the meanwhile and probably as a result of the work I had done as a Sergeant but in the appointment as Company Quartermaster Sergeant in Bahrain and Aden, here in Aldershot I was promoted to Colour Sergeant. The rank is usually that of an administrator but can be that of an Infantry Patrol Commander or Platoon Commander.

On promotion, for a short while I was, within 1 Para, posted to

122

Patrols Company to take up Malay and Signalling, First Aid and Ambush Tactics. The Company under Major Joe Starling, Captain 'Birdie' Martin and CSM Middy Campbell was training for Operations in the Far East. During extensive SAS type patrols in The Black Mountains and the Brecon Beacons over some days and long distances carrying heavy loads, it was found that my previously operated on right knee would not stand up to this severe punishment.

Interviewed by the Commanding Officer back in Aldershot, I was to relieve Colour Sergeant Kennedy of A Company on his posting as a Warrant Officer to the Lincoln TA Company. I therefore became the CQMS of A Company 1 Para. Taking over from the elderly, 'Nuff Nuff'.

Jack Kennedy was quite a character! Nicknamed 'Nuff Nuff', because he had always had enough of this, or enough of that. He had been in 'The Royal Welsh' during World War II and on the wall behind his stores counter he proudly displayed his citation of a 'War Wound'. Beautifully framed, behind glass, maroon border. I read it one day and it said, 'Grenade splinter, left buttock'. I jokingly told him that he had been running away! He went ballistic. We very nearly came to blows. I vaulted the stores counter and shot out of the door.

Jack ran a tight stores and his word was law; he didn't often slip up but when he did things could be spectacular. The Company had a night parachute descent onto Hankley Common and we had to meet them with breakfast at a pre-arranged RV. Jack told me to meet him at the RV by my own transport, he would have breakfast in containers in his ¾ ton Landrover, there was no requirement for me to come into Barracks as his storeman L/Cpl Linsey would help him. He wanted me there though to show me his way of feeding the Company in the Field.

So Jack's idea was of course to distribute the food from thermos containers, Landrover in a camouflaged re-entrant. Troops called a platoon at a time. Mess tins available but no noise. The Platoon of thirty or so lined up in the early morning light before the container lids came off. All at once.

I had the first Platoon all ready lined up, mess tins ready when Jack whipped off the lids. We were standing behind containers of sausage and beans, bacon, fried bread and eggs. There was no

123

activity, except within ten seconds, Jack belting the storeman. They had forgotten the ladles, serving forks and serving spoons! Jack rolled up his smock sleeve and dished out the sausage and beans by hand! No one laughed! Until I borrowed a couple of alloy airborne mugs to take over from Jack's hairy hand!

We were to meet again a couple of years later but that is another tale. When Jack, having parachuted in Aden, on training, had cause to pull the red handle on his reserve parachute, his main having had a malfunction. I was in the Sgt's Mess in Radfan Camp when Jack in 'Rambo' attire came into the Mess and threw the Reserve Red Handle behind the Bar. 'That's it,' he said, 'I've had enough.'

Change of Employment Pre-Aden Tour 1967

Early 1967, I was warned for a six month unaccompanied Tour of Aden in The Persian Gulf to cover the withdrawal. This was going to be a rough one but right up our street. However, on the 15th February whilst the CQMS of A Company the OC Major Farrell informed me of a PM interview with the Commanding Officer LT Col Mike Walsh. The CO had a surprise in store for me. I was to be posted into Headquarters Company and to the Motor Transport Platoon to assist the MTO, Capt Jeff Banks to run the MT during the Operational Tour in Aden. The MT Platoon would have a REME Light aid detachment and a Squadron RCT attachment as enhancements. The present CQMS administering the MT Platoon was found to be unfit to travel as he had developed stomach ulcers. Capt Banks had made the request to the CO for my posting and the CO had agreed.

Unknown to me then and certainly never thought of as a possibility for the future, after the Aden Tour I was promoted Warrant Officer, and then staying with the MT I took over as Motor Transport Officer of the 1st Battalion from Captain Banks, who was to be appointed Quartermaster. I held the appointment for a further two years, as the first Warrant Officer MTO ever. Having never been a, 'Petrol Arse', I was of course to attend an MT Sergeant's Course of eight weeks at Bordon in Hampshire. The Course was run by the Royal Corps of Transport Experts. It was true to say that after their expert tuition within two months I became a driving instructor, could take instructional lessons on various vehicle parts, the clutch etc and I passed examinations on fault finding and vehicle recovery. I even managed to win the Cross Country Driving Competition and this against Sgts who had been MT employed for most of their service.

The induction exam at Bordon was something that neither the Chief Instructor nor I will ever forget. I went into a room, sat in front of a 6 ft table on which were placed 20 items of vehicle interest (parts of).

The Chief Instructor said, 'Ok, Colour Sergeant, reel 'em off left to right.'

I said, 'I haven't a clue except one's an inlet or exhaust valve.'

He said, 'You are joking!'

I said, 'This is my first day EVER, in the MT world!'

He said, 'We have never failed yet! See you this afternoon.'

Thereafter during the working days of March, April and early May I travelled backwards and forwards Aldershot to Bordon, a half hour journey. Often of course staying nights at the Instructional RCT School.

Christine was busy being pregnant, Tanya at vital moments was cared for by Airborne friends. All was quiet until Sunday 7 May when I took Chris into the Louise Margaret Maternity Hospital in Aldershot. Taking Christine in at 1445, Tanya went to stay with 'Aunty' Sylvia Brown. The dog Whisky and the goldfish went to Aunty Val's. I then went back to the MT course and accommodation at Bordon for 9.30pm.

The next day Monday 8 May I telephoned the hospital from the Bordon MT School at 0745 and 1345 and then at 4.45pm when they told me that our second daughter had been born at 2.30pm. Calling in at Odiham on the way for flowers I managed to get to the hospital for 7.45pm where Chris was blooming. I was allowed to see Trudy our new daughter an hour later (much deliberation over name!). Then on the way back to Bordon and the MT Course I called into Aunt Sylvia's to let Tanya know that she had a baby sister!

Christine and Trudy came home on Thursday 16 May from the Maternity Hospital. I had been able to collect Tanya and Whisky the previous weekend from Aunt Sylvia's for a Saturday afternoon to

125

Frensham Ponds.

Finished the MT Sgt's Course at mid-day Friday 26 May. Saturday 27 May saw us as a family go to the 'White Swan' and Forresters, having walked Tweseldown with the dog. After lunch at home we went on to Queen's parade to the Horse Show, then at night I took Tanya to the Fair. Sunday was lunch at home, we stayed in at night. Trudy had a restful night, so did we.

Monday saw me leave for London and a VC10 TO Aden..

A Double Tragedy. Home and Abroad. June 1967

On the morning of the 5th June 1967 I was awakened within the tented lines of Radfan Camp, Aden by Captain Jeff Banks the MTO of the Battalion. He was my immediate boss and had during the night been given the awful news of the death of my Mother, Alice Godwin aged 51.

Mum had been killed as the result of the aircraft in which she was travelling running out of fuel whilst attempting a landing at Manchester Airport. The aircraft, a Douglas DC4 Airliner, was on charter to British Midland Airways and had been returning from the holiday Isle of Majorca. The aircraft had left Palma Airport at 5am local time and crash landed into the Hopes/Carr area, Stockport at 10am local, the 4th of June.

Travelling with my Mother was Christine's Aunt Mrs Elsie James, the landlady of The Three Horseshoes, where Christine and I had our marriage reception in1959. Aunt Elsie was also killed. The two Landladies were on holiday together as a welcome break from public house duties. The previous year they had been on holiday together to Capri, with Christine's mother Lois, on that event.

By pure good fortune Christine's Mother was not on this flight on the 4 June as leaving the 'Fox and Hounds' for a move to private accommodation had caused her to cancel this holiday to Majorca. Seventy-two people lost their lives in this disaster and only 12 survived, including the Captain who did a wonderful job in bringing the aircraft down on waste ground. The whole episode has been documented in a book by the Author Steve Morin, entitled 'The Day the Sky Fell Down'. The air crash has come to be known as 'The Stockport Air Disaster'.

Capt Banks had awoken my tent companions before awakening me at 6.30 and Ted Blundell the Signals Platoon Colour Sergeant and George Cook the Officers Mess Colour Sergeant had already disappeared when Capt Banks explained the Signal that he had received through the MOD in London to inform me of Mother's death.

What was not known to anyone was the fact that younger brother Christopher was also serving in ADEN as a Master Chef with the Royal Engineers in 'Little Aden', a half hour drive from where we were at Radfan Camp. I explained this to Captain Banks and to my ever grateful memory he put his Landrover, driver and escort at my disposal that morning for me to go see Christopher and break the awful news. I was also allowed time off all Operational duties to get my thoughts together over the next couple of days. Battalion personalities were all so kind, in particular the Padre and Sgts Mess Members.

My CO. Colonel Mike Walsh and the Chief Clerk fought at all levels to get myself and Christopher out of Aden on an indulgence compassionate flight back to UK for Mum's funeral and of course her two sons to support Father.

The Ministry of Defence back in London would only grant ONE compassionate seat on a return aircraft. Even recommendations from the Brigade Commander fell on deaf ears. Christopher and I therefore decided that he should return to support Father as I had seen both Mother and Father such a short while ago having only been in Aden for less than a week, having arrived here on 31 May.

Christopher had been in Aden a few months. So Christopher returned and I wrote letters to Father, Granny and Granddad Walton and Mum's sister Aunt Hilda.

This system of granting compassionate leave and travel arrangements had a profound influence on me in later life when as the Duty Field Officer at Berlin Headquarters I would move heaven and earth to assist soldiers of all ranks suffering in tragic circumstances.

THE INTERNAL SECURITY OPERATIONS
IN ADEN 1967

During the 60s as mentioned before, the Battalion was forever in and out of Aden in The Federation of South Arabia. Things of course really came to a head in 1966 when the then British Government (the Labour party), foolishly let it be known that all British Troops would be withdrawn in 1968 from Aden. This gave the two main Arab factions in Aden - The Front for the Liberation of South Yemen (FLOSY) and The National Liberation Front (NLF) - the Green Light to be visible contenders for political power from the announcement of the withdrawal in 1966.

FLOSY thereafter switched its efforts to a campaign of urban guerrilla warfare within Aden itself and the NLF provided troops for training its guerrillas in the Yemen, North of Aden. British troops now found themselves not only fighting these factions in the towns and areas of Crater, Tawahi, Ma'alla, Sheik Othman and Al Mansura but they were now subject to bombings, snipings and hit and run attacks on a daily basis. British Troops were also tasked to keep the two factions apart. A thankless task as 'Piggy in the Middle'.

1 Paras' task within Aden Brigade housed in a tented camp at Radfan Camp, North of Aden Town and on the border with South Yemen, was to deploy into the towns of Sheik Othman and Al Mansura thereafter to dominate, keep the peace and stop guerrilla incursions from the North. The Battalion took over the police station in Sheik Othman at the main crossroads and sited an OP. It of course became a favourite target. 'Checkpoint' Golf at the north end of the town and a position known as the Mansura Piquet, staffed by Para Companies, all came under fire after deployment by automatic weapons, grenades thrown and mortars fired. In no little time the Battalion fortified all positions by sandbags, concrete and sangers.

'Fort Walsh', as it was known was set up by the Commanding Officer Colonel Mike Walsh in Sheik Othman to be the dominating feature in the town. Literally thousands of sandbags were filled and transported from Radfan Camp over three days to make this vital OP position secure. (It was formerly a Mission Hospital). Messages were passed by the Mosque Tannoy system in Arabic to the guerrillas on the ground and even the Minaret was used as a firing point but the Battalion soon put paid to that.

A week after the Battalion had occupied these positions in Sheik Othman a general strike was declared by both FLOSY and the NLF. This cleared the streets and enabled the Terrorists to carry out co-ordinated attacks. 1 June saw an attack on a Patrol outside the Mosque. The OP opened fire, killed those terrorists, the patrol captured a fourth. All patrols were fired at during the day. OPs rocketed and the Battalion lost a soldier and another wounded. One OP had to be evacuated under the protection of C Sqn the Dragoon Guards with their Saladin Armoured cars. By 2100 hrs the whole situation had been brought under control and Sheik Othman was under Battalion Control.

Throughout June, July and August the Battalion OPs and Patrols were never free from attack. It can be said that the Battalion gave as good as it received and many terrorists would never again see the light of day.

On 24 Sept 1 Para handed over its positions in Sheik Othman to the South Arabian Army. Thereafter the Battalion withdrew to a position two miles north of Radfan Camp, thereafter to establish a defensive line called the Pennine Chain to protect the Camp and the nearby Khormaksar RAF Airfield.

During the first week of November the South Arabian Army declared its support for the NLF. On 27 November 1 Para embarked by air from Khormaksar Airport, seen off by 42 Commando Royal Marines who then left by ship from Aden Harbour.

My recollections from the main base at the Radfan Tented Camp was the never ending administering task to keep vehicles on the road and to supply the Battalion's Companies, positions and OPs with its vital supplies of ammunition, food, water and stores items. I was the Motor Transport CQMS and worked directly with the MTO Capt Jeff Banks, the RCT Squadron Sergeant, Brian Jones, his OC Lt Paul Miseroy and ASM Daniels of the REME whose repair team kept all vehicles on the road.

It was no joke to be out with a 3 tonner full of jerry cans of fuel in the Aden environment. Sod's Law sometimes prevailed as Colour Sgt Jack Kennedy found out when taking out **VITAL** stores one evening to a Company OP in Sheik Othman. At the main crossroads his Landrover was grenaded, vehicle overturned and driver killed all to deliver a 2lb tin of strawberry jam! Marked as Urgent over the radio by coded message!

Jack was to have one more narrow squeak. The Battalion had recourse to aircraft rigged for parachuting and Jack decided to do just one more descent before retirement into Civvy Street and to his civilian/military appointment as RQMS to the Lincoln Company T.A. This was two weeks before his final flight from Aden to UK.

In Radfan Camp, through the grapevine we had heard that during the morning jump and in dire need, Jack had pulled his reserve parachute! Most of us were in the tented Mess at lunchtime when Jack marched in, threw the reserve handle against the Mess bar wall and shouted, 'Fuck It, I've had enough!' (Some say that he had never let go of the handle since he pulled it!) Those of us who could, saw him off two weeks later happy to call it a day. Around his neck was the 1 Para Tie of Merit as a final accolade.

The main Radfan Camp was never attacked, mainly because it was not in a populated area and had the sea and Aden Gash Pit bordering on two sides and short sparse scrub on the others. The whole camp being wired and with sentry sangers at vital intervals. The Camp in area was about the size of three decent sized soccer pitches. It was a fact that within the outer perimeter Gash Pit area there lived an elderly Arab woman the 'Toms' called Annie. She lived within a makeshift 'House' of cardboard, carpet, netting material and scurried about all day after the Gash Wagons from Aden Town.

Our medics seemed to more or less adopt her and sometimes when driving past would throw her parcels of food. Well it takes all kinds to make a world and one of our off duty soldiers having had a couple of cans of Tennants one early evening decided to pay Annie a call. He was out through the main camp gate during daylight, bearing gifts. On his return, in the hours of darkness and not having properly booked out within an armed party of four, he decided to force his way through the Camp perimeter wire. He seemed to have been hung up at a last obstacle by the crutch when making more noise than necessary he was promptly shot through the chest by an alert sentry. He, a medic – did survive!

On the phased withdrawal from Aden, Camp stores holdings and vehicles were in the main to be handed over in situ to the South Yemen Armed Forces. The Battalion's mainly mined plated soft skinned vehicles, were to be driven to Khormaksar Airfield and were then to be handed over to a Government Agent to be sold there and then through the wire, a temporary exit gate, to any happy Arab owner for £100. This of course pissed off the Motor Transport Platoon which was in no doubt that these vehicles would find their way into enemy hands.

Such was the discipline and orders having been given that all vehicles had to be prepared for handover with full servicing and parts changed where necessary. As the MTO Capt. Jeff Banks had departed for UK to set up things for the Battalion arrival it was left to me as his second-in-command to have all vehicles prepped, driven to the a airfield and to be lined up in rows behind a large hangar adjacent to the 'Sales' gate.

My remit was then to have each vehicle with keys left in to be driven to the gate, handed to the sales agent, an RAF Officer who would actually conduct the cash sale. This I did, with a small number of 'ferrying' drivers and two REME fitters.

All the vehicles made it through the sales gate and were seen to be off up the coastal dirt road! With their Arab drivers! We wondered though how far?

Never underestimate the skill of the MT drivers and fitters when armed with screwdrivers, fine sand, water and a knowledge of what makes a vehicle un-roadworthy!

I cannot leave the memories of the final tour of Aden without telling the story of a remarkable event, the proof of which is housed within the Regimental Museum. One of our soldiers under fire in the Sheik Othman area took aim and fired his 7.62 rifle at a terrorist on the ground. At the same time, the terrorist fired at Cpl Ken Yoeman. The terrorist bullet head entered the barrel of Yoeman's rifle, split the flash hider and lodged side by side within the barrel, causing it to bulge (two bullet heads, one going out, one in). With the impact Yoeman was knocked on his back but otherwise unhurt. He was at one time in earlier years in my section and in my platoon. A super soldier and on this occasion a very lucky one.

Aden Tour 1967 and Final Withdrawal
Combined Services Entertainment CSE Shows

Performers who come out from UK to entertain troops really are unsung heroes. They are often housed in tented accommodation, hotels are usually out of the question and they perform in hostile areas, not free from attack. During 1 Para tour of Aden North we were visited by Bob Monkhouse, Tony Hancock and their supporting acts and dancers. The Bob Monkhouse stage was a boxing ring lit up by 3 tonner vehicle lights. He proved to be the quickest wit on two legs. We managed to build a makeshift stage for Tony Hancock and as many of the soldiers free from Piquet, patrol or guard duty as could be spared, attended.

Afterwards we entertained him for supper and drinks in the Sergeant's Mess at Radfan Camp. It was to be one of his last live performances before he went off to Australia where he fell ill and died.

On the bill that night in our camp was one Sylvia GODWIN! I got some stick as the 'Toms' thought that maybe we were related! Sister? Aunt? She was six feet tall and built to match in a skimpy costume that showed off all her assets. She was to give a performance as a 'Strong Woman'. Bending 6" nails with her bare hands, tearing up telephone directories and bending iron bars around her neck. The hairy arsed PARAs were invited onto the stage to straighten out her mangled ironwork and to tear up the Telephone Books – all failed!

God bless modern artists who give up their time like Catherine Jenkins, Jim Davidson etc.

1 PARA RETURN TO UK
Sporting Prowess 68/69

After the six month Tour in Aden and the withdrawal, whereby the CO. Lt Col Mike Walsh earned his DSO and the RQMS Tom Foster who acted as Quartermaster earned his MBE, the Battalion took up once again its sporting achievements.

The 1st Battalion had always been a sporting Battalion and in the 50s and 60s won the Army Cross Country Championship no less than eleven times. All the runners ran for their respective Counties. Sergeant Gordon Burt, later to be Major Burt MC was even an Empire Games Runner. The Battalion had a great athletics rivalry with the Cheshire Regiment when the 1 Para won the Army Athletics.

After Aden and within the year 1 Para were to win both the army football and the army boxing Major Unit Titles. We had however an absolute shortage of boxers in the heavyweight division. The upper limit for parachuting being really about 13 stones, 7lbs. So it was difficult to find a big lad to compete with those boxers from say, 'The Guards Battalions'. Our boxing trainer, Colour Sergeant 'Jones the Punch', trawled the Battalion and came up with Sergeant Barry Longbottom. Apart from milling in the ring for two minutes on selection he had never been in a boxing ring in his life.

Nevertheless for the honour of the Battalion and to earn one point for competing at the weight, Barry was prepared to give it a go. Of the eleven bouts to a match it was two points scored for a win, one point for a loss. One point could be vital in a drawn match. So Barry Longbottom went under training, was gutsy but really had no idea of the noble art of boxing. No-one at that time knew that 1 Para had drawn against the Irish Guards.

The match was held in the Military Boxing Centre in Aldershot, an old large Victorian building packed to capacity that night with the Battalions, 'Toms' and 'Micks', and officers and sergeants resplendent in Mess Dress. Barry was to fight one of the two Maginty Brothers. Both ABA finalists and the heavyweight the current Army and Commonwealth Champion.

Barry entered the ring sheepishly and looked as though he shouldn't be there. Maginty entered to a fanfare, a roar of approval and visited the four corners of the ring, soliciting cheers. He was 16 stones 4lbs and 6'4" tall. The referee called both boxers to the centre of the ring, the announcements were made whilst Barry watched the floor. The Irish Guardsman watched the crowd. Both went to their respective corners and the bell went. Maginty was still half turned and waving to his supporters as he was coming to the centre of the ring when Barry having shot across the ring at the bell hit him. Left/right, flush on the chin with 15 stones of pent-up fear.

The Irish Champion never got on his feet for a minute; the doctor was in attendance, seconds in the ring. Barry was like a jumping bean. The verdict was announced, LONGBOTTOM wins by a KNOCKOUT. The Irish were dumbfounded. 1 Para ecstatic – two POINTS!

Motor Transport Officer 1 1968 - 1971

At work one morning at Albuhera Barracks, Aldershot the MTO Capt Jeff Banks slid back the partition between the offices and asked me to come into his office for a confab. When I went in there he was sitting on the radiator under the window. 'Sit down,' he said.

'Where?' I replied.

'In the chair,' he said.

I said, 'That's yours.'

He replied, 'Not anymore, you are now this Battalion's Motor Transport Officer. I am taking over as the Battalion Quartermaster! You know where I am if you ever need me.' With that he picked up his briefcase and left.

The Commanding Officer Lt Col Walsh DSO sent for me that morning, promoted me to Warrant Officer and appointed me as MTO for the Battalion for the foreseeable future: The first Warrant Officer in modern times and certainly within the Brigade to hold the appointment. 2 and 3 Para Battalion MTO's were commissioned Captains. Later that week the Brigade Commander sent for me and re-enforced the appointment and mentioned that I had to let him know if any Commissioned Officer gave me any hassle! I must say in hindsight that no officer ever pulled rank or caused me any grief and I was to hold the appointment for over three years.

I had the most professional MT Platoon. The three tonner drivers won the SE Area Driving Championships, the MT drivers were all-terrain men and heavy drop riggers and the REME vehicle mechs and stores staff were first class.

During the next three years we were to support the Battalion with transport in UK, through France, Germany, Denmark and into Northern Ireland. We drew up vehicles in Canada on Exercise Pond Jump East, dispatched and recovered vehicles from Iceland.

The stalwarts that come to mind are the two Dixon Sergeants, Reg and Mick, Cpls Linkman and Fry the Details Clerks. Ned Sparks ex-

WWII and Stores accountant. Brian Hughes the REME Sergeant, Don Ellis former REME and now MT Stores and fountain of all knowledge MT.

I attended an MTO Course at Beverly in Yorkshire. I was already a driving instructor whilst qualified on the previous MT Sgts Course at Bordon in Hampshire. The qualification of MTO however gave me the authority to issue 'Pink Slips' as a driving examiner to those soldiers having attended the Battalion's six week driving course, who at the end, qualified on test as capable drivers. The MT driver then of course was able to drive a civilian car and exchanged my 'Pink Slip' for a Civilian License. I had a yardstick for drivers to be sent to me by their companies, no use sending me a below average soldier as you would get him back when qualified to drive your OC.

I had a most happy tour as MTO and indeed was to take over again years later, this time commissioned. In between times I was to be the Company Sergeant Major of Headquarters Company, the Regimental Quartermaster Sergeant of 1 Para. Then the Regimental Sergeant Major of 4 and 2 Para and of The Regimental Depot in Aldershot.

1 Para Visit to Mourmelon France & The Foreign Legion Visit to UK

The Battalion in the 60s, exercised with the French Army, with the Foreign Legion Paras who also visited our barracks in Aldershot, played us at soccer and rugger and had sterling nights in the Mess. We also exercised with their tank units at their base in Central/Southern France.

Our Battalion's transport went from March Wood, the RCT Port on the South Coast, by ferry. Around Paris however towards Rheims, by convoy packets, shepherded by a most efficient French Police Force. Motor Cycle Police at EVERY crossroads, blowing whistles to keep our convoys at maximum speed. The Battalion had two weeks in France. In off exercise moments we visited the First World War Museum at Verdun. Horrific, with the Museum built in hollow square around a preserved WW1 trench system, as it was at the end of the war.

We also visited the Champagne Cellars at Rheims and Eperney

135

and drank the French Sergeants' Mess dry one evening in two and a half hours.

When the Foreign Legion Battalion came to us in Albuhera Sgts' Mess in Aldershot, we had a night to remember. After a cracking curry supper and wines we were into the Mess games, Rugger, Tug of War, 'Out on the Bottles', and even Darts. Our RSM and the French equivalent Adjutant Chef called us to order in the Mess large ante-room and a large blanket was laid on the ground. We, in Mess Dress Blues were ordered to remove lanyards, collar badges, wings, and Warrant Officer and Sergeant Badges of rank. This took some little time as stitching had to be removed by safety blade! All accomplished, every item was thrown onto the blanket. The French did likewise with their accoutrements from their Mess Dress.

All Mess members then lined up, one pace from the blanket. French North/South, 1Para East and West. At the blast of a whistle blown by the Adjutant Chef all members would dive onto the blanket to retrieve a trophy. On the second blast from our RSM, all members would come off the blanket and all would hold up their trophies! Theirs to keep! In seconds it was mayhem. Apart from collecting a black eye I collected a lanyard with a brass ferrule at the end.

Later at the bar, wearing our new insignia or trophies I was approached by an old French Warrant Officer to inform me that I had won his Dien Bien Phu, Battle Honour (My God, the holy of holies). Tears were running down his cheeks as he spoke to me. I offered it back, but he would have none of it! 'Fair combat, on the blanket'. It hung in the bar of my Father's pub, The Crown in Ossett, for many years.

The liaison with the French Paras endured for a few years in the 60s/70s until the idiot De Gaulle who always had an axe to grind with the Brits, pulled French Forces out of NATO.

Canada 1969: Exercise 'Pond Jump East'

The First Battalion had an Exercise in Canada in forest and swamp areas, not only hard living but fighting the black fly! The main Base when off the training area, was a tented camp with a few permanent Mess, toilet buildings named, 'Petersville Camp' twenty miles north of the large Canadian Military base at Gagetown. We called on the

136

Military Base for transport facilities and I,as MTO, regarded the whole exercise as a costed one, accountable on return to UKLF Headquarters.

In the meanwhile, apart from controlling the MT, I acted as Main Base Warrant Officer working with our Quartermaster/Camp Commandant Major Jack Crane. We even set up the Mobile Bath Unit, water from the Creek, through a heating shower system. Gungy Toms in at one end, clean Toms out the other, all paddling through on duckboards.

In the camp one afternoon, the Battalion being out in the main on training, I was called on to deal with one of our attached ACC Cooks who had thrown a wobble on canned beer and local wacky baccy obtained from the part time local mess hands. When I got to the tent lines this clown was prostrate outside his tent, gripping the grass and shouting that he was going to fall off the Earth. Approaching from behind, the size 10 boot into the crutch soon brought him into the land of painful living. On entering and searching his tent I found that with a cook's knife he had stabbed a cat to death within. The cat was one of the rodent chasers, or had been.

The very next day I put the cook in front of the Battalion Second in Command Major Epplestone charging him with, 'causing unnecessary suffering to an animal'. Eppy fined him £40 and ordered him to bury the cat that I had produced in a plastic bag!

The area of Canada that we were in was New Brunswick and bordered the Bay of Fundy. This bay has the highest tides in the world. The town of St John that I visited on Saturday had a unique phenomenon, the view of the River St John, from the town's bridge saw in 12 hours, the river running both ways. Out to sea in the Bay of Fundy and inland to fill the inland lakes. Over 40 feet tides!

In the evening from the Camp it was not unusual to go out trout fishing. One evening after a 20 minute hike through the surrounding woods with the local fire chief, he took me to a creek with a dammed up Beaver Pond and we caught 14 brook trout in 20 minutes on silver paper!

Brown Bears came to visit the Camp gash pit at intervals and when the Toms were in Camp it was not unusual for them to feed the bears loaves of bread, by hand! Soon all bears for miles around were coming to PICNIC and we had to forbid the practice on Unit orders.

When we first arrived at Petersville Camp I had a work party erect the Sgts Mess Tents within what had been an orchard area. A parallel row of tents, entrances inwards with the Regimental Sergeant Major's tent at a little distance away as befit his rank! On seeing the position for the first time, he wanted more space so we had the tent and duckboards moved 12 feet.

During the first night of occupation his tent was entered and he was awakened by a drumming on his duckboards by a most irate PORCUPINE! The RSM had encroached upon its sleeping patch. The RSM took up his camp bed and sleeping bag and sought solace within the Mess. We moved the tent the next day!

At the end of the Exercise period the whole Battalion was allowed four clear days off before returning to the UK. Some Toms even went into the USA, as far as New York.

I had plans to canoe the St John River from Mataquack Dam, some 70 miles away, down toward St John. WO2 Beveridge was to come with me on the trip as we had on loan a 20 ft aluminium canoe from the Gagetown Forces Gymnasium. With one day to go, Hugh Beveridge pulled out through ill health. It was too late to get anyone else to take his place so I decided to go it alone.

The Motor Transport 3 tonner dropped me off and using a double paddle (i.e. two taped together) the journey began. I canoed down river, in parts it was over 600 yds wide, river traffic was often seen of log booms being towed by barge.

To keep me going I had a 10 day ration pack, water cans, primus stove, sleeping bag, mossy net and bug cream. Suit and tie and shoes in a plastic bag. Two bottles of Scotch and a case of beer. The first night saw me pitch camp on an island in the middle of the river with cattle for company. I slept under the canoe with a machete.

The second day and afternoon saw me walk a jetty to a camp landing where having bought fruit I was invited not to hang around as the camp was a late summer one for Girl Guides aged 14 to 18. The Akela saw me off.

I canoed into Fredrickton Harbour on the St John River in the early evening and found to my delight the Fredrickton Militia Mess. Rather like the British Territorial Army, the Sergeants Mess Steward was, believe it or not, 'Ex-Black Watch'!

I was invited to stay the night in the Mess, leaving the Canoe in

138

the Yacht Club in the Harbour. It was Saturday night, there was a dinner/dance on and I was made more than welcome by their RSM and his charming wife.

The next day saw a full day's paddling once I got off, and camp was made in Oromocto Park some 20 miles down river. Just after midnight the canoe was upturned, a light shone into my eyes and the local police paid me a call looking for druggies! I explained who I was and they knew of me as, 'The Brit Nut on the River, with the double paddle'.

On my last day before my transport picked me up in the afternoon I met the Canadian RMP, the River Police, before I had recourse to enter the Great Lakes. They from their launch invited me to spend the night at their Riverside Headquarters and camp on their lawns. This I did and was picked up and returned to Petersville Camp the next day.

A most remarkable River Holiday.

ULSTER NORTHERN IRELAND 1969. 1970-73

In the 70s and 80s a fair amount of my Military Service was spent in Northern Ireland, or Ulster as the Protestant population would have it. I had four months in 1969 when the Battalion in a Hearts and Minds Campaign was sent to keep the Peace between Catholics and Protestant factions in Belfast over Civil Rights issues. Later in 1970 to 1973 when things took a turn for the worse and the population criminal element, the thugs and terrorist factions had a murderous hatred for each other we, the Battalion and the British Army,were really up against it keeping the peace. The whole affair was fanned by the local politicians, the Protestants who wanted Ulster to remain under rule from Westminster and the Catholics who wanted Ulster to be absorbed into the South (Eire) and ruled from Dublin.

The British Army, of course, in keeping the peace between factions and upholding the rule of Law were, 'Piggy in the Middle'. The Tour of over two years 1970-1973 was an accompanied one and the Battalion 1 Para worked from the permanent and guarded base at Palace Barracks, Holywood, three miles or so out of Belfast.

Christine, Tanya, Trudy and I, as the Company Sergeant Major of Headquarters Company, took up residence at the Married Quarter within the Camp at No1 Lindley Drive, a modern three bedroom semi-detached house overlooking Belfast Loch.

Ulster was a most complex situation and still is, fuelled by this religious hatred going back centuries. History books and television programs still record the dividing differences and it is far from me to have a finite opinion. All I know is that in my years of Service there I witnessed bombings in public places, assassinations, car bombings, ambushings and the treatment of one human being to another that I never thought possible. Victims without limbs, others mangled, knee-capped, strung up with barbed wire merely for wandering into the wrong street. For me, Northern Ireland was and is a most beautiful place, destroyed by the poisonous thugs and religious bigots who live there.

In 1969 the Battalion was committed to Northern Ireland for four months and 1 Para set up company bases in various locations in Belfast to keep the peace between Protestants and Catholics. There had been shootings and intimidation from within the sectarian areas of The Falls Area (Catholic) and the Protestant Area, The Shankhill.

The local Politicians on both sides asked Westminster for help to 'Keep the Peace'. We occupied a school, 'St Congalls', a bakery 'Snugsville', a mill, a police station, 'The King's Hall' and really made a peace line of permanent bases and patrolling 24/7 by vehicle and foot through the streets. We even had a Club built by the Royal Engineers, a large wooden structure complete with bars and a disco set up. This, 'The Paradise Club', actually straddled the 'Peace Line' with an entrance from the Catholic side and one from the Protestant side. All went well for two weeks! The young people came in and fraternised. It however was not to last. The Godfathers on both sides had the place burnt down.

So we carried on and set up bars and discos within the Company positions that we occupied. A 'Frat Dance' once a week. The off duty soldiers had a ball with the local girls. After four months our Battalion Tour was over and we went back to the UK and to Aldershot.

As I remarked before, things in the late 60s were really taking a turn for the worse and the British Government were thereafter sending Infantry Battalions into Ulster on a two years' Tour basis. 'The Troubles' had begun.

140

Palace Barracks 1970-1973

The First Battalion the Parachute Regiment was posted into Northern Ireland into Palace Barracks to assist the Ulster Police and the four month tour Battalions in keeping the peace, mainly in the Belfast Area. From our permanent base we usually had three companies on permanent call. The first at twenty minutes, bombed up and ready to dash into Belfast, the second on 45 minutes. The Units in the town were not slow in asking for assistance, some, every night of their tour.

Even Headquarters Company of which I was the Company Sergeant Major had a part to play when the Battalion got stretched and we formed an armed force called 'Guinness Force'. I remember being called out to assist 'The Green Howards', who went through a rough patch in the Divis Area in town and had four soldiers shot and murdered within the week.

1 Para of course were known to be fast moving in stripped down Landrovers and hard hitting in riot situations, pick helves as opposed to soft soap so we were always a welcome answer to a down town punch up in any area.

In rotation we did have time off, with one company always off 24/7 for administration and the other training and where possible we had time off for our families and went out on private and organised trips to shopping in Belfast, markets in Bangor and days out in the 'Safe Areas', Ards Peninsular, Giants Causeway etc.

Chris and I with the girls had a favourite Loch side area some 20 minutes away in the village of Crawfordsburn. Delightful walks, a golf course and a lovely pub.

Tanya our eldest went to Holywood Junior School, a mile or so up the road from camp and a super school it proved to be. Trudy our younger daughter went to the in camp Nursery School a couple of days per week.

We had in camp excellent Messes, dining facilities, a super Gymnasium, Squash and Badminton Court facilities. The 'Toms' had a cracking well-staffed NAAFI Club and the facility of a DISCO DANCE every Thursday evening, for off duty soldiers who flocked to attend! There were Wives' Clubs, vehicle maintenance classes, sailing classes at the Loch Maint Military Base three miles away, and

141

a host of smaller activities, library etc. In all, it led to a most happy Battalion. Travel back to the UK for family was easy, by ferry Larne/Stranraer or Belfast/Liverpool. By air from Belfast or Aldergrove Airport. There was sailing in Strangford Loch, Fishing and Golf everywhere.

During my time at Palace Barracks I was promoted Regimental Quartermaster Sergeant taking over from RQMS Middy Campbell, later to be RSM WO1 MBE of the 3rd Battalion. In this role I worked directly for the Quartermaster Major Jack Crane MBE, later to be LT Col, MBE, the Regiment's Senior Quartermaster.

The Battalion Guardroom: 'Coughtrees Own'

The Commanding Officer Lt Col Mike Gray could award up to 28 days detention into the Unit guard-room for those soldiers brought before him on discipline charges i.e. absent without leave, falling asleep on duty, drunkenness etc. He of course was loath to do so as it took soldiers away from their primary duties and here their Operational duties and as members of a team each man was vital. A tough jail/guardroom regime was therefore called for whereby there would be no repeat offenders. Such a guardroom was set up within Palace Barracks by Sgt John Coughtree. He was empowered as the entitled, 'Provost SGT', to run the jail and this he did, the regime was HELL. He was ably assisted by junior NCOs who were all members or past members of the Battalion's boxing team, fitter than most and hard as nails. They were tutored by Coughtree to be mean.

The soldiers under detention ran everywhere! To meals, from meals, to and from showers, training gymnasium, work and menial tasks in and around the camp. They wore PT Kit, light battle order or on daily runs, full battle order. Outside the guardroom they wore steel helmets and not berets. The first exercise for the day and before breakfast was Log Drill. Rain or shine, wet or dry. On their backs on the tarmac of the Guardroom. Old telegraph pole pieces; Up and Down, Up and Down. Standing up, legs apart – logs, up and over, up and over. Squats with logs, knees bent – Down and up, down and up. All with helmets on.

After breakfast and much polishing and kit cleaning, it was into full battle order, pouches and packs filled with sand, within plastic

142

bags to an appropriate weight, then it was off on the morning run. Every morning! Seven days a week.

The run was known as 'Coughtree Hill'. From Barracks to the east it led up an escarpment some 600 feet towards Stormont Castle. On top the prisoners were then encouraged to make best speed down to return to flat ground then cool off by running around the Unit soccer pitches. Beasted by the mean provost staff there were no idle soldiers. As the Sergeant Major of Headquarters Company and an occasional visitor to the Unit guard room I can never recall any repeat offender into Sgt Coughtree's Jail. Once was enough!

Palace Barracks: The Thursday Nights Dance

Those base soldiers and the Company 'Toms' off duty, attended the in-barracks NAAFI CLUB DISCO on Thursday nights. The attraction was plain to see.

We had attached Arms with us of course as did every major Infantry Unit. Cooks, drivers, medics, signallers, clerks. Not all Para; we even had dental technicians. This helped to swell the ranks and for the local girls from Bangor and Holywood and even Belfast. The Thursday night disco at Palace Barracks was the place to be. The girls came into barracks and were searched by female provost staff at 7.30pm. Escorted by the Toms from the guardroom to the large NAAFI building to the bars and the disco the action was to be until 11.30pm then the girls were to be clear of barracks by MIDNIGHT. Many of the girls were regulars, so much so that when the Battalion left after two years it took with it 30 or so wives.

Chris and I did have the occasional giggle as on each evening about 10pm we walked our West Highland White 'Dougie' around the perimeter of the Unit sports pitch. Sometimes on Thursday summer evenings we were tripping over the odd body or two prostrate in the grass.

On occasions, in uniform as the Battalion Duty Officer, I had to ensure that the ladies were actually all out of barracks by midnight, so after 1130pm I did the rounds. I was as crafty as they were and in the last hour or so of the Thursday Dance I found couples clinched in farewell in the most unlikely places. Any MT vehicle was most attractive, the Unit Ambulance even more so. Behind the main

143

kitchen wall was a favourite as the wall was always warm due to meals being cooked 24 hrs a day. Gymnasium changing rooms, gym matting – all favourites. The Barrack rooms were absolutely out of bounds for security reasons, the Toms knew this and 14 days jail would have been the penalty.

Armed with a powerful torch one evening and creeping around the wall of A Company Barracks accommodation I came across a rather older woman than was usual looking at me, coat open propped against a wall, chewing gum. The Para, 'Tom' with his back to me was completely oblivious to my presence. I said to the lady, 'It is ten minutes to Midnight!'

She said, 'Let me finish!'

On this, the soldier turned and I recognised him as L/Cpl Gorgiou of A Company. The *only* Greek Cypriot soldier we had in the Battalion. He was later to be the ill-famed, 'Colonel Callan' of the Congo and to be executed by a fellow ex-Para from the 3rd Battalion. On this occasion, he had a happy evening although it did finish before midnight.

Sunday Lunch and the Sergeant's Mess

Whilst off duty one Sunday I called for a long standing pal, C/Sgt Aussie Fotheringham of four doors away at Lindley Drive. His wife Doreen, a Lancashire Lass, was the 'Brown Owl' and ran the Girl Guide Pack. She also ran Aussie!

Lunch at home at our house was usually scheduled for 3pm, give or take half an hour. The Yorkshire Puds actually went into the oven when I arrived home. Aussie and I went to the Sergeant's Mess about 1 o'clock in good form for darts, banter etc. We were onto a third pint about 3pm. The Mess telephone rang, Aussie was asked for and he came back to me after his conversation and said, 'I have to go, that was Doreen, dinner's ready.'

I reminded Aussie that he had a freshly pulled pint in front of him and that he should drink it. Twenty minutes later and as the pair of us were saying our farewells, the Mess bar entrance door was kicked open and in marched Doreen, Aussie's wife, two plates in her hands. One full of Sunday Roast, spuds, veg and gravy, the other as top cover. She came between us, plonked the plates on the bar and said,

144

'If this is where you prefer to be, eat your dinner here.' With that, she turned and marched out. Although the Mess was quite crowded, no-one said a thing.

Aussie said, 'Well, I may as well eat it!' and did.

Palace Barracks. A Colonel Worth his Salt

This was the day when the shit really was to hit the fan, and of all the fine Commanding Officers I have ever had, who else would have had the balls, the presence and the wit to carry this off. Our CO at the time was Lt Col Mike Gray, later to be General Sir Michael Gray and highly decorated. I make no wonder.

In the RQMS Office one morning at about 9am, the Quartermaster away from the Office at daily, 'Prayers' with the CO, 2 i/c. Adjt and those Company Commanders in Barracks. I had a telephone call from the Company Sergeant Major of one of the Companies. He asked me to bring over the Special Stores Arms Register. A book that I kept in a safe, as it was the register and record of every weapon held within the Unit account, in what state and issued to whom. I took the Register over to the CSM and we checked every 7.62 rifle held on his account within his Company Armoury. No rifles had been issued that morning as the Company was stood down for 24 hours. The rifles under repair were accounted for.

It became clear after our careful check that a total of six rifles had been unchained from their holding racks and were missing. There was a suspect thief as it was known that an NCO who was proven to be absent was seen to have been loading sacking bundles into his private car at daybreak. He had legitimate access to armoury keys. He was now though as a single NCO found to be absent.

Once the weapons were found to be missing and proven, the CSM and I wasted no time in informing the OC the Quartermaster and rushed over to the CO's office to give him the bad news. The Battalion think tank was assembled: Commanding Officer, Adjutant, Intelligence Officer, The Company Commander and the COs Operational heavy gang. RSM, escorts, bodyguard.

The missing corporal's history was gone into: friends, Toms, other NCOs quizzed, and during the morning the Commanding

Officer and heavy gang in stripped down $^3/_4$ ton Landrovers roared out of camp. Into the heart of the Protestant Shankhill and to a private unlicensed club went the CO and his party. There the Godfathers were told in no uncertain terms that the Shankhill would have no rest from the Battalion, from being turned over day and night 24/7 unless the rifles were returned that day.

Within three hours a coded message was received, the heavy gang left camp to a pre-arranged spot and the six rifles were back in 1Paras' hands. The CSM and I checked them back into the Armoury by registered number stamped on each weapon. All were correct.

It was rumoured that the selling price to the soldier was £750. He was and still is absent! He, as an Ulsterman has never been seen since and never on the Para net.

The soldiers' perception of their Commanding Officer went sky high after this. Higher Headquarters was never informed. Except for the absentee, now classed as a Deserter and has been for many years.

The Bangor Post Office Heist

A film should be made of this one.

Once a week soldiers were taken to RAF Aldergrove for various reasons: for flights to UK, to attend courses, to take leave and to terminate their service etc. 1 Para had a white 30 seater coach with armed escort to use as Unit transport for this task.

One Wednesday afternoon such a journey was made from Palace Barracks. There was no-one to return to the Unit Lines late afternoon and so the Military coach driver and three escorts made their way back to Palace Barracks. On this occasion they decided to make a detour, past the 1 Para Barracks entrance, and carried on towards the coastal town of Bangor, a few miles away.

They must have had a cunning plan as, at the entrance to Bangor, they pulled up at the local post office. Into the post office went two of the armed escorts, held up the lady postmistress and came out with bags full of cash, frightening the dear old girl half to death. The escorts hopped back onto the coach, the white coach reversed from whence it came and was driven back to Palace Barracks.

The postmistress being switched on, recognizing an Army 'White' coach when she saw one, rang the Military – 1 Para Unit guardroom! Sgt Coughtree the Provost Sergeant had a reception party waiting as the coach drove into Barracks. Escorts were disarmed and put straight into cells. Clang!

The Guards All Arms Drill Wing
Surrey. 6 Weeks Bullshit

Elevated to WO2 rank and holding the appointment of Company Sergeant Major within the 1st Battalion, it was decided by the powers that be and to enhance my career, that I should attend a drill course at the famed All Arms Drill Wing at The Guards Depot, Pirbright in Surrey.

Bullshit and drill for six weeks. Living in the Mess accommodation within their camp where morning inspections of each student bunk before first parade was paramount: 'Dust on Mirror', 'Unmade Bed' (where one could not bounce a coin off the cover). 'Unpolished Floor', where some students had been up early to actually 'Black and Decker' the bloody floor. 'Water in Sink' (where the student had washed his hands and not mopped up a drip).

It was then, out on parade, formed up in teaching squads and inspected: 'Boots not highly polished - Showclean!' 'Fluff on Laces – Showclean,' 'Unpressed uniform - Showclean!' 'Loose thread - Showclean.'

The 'Showcleans' took place at the guardroom each evening at 1830 hrs where the offending item or article would be shown.

The day was then spent under instruction on the Square, of usually three drill periods in the morning and two in the afternoon under the tuition and eagle eye of a Guards Drill Sergeant. Our Squad of ten students to start with, had Sergeant MacConnell of The Scots Guards as our instructor. Excellent in tuition he took no prisoners. He had previously taught at The Mons Officers' School.

Over the six weeks we were taught each movement of foot drill within the Drill Manual and after three weeks we were then taught how to teach! I can still remember the pre-amble to each drill lesson, even after 40 years:

'Squad,' 'Squad Chun,' 'Squad, Stand at Ease,' 'On my Word of Command - Stand Easy!' 'Relax the body and look this way!' 'Stand Easy.'

147

'I am now going to teach you, "The about turn in quick time". The reason that this movement is taught is to enable an individual or body of men to turn 180 degrees without first being halted.'

'Continue to look this way and I will demonstrate the movement!'

It is fair to say that after six weeks I could have taught the golf swing using different irons this way.

We the students were taught the protocol of Pace Stick Drill, Rifle Drills, Funeral Drill. Quick and Slow Marching. Various parade formations i.e. Muster parade, forming Hollow Square, dressing, forming divisions, two ranks from three and three from two. The course, on the feet and knees was most demanding with all the constant pounding on the tarmac square.

Our Squad Senior Student and Royal Signals Warrant Officer soon left us and the course when putting his back out on the third day whilst, 'forming two ranks from three!' He was carried off the Square on a stretcher. Yours truly was then made the Squad Senior and had thereafter to help tutor a Malay overseas student who spoke no English.

We were assessed half way through the course on our personal drill, then at the end of the course on our teaching skills. I came away from the drill wing with a 'B' Grade. Remarkable for a muscular Para.

The course was to stand me in very good stead in later years in my appointments as the Regimental Sergeant Major of 4 then 2 Para, then that as Senior RSM at the Regimental Depot, where I was instrumental in the presentation of New Colours, the parades for Royal Visits and the burial of a Knight of the Realm and of Senior Generals. one, our ex-Para Brigadier.

For the Guards Instructors on this course I had great admiration. The Senior was WO2 John Ford, a Coldstream Guardsman with an excellent sense of humour. My own, Sgt Al MacConnell, helpful, smart as a button stick and, although we had been near neighbours in married quarters in Aldershot, pre-Northern Ireland, we became firm friends when we all lived in Cyprus as retirees years later. He with his charming wife, Laurie, and daughter Julie on many visits from the UK. We lived in the hills north of Limassol in the village of Kalo Chorio, they a few miles out of Paphos on the west coast. We met up frequently.

On the Drill Course, we did have our lighter moments. The Sergeant's Mess held a lively weekly dance usually on a Thursday evening. The Drill Sergeant's wife, a lively bird, used to dance the sore legs and feet off the students. The birds came from miles around as a ritual. What an excellent Mess.

A couple of Saturday mornings we were, as a course, invited to take part in the Guards Depot Drill Parade for their recruits. The parade was conducted by their Senior RSM, aptly named, 'The Blade', who stood on a rostrum in the centre of the main square and had recruits, permanent staff and our course march and circle around him like ponies at a circus, all exercises to the beat of a drum. We had never experienced anything like it. One daren't laugh but it was so comical to us senior ranks. After half an hour and before we marched off my inner cheeks were bleeding with suppressed laughter. Billy Smart's Circus had nothing on this one!

RETURN TO ALDERSHOT 1973.
Salamanca Park Mons Barracks

After a hectic Tour in Northern Ireland the 1st Battalion returned to Aldershot and took up accommodation, not within the old lines but at what was formally the MONS OFFICER TRAINING SCHOOL. This used to cater for short service potential officers, Sandhurst being really for career long service or regular cadre officers. From 1972, ALL OFFICERS were to be trained at SANDHURST. The barracks, stores and offices easily accommodated the single officers, NCOs and Toms of our 1st Battalion.

The family, Christine, Tanya, Trudy and the Dog took up residence within Salamanca Park, modern army housing on the outskirts of Aldershot Town – 400 yards away. 364 Salamanca Park. The Mons Barracks were a mile's walk away. Once the whole Battalion had returned from Northern Ireland, initially the Quartermaster Major Jack Crane had remained there to effect a handover of Palace Barracks to the next Unit. Jack and I used to walk the mile to work together. I used to, 'call' for him, from his quarter in Knollys Road. We were a formidable pair walking the Queen's Avenue on the way; as idle soldiers failed to salute Jack, the Major. Iit was up to me as a Warrant Officer to admonish them of

149

the error of their ways, 'Soldier!! Come here you idle man etc. etc!' After a time the Queen's Avenue seemed to be devoid of soldiers between 0830 and 9 o'clock! I wonder why?

As I have remarked before, Major Jack Crane MBE remained in Northern Ireland with his team to effect a handover of barracks and I as the RQMS came back with a small party of senior ranks to take over the barracks, buildings, furnishings and officers' and sergeants' messes. The Officers' Mess had all the trappings of a previous officers' training establishment and there was within some very smooth furniture.

The very first Saturday of our occupation those of our Subalterns and junior officers who had returned to Aldershot christened what was now their Mess with a riotous party. I was to find out on the Monday morning following, when at 9 o'clock I arrived for work and in the office I found the Officers' Mess long standing Manager waiting for me! He was in bits and so upset. He asked me to go over to the Officers' Mess to view as he put it, 'The debris!'

In the main opulent dining room the highly polished 19th Century tables had been pushed together to form a runway to a large Victorian ground floor window, open to the flowerbeds. The idea after dinner on the Saturday evening must have been to mount the tables, run through the glassware and table trappings and dive through the windows one after another, as a carousel. The idiot diners no doubt achieved their aim but what they could have never known was that all the dining tables had been refurbished at 43 Command Workshops at great expense and before our Battalion's occupation. I took one look, told the Mess Manager to arrange for immediate repairs with PSA and pick out the chards of glass from the table tops before collection, and I rang PSA for them to raise all charges to the Officers' Mess Account, the Battalion being back during the week. I then telephoned the Brigade Major as there was no senior officer of 1 Para yet back in barracks.

To my absolute surprise, within the hour the Brigade Major attended the Mess together with the Brigadier. Neither was amused. The bill raised, within the four days that it took to refurbish the tables came to £750. It was paid for in total by the idiot diners who caused the damage. I was not popular for raising such a bill but it did set the tone.

150

One officer did come to see me about his bill a couple of weeks later, when the whole Battalion had returned and we all took well-deserved leave in the UK. It was a Friday evening about 5pm in my office when this irate captain just had to have 'Words' before he drove off to Scotland in his smooth car. 'Short of Funds' so he said, thanks to me. His words were, jumping into his car outside my office,

'Well, Fuck you then RQMS.'

He started the car, rammed it into gear and then yelled as he waved the stubby gear lever at me, through the open car window,

'Look what you have made me do now!!'

I went back into the office, came out and gave him a garage breakdown number, local on 24 hour call. The Captain and I, by the way, are still friends.

Mons Barracks 1973. The RSMs Farewell

WO1 RSM 'Dinger Bell' had been with the Battalion through the tour in Ulster and now back in the UK, he had come to the end of his two year tour and had indeed been selected for an officer's commission. It fell to me as the next Senior Warrant Officer in the Battalion to arrange his, 'Dining Out'.

At a Mess meeting within the Mess, which I chaired, it was decided to have a formal Mess Dinner, in Mess Dress, on one Friday evening. A stag affair with all Mess Members present including attached arms, about 75 of us in all. Dinner half past seven for eight: Toasts, short speeches and a suitable farewell present to be handed over. A stripper was to be engaged to entertain and focus her attention mainly on the RSM.

The dinner went off as planned and the wine flowed. Dinger gave an excellent speech and he actually received his Officer's Commission that evening, so at midnight he left the Mess then knocked on the door in Captain's Mess Dress and asked to be allowed into the Mess as this time an ex-officio member. Permission was granted and we all assembled in the large Mess ante room to form the seating into a semi-circles to leave an area for the stripper to perform her 2 x 5 minute slots.

She came with a, 'Minder' and he heard me brief the members

151

that everyone should remain seated and that there would be no touching 'unless invited'. The lady was an absolute stunner. As she disrobed she threw the bits and pieces to the 'Minder' who stood to one side. We had seen a good four and a half minutes of what was a glorious performance, to music, and dance. The Mess went wild with applause throughout. At the finale the lady chose to turn her back to us, bend over and expose the most glorious arse. Then with hands on hips she gave it a wiggle.

One of our front row members on hands and knees scampered across forbidden ground, kissed what he saw as a Centrepiece then bit the lady's arse. The Minder minded, and our Romeo was belted. We did not get a second 5 minute spot although I had already paid the fee, up front. Lady and Minder left in a huff.

Some days later Bill Bell came to see me brandishing a letter addressed to the RSM. As he was now commissioned and the contents of the letter were of no concern to the new RSM (if it had to be addressed?) it therefore fell to me!

The lady stripper claimed £50 for loss of earnings for the week as the bruises on her delectable backside stopped her working, at least for the present. (Some say that those teeth marks would have added to her display!)

Anyway, I quickly called an extraordinary Mess meeting at lunchtime and all members sanctioned the payment of the £50. All agreed that the dinner, dining out and entertainment had been well worth the extra cost.

UNITED NATIONS TOUR: Cyprus 1973

In mid 1973 the 1st Battalion were sent to Cyprus on a six month UN Tour to help keep the peace between the Greek and Turkish Communities. The Battalion occupied in company groups, strongpoints along a recognised 'Peace Line'. Other Units in Cyprus straddled other areas such as in divided Nicosia.

Our areas were mainly in the south and to the east of Limassol, Zigi, where the main Island and BBC communications were. Stavarouni, to the west of Larnaca, commanded a 2000 ft high view. The Line east, running up toward Famagusta.

All ranks had to discard their maroon berets and wear the blue

UN Beret and UN Cap Badge for the length of the six-month Tour.

The Battalion Headquarters and Headquarters Company were housed within Polemedia Camp which was on an escarpment three miles north of Limassol and had been a military base since the 1880's. The camp was a comfortable one to operate from and had been improved much over the years. The accommodation for all was hutted, with well-appointed Wet canteens, a Naafi and attractive Officers and Sgts Messes. Good MT and Medical Facilities.

I was the RQMS by appointment and Warrant Officer 2 in the ranks, with the Quartermaster providing and seeing to the Battalion's administrative needs. I took on various contracts to civilian contractors for the laundry and footwear provision, detailed much of the camp workforce, electricians, gardeners, refuse collections and the like and all soon ran to a well tried and satisfactory conclusion.

The main laundry contractor with a large remit all over the Island and not just with the Military was the firm of Loukasan. Half way through the tour the owner invited myself and another Warrant Officer to his daughter's wedding in Agros, a mountain village up in the Troodos Hills. Although an old EOKA stronghold, on the day as we were in uniform and were wearing 'Wings', we were known to be Para, the village elders made us more than welcome with food and wine.

The whole tour in Cyprus in 1973 was rather a jolly one, much different from a year later when the Turks invaded Cyprus in the North and really divided the Island with murder on both sides. In the meanwhile in 1973 we enjoyed weekend Mess Parties, liaison with the UN Police (Aussies) out at Paphos, sporting, training and Indulgence RAF flights out for families who wished to come out on holiday. Swimming at the Curium Beach and band concerts at Curium and Salamis at Famagusta were the order of the day.

My widowed Father who ran the 'Crown' at Ossett, Yorks, left sister June in charge and came out to Cyprus on a ten day holiday at the five star hotel on the Limassol sea front called The Apollonia. He was gracious enough to fly civil aircraft from London and brought out with him, Chris, my charming wife. Major Jack Crane the Quartermaster gave me the afternoons off and I too stayed in luxury with Chris at the five-star. She was due to come out on a booked holiday by RAF in later weeks and so we really had two holidays before I left the Island for good.

Father, I will say, was always a most welcome member of the 1st Battalion Sergeants Mess. In his late 50's, all Mess Members treated him with the reverence given to an old RSM. A number of Mess Members and the odd officer had visited his pub of course up in Yorkshire. When in Aldershot and even now in Cyprus he was always invited to attend the WOs and Sgts Messes.

It was so, in Cyprus when we had a Sgts Mess party in the Diana Restaurant in Limassol Town Square, dinner 7.30pm for 8pm and taxis out at midnight. The Battalion Band played, those wives who were out on holiday danced and so did girlfriends. Father, at the head of a table, declared the Keo Beer and Keo Brandy, 'Gnats Piss' and had to be helped, almost carried out at midnight! He was also fortunate to attend the Band Concert at Salamis, the old Roman Theatre outside Famagusta. A super holiday in super surroundings.

When Christine came out on the second holiday we stayed in an empty married quarter, one of a number taken over by WO2 Charlie Hodgekinson in his role as PRI Warrant Officer (Welfare) on short term contracts for the holiday season. I was friendly with a number of the Cypriot camp staff and locals and Christine and I were made most welcome in the house of PAMBOS the Head Electrician.

My tour was a short one, as after three months I was due to hand over the RQMS appointment to WO2 Ron Lewis, a Mess pal I had known for years since the Bahrain days in the early 60s. Before I left, Major Jack Crane, who I had worked with for the past four years, as his Company Sergeant Major and as his RQMS, sent me a written note to invite Christine and me to my farewell party and dining out at ARIFS Restaurant in the Turkish Quarter. Jack's wife Ursula was out on holiday with one of their children from Aldershot. This invitation was a great honour for me. I had the greatest admiration for Jack, as a soldier, a father and as a Comrade in Arms. Awarded by HM, the MBE, Jack for many had an unknown past.

Although now, as he always came over as a polite Commissioned gentleman with a clipped military accent, few knew that as a Sergeant and Commissioned from the ranks, he was at one time an out and out Scouser and ex-Battalion and BAOR heavy weight boxing champion!

The evening was a most pleasant one at Arifs and Jack even took

154

the time to stand and say a few words and present me with an inscribed solid silver ashtray! Ursula had brought it out with her from Aldershot.

We parted on more formal terms in camp a week or so later when, after a session in his office and accounts formally handed over to my successor WO2 Ron Lewis, I left to have an interview with the Commanding Officer. There it was confirmed that I was to leave the Battalion to join the 4th Battalion in the appointment as WO1 Regimental Sergeant Major.

REGIMENTAL SERGEANT MAJOR. WO1 PROMOTION
4 Para. The Territorial Army Volunteer Reserve

The TA, as it was known then, the IVth Battalion The Parachute Regiment as it is known now, but still the Reserve. The most professional of all reserve units. Unequalled as Service in The Gulf and Afghanistan proves.

When I joined the Battalion in November 1973 the main Battalion Headquarters was in Pudsey in Yorkshire. The Companies making up the Battalion were based in TA Drill Halls at Oldham, Liverpool, Gateshead, Norton and Leeds. A split of the old 12/13 Para. Yorkshire and Lancashire Battalions.

The Companies were staffed with Regular Warrant Officers and Sergeants and their TA counterparts really took over at drill nights and weekends. The Regular Army WOs and Sgts were known as PSIs i.e. Permanent Staff Instructors. They normally did a two-year tour away from the Regular Battalions.

The volunteer soldiers who were committed to attend so many drill nights and shooting, parachuting weekends and attendance at annual camp for their bounty, were keen, enthusiastic and as, 'Para' as the normal 'Para'.

Many were ex-regular, whose wives did not want a full time commitment for their hubby but didn't mind him 'Playing' soldiers once a week and at the odd weekend. The other single volunteers were fit, motivated, loved a crack at getting fit, parachuting and the camaraderie. In the main, all were employed.

The Regular Officers were mostly at The Headquarters at Pudsey. The Commanding Officer when I was to take up the appointment as

155

RSM was firstly Lt Col John Rymer-Jones later Lt Col John Kent. Both I had known for years. The Adjutant was Captain David Roberts, sometime after to be Colonel Roberts. The Second-in-Command was Major Ben Arkle MBE later to be Colonel. At one time he was an ex-Regular Officer of the 1st Battalion and OCD Company,and was now to be a volunteer and retired from regular service. The Quartermaster Charles Storey was a Regular Officer as was the Chief Clerk a Regular Warrant Officer, John Bullas, a fanatical Aston Villa supporter.

The MTO Captain, 'Rocky' Small, was an ex-Regular Warrant Officer, now a reservist but with the distinction of having been awarded the George Medal for Gallantry whilst a Sergeant, saving recruits whilst parachuting from a balloon. He, the dispatcher, threw out the recruits at 800 ft when the balloon exploded in the air before lying on the floor of the balloon to make the crash landing. He at the time was severely injured. The four recruits survived with only one injured.

At The Headquarters there was a crop of ex-regular NCOs who really made the place tick over. C/Sgt Larry Grimshaw and John Fargin an ex-army boxing and cross-country champion. Harry Burns now the Pay Warrant Officer. Sgt Lyn Purnell was a regular PSI who picked up the administrative tasks daily and even ran the Sgts Mess Bar, stock and accounting as an extra!

The Adjutant, Capt David Roberts, and I, in tandem, usually in my car an 1800 Morris 'Staff Car' maintained by the MT Fitters, were usually on the road Tuesday and Thursday nights visiting company drill nights at their locations. Tuesday – Oldham and Liverpool, Thursday – Norton and Gateshead.

In TA life most weekends were busy as the Battalion's soldier's really were Weekend Warriors. There were companies training at Altcar and Strensall and Catterick Ranges, parachute ballooning at RAF Church Fenton, Temple Newsam Park, Leeds and Roundhay Park and field training at Leek in Staffordshire and Appleby in Westmoreland.

Summer two week camps whilst I was with the Battalion were taken at Crookham Camp near Aldershot and Barry Budden up in Scotland.

Mondays therefore were usually taken as a day off. The days when Christine and I would go into the Yorkshire Dales and take a pub meal or into Derbyshire to Castleton and the Blue John Mines etc; Bolton Abbey, Skipton, Ripon, York and Scarboro' were our particular favourites. We did find time even on some weekends to take our two girls, Tanya now 14 and Trudy aged 7 and their friends to the coast.

As most weekends' training usually finished by 12 noon we often found time, late afternoon early evening to visit our Grandparents George and Mary Jayne at Brighouse, but 40 minutes away. Father's pub, 'The Crown' at Ossett, another favourite, was only 15 miles away, as were my two sisters houses.

As a family we took over a married quarter within a small pleasant estate on the southern outskirts of Pudsey Town. No 43A Roker Lane was our home, a three-mile drive to Battalion.

The Headquarters were at Thornbury Barracks halfway between Leeds and Bradford and just off a large roundabout on the main road.

The Passing of my Father and the Family Funeral

Father had not been well over the Christmas of 1973 and as a result was admitted into the hospital in Wakefield in February 1974. My sister June and brother-in-law, Albert Kendrick, actually ran Father's pub - 'The Crown' at Ossett - and Father, a widower, was really a sleeping partner.

Father had a dickey ticker and this took a turn for the worse. On the night of the 14 February, an appalling evening weather wise, I had attended a drill night at one of the drill halls and with Christine I looked in on Father mid-evening. I remember walking into the Pinderfields Hospital in Military Uniform, white WO1 Mac and maroon beret and standing at the foot of Father's bed and saluting him. I took off the mackintosh and shook it, sat down and asked Father how he was.

He replied, 'I'm knackered lad!' (Typical Father).

Chris and I spent time with him, and I sought out the senior doctor before leaving to ask of Father's condition as he was in the Intensive Care ward. The doctor told me that, 'He would not come out of this one!' His whole body was shutting down.

157

Father died on the morning of the 15 February, the very next day. Thank God that my younger brother Christopher was at his bedside when he passed away. Sister Melanie was at hand in the car in the hospital car park.

All we siblings then held a meeting in 'The Crown' at Ossett and it was my duty to inform our Grandparents at Brighouse and Father's relatives and friends at Keighley of Father's demise.

The funeral was held at the church next to 'The Crown' in South Ossett and the turnout was tremendous: Customers, members of the West Riding Constabulary and hosts of Father's friends – and girlfriends. Two Para Sergeants attended from the 1ˢᵗ Battalion with a Sgts Mess tribute wreath, and, together with my brother and I, and two of Father's closest customer friends, acted as Pall bearers.

We saw him in and out of church and to the cemetery in South Ossett but a mile away, to be buried within the same grave as Mother Alice, who had died some seven years before.

The Wake was held that afternoon immediately afterwards in 'The Crown', courtesy of sister June and hubby, now landlords. Within two hours one would have thought that it was a wedding celebration. The food appeared, the booze was never ending and tales were told, as Father had been a character 'Copper' and Landlord. Even as a widower a bit of a rogue. His THREE girlfriends were seen to converse together, shedding a hung-over tear and saying, what a lovely fella he was! One lady 57, one 27 and the barmaid 19 years of age. Father would have been most pleased and proud of the party.

My wife Christine, helping out with the carriage of eats from kitchen to bar, said to me, 'I have just seen Father in the lounge sat on the radiator!'

I said, 'What did he do?'

Christine said, 'smiled and nodded!'

I never saw him!

For years afterwards and a succession of landlords, Father's presence was known to be within 'The Crown'. After a couple of years, sister June gave up the tenancy and a Huddersfield couple took over the Pub. Christine and I when visiting the area and calling at sisters a two minute walk away, always went into the 'Crown' for a drink. On entering the Pub I always said, 'Hello' to Father and on leaving, 'Goodbye!'

The now Landlady said to me that Father was still in the Pub and she said that he didn't frighten her. I said, 'What does he do?'

She said, 'He wafts the bedclothes in the bed. Sometimes I see him in the cellar sat on the beer barrels!'

Jack Ells, a following Tenant was sitting on a bar stool with his lower leg in plaster when one day I called in for a drink. I asked Jack about the leg and he said, 'It's your bloody old man's fault! I went down the cellar, clicked on the light, and there was your old man sat on a barrel! I fell the last two steps, broke my ankle and the bugger disappeared.'

His last reported presence, as I recall, was when one sunny lunchtime whilst North on leave from Aldershot, I called in for a pint. The sun was behind me as I walked through the door. Of the three at the bar - Jim Law a salesman, Charlie Wilkinson, the butcher and Byram, Coop manager - one remarked, 'Tommy Godwin. Bloody hell, we thought it was your Father.' Over pints we all told tales of Father as his close friends and customers would. Suddenly a 4 Horse Brass and Leather Martindale on the wall fell onto the FLOOR. It shouldn't! It was on a HOOK!

The Presentation of New Colours to 1, 2, 3 and 4 Para
Rushmoor Arena Aldershot 1974

On the 15 July 1974 the First, Second and Third Battalions and Fourth (Volunteer) Battalion of The Parachute Regiment, (as we were titled), were presented with New Regimental Colours by Her Majesty the Queen within Rushmoor Arena, Aldershot, the home of the British Army and of The Regiment.

Two Colours for Infantry Battalions; One Regimental, One Queens, are usually changed between 25 and 30 years of age. Old Colours are usually 'Marched Off' and The New Colours are consecrated, paraded through the ranks and all on parade swear to uphold old traditions and to renew their allegiance to The Crown. It must be remembered that all officers and soldiers swear to fight for Queen and Country on enlistment.

The Territorial Battalion, of which I was the Regimental Sergeants Major, was fortunate that its Colours were in the same time frame for renewal as the three Regular Battalions, and so were given the honour of renewal at the same parade.

The Battalion took its two week annual camp at a Barracks at Crookham Camp, some four miles away, and there we paraded in company groups, and there, as a Battalion exercised the drills required for the parade. Officers on Sword and Colour Drill. Soldiers on Arms and Foot Drills. As the RSM much of course was my responsibility. Much was achieved, and on the actual parade in front of Her Majesty, the 4th (Volunteer) Battalion performed well.

Afterwards I received a personal letter from the overall and Regimental Senior RSM, Peter Longley, to say that our Territorial Battalion on parade was indistinguishable from that of the regular three Battalions. This accolade pleased me no end.

The weather however was awful and we were drenched throughout the parade, which was almost a two hour one from March On. Her Majesty throughout seemed to be under umbrellas.

All brightened up of course within the large marquees afterwards, and Christine and I, together with the other parade RSMs and their ladies, were formally presented to Her Majesty. We, the Senior Warrant Officers then had a photograph taken indoors, under a large parachute canopy together with the Queen, seated. Refreshments at Rushmoor were provided for all ranks, then it was transport to return to Crookham Camp, then party time within the various Messes.

On the Sunday following, with a select Guard of Honour, we laid up the Old Regimental Colours at The Garrison Church in Aldershot. The Guard then marched off to disperse down Wellington Avenue. The Guard Commander was the Battalion 2 i/c Major Ben Arkle MBE. The Guard, drawn from 'A' Company, Liverpool. CSM WO2, was Trevor Brownrigg.

My New Colours Party on the day of The Parade at Rushmoor was: The Queens Colour, Lt. I.G.Stancombe. The Regimental Colour Lt. R.R.B.Evans. Close Escorts CSM R.Devlin, C/Sgt S.D.Bright and C/Sgt. P.McGarry. The Commanding Officer on parade was Lt Colonel John Rymer-Jones, with his Adjutant Capt David Roberts MBE. This Presentation of New Colours was to be the only one honoured during my whole Service.

The Battalion Provost Sergeant and the Cockerel

During the Summer Camp at Crookham we were awoken every morning by a raucous local cockerel. It really was a noisy sod and lived over the Sgts Mess accommodation fence and could be seen strutting around. Various members of the Mess tried to entice it with food into grabbing distance, but to no avail. Into the Arena strode, 'Dickie Dunn', the Battalion Provost Sergeant. A TA Volunteer, Dickie's day job was that of a professional boxer. He was soon to be the British and Commonwealth Champion. He fought against Mohammed Ali once for the World Heavyweight Championship. Although dropping Ali once to his knees in the 4th round, he was outclassed and eventually KOd.

However, here at Summer Camp with the Battalion, Dickie worked hard, trained hard and wanted his sleep. The cockerel had to go! It took all of 13 days. On the night of the Sergeants Mess wild party following the Presentation of Colours and at about midnight, Dickie ran through the Mess whooping in his pyjamas, swinging the bloody cockerel around his head, in through one door, out through another. So we did thereafter have one quiet morning and the Mess a supplement to its Sunday Lunch.

Horbury Road, Ossett – A Change of Accommodation

My sister June and brother-in-law Albert with their two children lived in the cottage attached to The Crown Pub, tenanted by Father. When Father fell ill and things were deemed to be serious, they moved into The Crown really to run it. After Father's death in January 1974 they took over as licensees from the Tetley Brewery.

With the cottage becoming vacant it seemed a good idea for Christine and I as a family to move to Ossett from Roker Lane, Pudsey. Daughter Tanya could continue to go to school at Pudsey, whilst Trudy of tender years could attend the Junior School at Ossett some 100 yards away. So in the late summer of 1974 we moved into the three bedroomed cottage. Tanya persuaded a local builder Frank Callaghan to rent her some old out buildings half a mile away, where she kept hens and sold the eggs to her Mother.

As life with the TA was very stable it was no problem to drive the

15 miles to work as required. Late drill nights and commitment most weekends was the order of the day anyhow, so the move would give Chris and the girls stability and a busier friendlier outlook on life. We had many friends as customers who used 'The Crown' and there was much life and enjoyment outside strictly military circles.

The Crown Hotel, Ossett

Father had taken over this Pub when he retired from the Police Force in the 60s from an elderly tenant who did but two barrels of beer a week. It soon became a lively venue under Father and Mother and in no time was up to nine barrels of bitter per week. From there, were Easter Walks, Hat Nights, and late nights when Father's police pals rolled in!

There was Country Music one night a week, darts, dominoes, ringing the Bull (a hook on the wall). Fancy dress nights and music on a Friday evening. 'The Piscadors' met on a Friday evening, those lovers of Tetley's Bitter, sporting fish and good company. I was a member! We wore regalia, made up of a necklace of bottle tops, with our photo at the end encased in plastic. Funny hats were worn, usually Bowlers. Each of us 'played' a musical instrument and/or, we sang!

Malcolm Marriot, a member, ex-Korean Vet and an eight pints a session man was a member of the Huddersfield Choral Society and a fine tenor. Neville Himsworth; he played drums. 'Uncle Baggie' played a guitar. Tommy Tarny – a Jew's Harp. Albert – a 'Tommy Talker' or 'paper comb'. Yours truly played a mouth organ or tried to sing, after four pints. Other customers would join in! The best of the rest would be 'Lady Patricia' Lamb, wife of David, lover of ale and sporting fish. Lady P had a trained choral voice, as another member of the Huddersfield Choral Society.

When the 'Easter Race' ran from the Pub it was a circuit down and around the nearby Storrs Hill. The winning gent won a stainless steel bucket of beer, the winning lady, a pair of kippers.

0The Piscadors

As I remarked before, they used to meet in 'The Crown' on Friday evenings. There of course it was decided where the next fishing trip was to take place. This was usually on a Saturday or Sunday, once a month at least. After trout and/or grayling in season. An early morning start, usually from 'The Crown' at 0530, to the venue by 7am. fishing until the Pub opened at mid-day. I was lucky to join them on two occasions when the TA had weekends free and I had no military duties.

On the first memorable occasion the venue was just north of Pately Bridge, along Howsteins Beck in North Yorkshire. It was Bradford Angling Society Water and we had the Rights. I teamed up with Malcolm Marriot and the idea was to have a 'toast' on each trout caught. We took a bottle of Brandy and bottle of Coke.

By 12 o'clock and into the Pub, we were plastered. We had caught 13 fish. All brook trout. How did we get home? Well as always the Piscadors travelled in a large painter and decorators' van owned by another 'Malcom', A tee-totaller!He Loved fishing with us as mates and was quite happy to sit in the Pub with lemonade and a pie!

The second occasion that I took off early with them for a day's fishing we had a poor morning. Few fish about, and brother-in-law Phil who had joined us for the experience was set off on the river bank to stamp up and down in his size 13 boots to draw up worms as an alternate bait! All to no avail. The seven of us had only caught three fish all morning and so at 11 o'clock it was decided to drive down to Pately Bridge and go into 'The Crown'. The seven-mile drive there would see the place open by 12 o'clock. Well, we made it. In a lively mood we ate hot pork pies from the local butcher, the like of which I have never again tasted. We played the locals at darts and sank to my absolute knowledge 13 pints over the four hours whilst we were there (each!).

On the way home we had numerous pee stops and I recall picking enough roadside daffodils to satisfy our wives. When I was tipped from the van at home I could barely climb the three steps leading to our front door. Chris had to help me undress and shower, and I remember to this day her saying,

'Never mind the daffs, where's the FISH?'

163

Walking, 'The Pennine Way'

Drinking in 'The Crown' with good friends brought out all kinds of ideas, and one of mine was to walk the Pennine Way or at least a part of it. Not from south to north though, i.e. Edale in Derbyshire to Scotland, but north to south.

I knew the area in the south too well and the challenge for me would be from the north, from Kirk Yetholm. The first leg of 34 miles, a night's kip in the heather between, would see a challenging 'Tab' with not a dwelling in sight. The journey was planned to be taken during 4 Para summer leave.

beforehand I persuaded two companions to do the walk with me, and much preparation and planning was done in 'The Crown' over pints of Tetley's Beer. One intrepid walker was my brother-in-law Philip Smith, twelve years younger than me, a fit lad who was a cricketer for College Grove Wakefield and an in tandem fast bowler with Imran Khan. The other was business director David Lamb, more of a par with me in age but very fit, having once been an athlete in his Royal Air Force days of National Service.

I loaned them boots to break in beforehand and Bergans and sleeping bags to get the feel of and a few weeks of 'tabbing' beforehand was the name of the game.

We had a remarkable send off from 'The Crown' as we formed up in full marching order on the car park before boarding military transport for the journey north to our drop off point at Kirk Yetholm. We were inspected by, 'Captain' Malcolm Marriot, ex-Light Infantry and Korean vet. He was mounted on a spirited white cob as he reviewed his troops!

Complete with Fez and we in full marching gear a photograph was taken by the local 'Ossett Observer' reporter and on publication we were famous locally for a week. Dropped off in Scotland mid-afternoon we set off south at once, self-contained and making best speed, some 17 miles over the moors to finish before night-fall at 'The Hen Hole'. This was an old Railway Carriage dropped by helicopter on the Pennine Way to offer refuge to walkers in really bad weather. Well, the first leg was kind to us even on these bleak hills and so we slept in comfort in the heather in sleeping bags.

The next leg saw us into Cumbria and although self-contained we

164

decided to bluff our way into a Youth Hostel and make use of the nearby pub for 'Steaks and Ale'. Returning to the Youth Hostel before 10.30pm 'lights out', we were met by the irate hostel caretaker. She told me that the booking in number that I had signed in on was a military identification number and not a Youth Hostel one! She was of a mind to kick us out. David, a much smoother talker than I, took over and calmed things down with fine words and a bar of chocolate. So much so that the dear lady booked us into the next Youth Hostel for the following night some 20 miles south.

We laughed our way along and thereafter no leg was more than 17 to 20 miles daily. We found discarded sheep's balls on the moors, discarded socks often and even discarded boots. Also, all manner of clothing.

A couple of days saw us meeting up with a scout troop and other travellers on the Pennine Way, usually in the early morning as we always seemed to be in the next village hours hence at one time seated on a wall eating ice creams when the scouts 'trooped' past which caused David to say to me, 'Tha reads a map better than I read Daily Telegraph.'

On one particular day's walk, and it was in awful weather, I planned for us in crossing Hadrian's Wall to hit the only pub for miles. We did! In sight after a miserable day we arrived at 'The Twice Brewed'. We had come out of the Forest of Bowness and didn't fancy sleeping there in our sodden and muddy state so engineered, 'a cunning plan'.

In the nearby roadside bus shelter we had David change into slacks, shirt and pullover, run to the pub and secure a room for the three of us! It worked. You should have seen the landlord's face when we then all went in with the sodden Bergans and gear. We were put into a family room and after I had played doctor on blistered feet, we changed and went into the dining room for a most pleasant meal.

We were in a drinking mood later and the landlord, enjoying our company, kept late hours until after midnight when 'her indoors' came in, ordered the bar to be closed and saw us off to bed.

Next morning, a good breakfast was taken, served in silence! Bill paid, all gear dried and we took off to see the nearby Roman Fort on Hadrian's Wall before continuing our ambles along the Pennine

Way.

I had pre-arranged with my brother Christopher, a master chef in the Army Catering Corps, to offer us transport when we reached Horton - in Ribblesdale in Yorkshire, the area of the famed, Three Peaks Circuit: Ingleborough, Whernside and Penyghent. In contact by telephone he told us to meet at the 'The Red Lion', mid morning, where, with the kind permission of the landlord, he cooked us a full English breakfast in the pub car park and out of the back of his estate car. Whilst he did, we got the beers in.

From there we were driven home to arrive back at 'The Crown' in Ossett just in time for bar opening and for us to recall our tales of our part walk of The Pennine Way.

The 4th Battalion - Boxing, A Way of Life

The 4th Battalion being at that time a volunteer unit used to draw its recruits from across the North of England. It was as sporting a unit as its regular counterparts and even more so in boxing. Soldiers were recruited, went through pre-fitness training and recruit training then, if motivated enough, and some were through boxing club contacts, they joined the Battalion boxing team.

The team was formidable. Boxers were from St Pats Club in Leeds or The Golden Gloves in Liverpool and we also had boxers from Skipton and Gateshead.

The team of course was sanctioned by the CO, who, giving it full support, expected the points gained from boxing (TA Champions for eleven years) to be added to the other point collectors of cross country running and shooting which would then give the Battalion the advantage of overall Territorial Army Champions. A handsome trophy was at stake and a cash prize for the Unit's PRI to be spent on sports kit.

The Battalion had indeed won this trophy for the past eleven years prior to 1976. As the RSM, and as my predecessor had been, I was expected to manage the team. Not a difficult task, just the organisation of transport, accommodation at boxing venues and messing. Sometimes welfare, keeping boxers entertained on waiting days at competitions i.e. London White City etc. Cinemas featured, pubs did not.

166

I sometimes acted as MC in the ring, on one occasion when the whole TAVR Team beat the Regular Army Team., a feat never repeated and 4 Para provided five boxers on the night.

The boxing side of life was left to the boxing professional trainers in an amateur sport. Mr John Devanney, who had two sons in the Battalion, both boxers, was a most remarkable trainer.

We did have a full sized active boxing ring within the Battalion Headquarters drill hall at Pudsey and on drill nights and weekends it was well used. Mr Devanney's son-in-law happened to be, during my tour, the British and Commonwealth Heavy Weight Title holder and I was privileged to see two of his title fights, both at The White City, London.

Richard (Dickie) Dunn made full use of our boxing ring and helped condition and train our boxers. He had a perfect right to do so as he was the Battalions Provost Sergeant and a trained parachutist. His wife Janet was a formidable lady, if she thought that Richard wasn't training hard or motivated enough she would give him stick at ringside.

Some boxers as I recall were Cpl George Fitt at Liverpool, Pte Molinary from Skipton, and the Feeney brothers both ABA champions from Gateshead, both later to be professionals.

Farewell to the 4ᵗʰ Battalion, Dining Out 1975

The Commanding Officer Lt Colonel John Rymer-Jones and Avis his lovely wife were dined out by our Sergeants Mess Members in late summer at the Swallow Hotel, Wakefield City. The Mess took over much of the accommodation and the ballroom. We had a super dinner/dance, speeches and a suitable presentation and flowers. It was a memorable evening made more so when most of us ended up on the hotel flat roof sitting on empty beer barrels having a nightcap, the Colonel and his lady included!

Later in the year at the end of our two-year tour, Christine and I were dined out at The Lumley Castle Hotel, Chester-le-Street, Durham. A once in a lifetime experience, all arranged by WO2 Peter Hodgekinson and Jean his wife, they really did us proud.

We occupied the 'King James Suite', panelled and with a

magnificent four-poster bed. We were piped down to dinner to join all Sergeants Mess Members in the magnificent dining room, ancient and sporting its fantastic marbled fireplace.

This gracious 13th century castle stands amidst beautiful parkland and was the ancestral home of the 12th Earl of Scarborough. What a night, we ended up having mock fights in the early hours of the morning on the battlements! Breakfast was taken next morning at 'The Black Knight' restaurant: What a fitting and memorable end to a most enjoyable time with the IVth Battalion.

In this year 1975, indeed, as in the previous year, we as a family had time off during the summer and visited the West Country. camping one year and towing a caravan the next. Happy times were had at Newquay, St Ives, Polperro and visiting Land's End and the Cornish Coast. We were also able to keep in close contact with Christine's parents at 'The Fox and Hounds' at Shafton and to visit our Grandparents at Brighouse, often, mostly during Sunday afternoons.

Now coming to the end of our tour with 4 Para I was posted back to join a regular battalion back in Aldershot. I had hoped to take over the RSM post of the 1st Battalion and thereby to satisfy an ambition of holding every rank from private soldier to WO. This however was not to be and I was posted to the 2nd Battalion The Parachute Regiment as its Regimental Sergeant Major.

Returning to Aldershot late 1975 I took over a married quarter at 53 Alamein Road on the Waterloo Park Estate, a modern three bed-roomed house not more than half a mile from Aldershot town centre and a mile from the battalion lines at Albuhera Barracks.

Christine and the girls stayed in Yorkshire for a few weeks whilst Tanya completed her exams at the Pudsey School.

2nd Battalion, The Parachute Regiment Regimental Sergeant Major

Never having much to do previously with the Battalion except to say, 'Hello and Farewell' as Battalions passed each other on tours in the Gulf and in Northern Ireland I had to learn of the Battalion's strong links with its wartime Scottish roots.

'Burns Night' was a must, as was the old 2 Para 'Old Comrades'

168

Wartime Club.

The Commanding Officer was Lt Col David Taylor a large, rugger playing, pleasant Commander, who I was to get on with extremely well.

The Adjutant was Capt. Farrar-Hockley and later John Reath, both later to be Generals. I had the utmost regard for these two as Adjutant in a regular battalion is one hell of a job and in Dair Farrar-Hockley's case even more so as his father was the Brigade Commander and later to be the Commander of The South East District. General Sir Tony Farrar-Hockley, Korean vet, highly decorated and an author in his own right.

During my appointment with the Battalion we were busy on UK Exercises, host to overseas visitors, exercises overseas and a four-month tour back to Northern Ireland and 'The troubles', where we were to spend Christmas 1976, Battalion Headquarters being within the Springfield Road Police Station.

We even, 'Trooped the Colours' on Airborne Forces Day on Montgomery Square, under the Eagle Eye of General Sir Roland Gibbs. The Colonel Commandant. The one occasion where I actually drew my sword!

The Ulster Tour with the 2nd Battalion 1976

The Battalion headquarters this time were housed within The Springfield Road Police Station in the heart of Belfast, a well-defended area as one can guess. The Companies were keeping the peace between the usual warring factions of Protestant and Catholic, and were housed in derelict buildings in and around the divided City. The Ballymurphy area being the most of our focus. We had our casualties and our successes.

My usual working day was a shift of four hours on the Operations Desk at which I learned that the duty Police Constable on my left was earning twice my salary, for the same shift. This was followed by a daily round with the CO and escorts either vehicle or foot patrol, to visit all the Company locations. We were lucky to be in bed before 0200 then up at 0730 hrs. Oh that politicians worked such hours or even knew what it was all about! Bed was a camp safari bed within an office.

169

We did have a 'lighter' moment to remember on Christmas Day! Making the best of a traditional Christmas Lunch our Headquarters Sergeant Mess Members of which there were a dozen of us, WOs, Int Sgts, Signals, MT Sgts etc., were seated at a long table, yours truly at the head, when some wag passing the police station on the main road, chose to heave half a house brick though our canteen window.

I served with some cracking senior ranks during my time with the Battalion, friends to this day.

The MV Bolero, a South American Cruise Ship

2 Para was sent to Norway to Exercise against the Norwegian Army. Simple you may say, from an airfield in Southern England, a drop north of Bergan, a rally, then into the Tundra to cause havoc to opposing troops! Not in this instance. Hard to believe but the Battalion Group went by ship. The Government could not find the aircraft for the Drop as most Transport Aircraft had been sent to Africa for the delivery of food, to some crisis. So at great expense firstly of a move by rail up to Newcastle and a port, we then joined the MV Bolero for the voyage to and from Bergen in Norway.

What a novel way to go on Exercise. Dry on the way out, party time on the way back. After a pleasant cruise through the spectacular Fiords spotting jellyfish as big as dustbins and marvelling at the nights 'Northern Lights', we disembarked at Bergan to be transported north by Norwegian army trucks into the Exercise Area. There we saw Tundra, tabbed miles, dug holes, set up ambushes and after ten days were declared, 'The Winners'.

So to our great delight it was back to the ship, 'The Bolero', and back to the UK. Now this was no ordinary ship, this was a luxury liner. Commissioned through trade to transport us, it had just finished a cruise around the shores of Central and South America and had the same crew and facilities on board.

There was a large ballroom with an organ that rose up through the floor, numerous bars, swimming pools and a most delightful male and female crew.

As the RSM and keeper of the Peace so to speak, I had arranged with Major Wood, the Battalion 2 i/c and the Adjutant Capt. Farrar-

170

Hockley that the soldiers be allowed to drink on board the evening of embarkation in the bars within the large ballroom lounge. My reasoning was that if declined the soldiers would drink their duty free spirits, already purchased for home, in their cabins, a recipe for disaster! Paras are Paras and it would have ended with idiots on deck, walking the handrails for fun.

The bar opening times were announced by tannoy! 8pm till midnight! Thereafter, no-one was allowed on deck. Beer, lager and soft drinks only, no spirits to be consumed. A terrific evening was had by all. The organ played the music, we had on stage our own compere, Colour Sergeant 'Stovey' Cornwall and enough comedians and singers from our 800 strong Battalion group to even keep 'The Palladium' entertained.

What really brought the house down was seven 'Toms' in hats as Seven Dwarfs, wearing boots and socks and nothing else doing exit drills across the stage to music. One of course behind the other, hands on shoulders.

The mainly Bolero Male Crew loved the Spectacle. I called a halt to the evening at midnight on stage with a gang of senior ranks, singing 'Old MacDonnell's Farm', gave all ten minutes drinking up time, then the Order, 'Bugger off to Bed.'

We disembarked the next day and bade the Bolero crew farewell. The Purser remarked what a pleasure it was to have us on board, no drama, no damages and the profits made on his bars were unbelievable.

He said, 'You had some Party last night. Your Battalion drank 16,000 cans of beer and lager!'

As a footnote, the Commanding Officer Lt Col David Taylor didn't join the ship on its return journey from Bergan! He chose to leave by air! Wonder why? What a Party!

Farewell to 2 Para
A Surprise Party

Well into my second year as The Regimental Sergeant Major of the 2nd Battalion I was looking forward to being with the Battalion on its forecast posting into Berlin. A two-year accompanied Tour.

A surprise telephone call to my office led me to an interview with

171

the Regimental Colonel at The Parachute Regimental Depot at Browning Barracks, a five-minute walk away. Before leaving, I rang my CO, Colonel Taylor, and asked him if he knew of my being summoned. He said, 'No, has anything happened in Aldershot over the weekend. Let me know what it's all about.'

Reporting into the Regimental Colonel's Office, Colonel Mullins greeted me warmly and offered me a seat and a coffee! (Always a bad sign I thought!) Then he gave me the surprise. I was to leave 2 Para within the month. The Present Depot RSM had been Commissioned to do a particular job that required Captain's rank at short notice. The Regimental Depot was therefore short of The Senior Warrant Officer's Appointment. I was to be the Senior RSM. Post Haste!

Thanking him for the appointment but, from a family point of view, I asked if I could stay with 2 Para and accompany them into Berlin. He replied that it was more important to the Regiment that I take up the mantle of Senior RSM.

He then said that having carried out the appointment for a couple of years and with recommendation, I would be Commissioned as a Captain and within the Regiment, take up a Quartermaster's Appointment.

The interview over, the Regimental Colonel remarked that by the time I had walked back to my office in Albuhera Lines, he would have telephoned my CO, Colonel Taylor, to give him the news.

My successor into 2 Para was to be WO1 Jackie Henderson. I indeed knew Jackie well, he had taken over from me in 1 Para as RQMS. Of course I could not see, at this time, into the future, but in later years he was to follow me as Senior RSM then take over 1Para as MTO from me, on Commissioning.

Returning to 2 Para Lines I saw my CO at once and he was as surprised as I was at the move, even he had no prior knowledge.

Senior Regimental Sergeant Major. Depot

The duties were various. The tone was set at The Depot by the quality of the instructors, the continuity of training, the high standards of physical wellbeing and the camaraderie of all ranks. I felt that I was the guardian of the past and the future, fortunate to

172

play a part I had a super Commanding Officer, Lt Col Graham Farrell MBE.

We had served together years previously at 12/13 Para when he the Adjt and I was a Sgt PSI. Later, and in 1966 when in 1 Para, he was the Company Commander of A Company 1 Para. I was the CQMS and often his Sergeant Major whilst CSM George Brown the incumbent was away on duty.

I had the backing of an outstanding Sergeants Mess, most of the members I had known over the years. They were drawn from all three parachute battalions. We also had an attachment, WO1 Ralph Weaville RAF, the resident PJI, an instructor from the School of Infantry and an exchange Sergeant from The Royal Marine Depot, Dougie Richardson RM.

The Chief Clerk WO1 John Carruthers was ex-1 Para, my formative Battalion, as was RQMS Peter Hodgekinson, Band Sgt Major Brian Buddle, WO2 Dick Goldspink, and WO2 Bob Hainey. C/Sgts Fred Shaw, Bill Hickie and C/Sgt Len Sara. Also as Sgt Instructors ex-1 Para were Sgt Phil Atkinson, Mick Skelton, and ex-2 Para legends Sgts Frankie Pye and John Weeks. We had a most super Master Chef at the Depot. WO2 Bill Masterson of the ACC, who masterminded the whole catering business throughout the Messes and the main kitchen.

The Regimental Depot was high profile. We had Royal visits, overseas visitors, Passing Off Parades, Regimental Days of parade and spectacle. We hosted the annual Warrant Officers and Sergeants (past and present) Dinner Club of which I was the chairman and hosted the local Aldershot Branch of The Old Comrades Association.

Annually the selected Depot Staff had a 'jolly' and parachuted into St Helier Harbour in Jersey to take a part in either the 'Battle of the Flowers' ceremony, or Armistice Day Parade.

We were sometimes called upon to provide teams for charity or to keep the Regiment in the public eye, so we fielded Sergeants Mess teams in the Surbiton Pram Race (14 pubs and 4 miles) and swam for charity for the British Heart Foundation. We hosted summer balls and Mess dinner nights, once a month. The Red Devils dropped in on one occasion.

Annually and over my two years I chaired a three day conference and dinner night for the Regiment's Senior Sergeants Major this usually took in the Past and Present Dinner Night. There was also a Ladies Dinner.

The Depot was asked on the odd occasion to take part in some unusual requests, usually by letter to the CO and passed to me, to fix! One came from a widow to scatter her husband's ashes on the main parade ground square! We did rather better than that. With the Padre, the CO and Sgts Mess Bearer Party we had the widow see the ashes 'planted' in The Red Devil Rose Garden surrounding the Regimental Flag Pole. After the ceremony, there was lunch within the Sergeants' Mess. Mr Edwin Beech was given a true airborne send off.

DEPOT THE PARACHUTE REGIMENT 1977
Off Base at home, Vine Close

The Montgomery Lines and, at Browning Barracks, The Regimental Depot, Museum, Parade Ground, accommodation and Messes, flanked the Fleet Canal. Across a bridge was Queen's Avenue and acres of sports fields and a parachuting drop zone for ballooning and the Regiments free fall team, The Red Devils.

Christine, Tanya, Trudy and I moved into the nearby married quarter of Vine Close, alongside the main Farnborough to Farnham Road and overlooking Queen's Avenue. A super private estate of semi-detached houses with fruit treed gardens it was occupied by Officers and Warrant Officers only. Near to the Fleet canal tow path for lovely walks, adjacent to the army golf course and with a view over the Farnborough Airfield at Air Show time, the accommodation was ideal and we grew to love it.

Whilst here for a couple of years we had many visitors, friends from Yorkshire and German parachuting friends and their families. Tanya had a particular liaison with the Quartermaster's daughter of 272, Battalion based at Hildesheim in Germany. Major Hartung, the Quartermaster, and his family, Heidi and friend Wolfgang made exchange visits and Tanya was able to take holidays in Germany.

Whilst in situ here, Tanya having left school took up an appointment as a Pharmacy Technician at Frimley, then Farnham hospitals.

I joined the Army Golf Club, continued to play cricket and shoot

174

for the Depot Team. Christine secured a part time job with M&S and also took up wine production in a big way. We had gallons in demi-johns in the garage and shed, all bleeping away. This we bottled and even had labels printed 'Chateaux Vine Close'. After all, that is where we lived.

My brother Christopher, who as a master chef at The Army Catering School in Aldershot, took up the appointment as WO1 of Technical Training. He and Anne, his wife, and their four boys Andrew, Jason, Stephen and Martin came to live in Vine Close as neighbours. We were to look after their West Highland White dog, Dougie, when he was posted eventually to the Far East.

I took him up in a parachuting aircraft once as an observer. We flew from Odiham on an evening drop to Frensham DZ, not above ten miles away. The aircraft after the drop returned to Odiham, only five miles or so from Aldershot, to allow the RAF dispatchers and brother to return home. I was No1 that evening, going out of the port door and seeing him with harness on standing at the side of the dispatcher, I gave him a smile!

He said to me the next day, 'You looked scared going out of that door!'

I said, 'So would you, leaping out at 1000 feet.'

Ballooning on Queen's Avenue. A Surprise for Tanya

Usually, once a quarter, the RAF Balloon Crew with balloon, suspended cage and winch vehicle, appeared on the Queen's Avenue playing fields adjacent to the Depot. There the Depot Staff and Paras from the Regular Battalions in Station were able to keep up their parachuting skills over a few days at little cost. Up and down for hours went the balloon, each time holding four jumpers and a dispatcher. 'Up 800, four men jumping' was the order.

One Saturday morning from our house in Vine Close, I saw the balloon flying some 400 yards away. I put on uniform, boots, puttees, jungle green trousers and jumping smock and, carrying my helmet, I made my way onto the jumping area. I asked daughter Tanya to come with me, with the intention of going up in the balloon cage to watch me jump. Our resident RAF Depot PJI had no objection to Tanya going up in the balloon with me, as he knew on a previous week she had jumped with the Red Devils over their weekend course.

Guests were sometimes allowed up as observers, indeed my Uncle Stanley, an ex-WWII Bomber Crew member, had made such a previous ascent.

We had Tanya change into overalls in the drop zone ambulance and she borrowed a helmet. She was then fitted with a military parachute and reserve and in we went into the balloon cage together, with two of my Depot Sergeants and the RAF dispatcher Sgt Blackburn. Up we went to 800 feet, the balloon settled and our two Sergeants jumped out. I then invited Tanya to stand at the open door to see what things looked like.

I said to her, 'You jumped with the Red Devils, if you fancy it, jump out now and I will follow you out.' The instructor nodded having seen all was clear below. Then to my amazement Tanya jumped! I followed her out. Being somewhat heavier we both landed more or less together. The junior lads were on duty to assist jumpers in rolling up their parachuted, they had quite a surprise when Tanya took her helmet off. I heard one exclaim, 'It's a **girl!**'

I went back home to enjoy the weekend, and a very proud Tanya, changed and went off to work at Farnham Hospital Pharmacy. The next working day, the following Monday, I did get a bollocking from Flt Lt John Cole the Senior RAF Instructor, who had been away over the weekend. Tanya jumping from the balloon was not on as she was not a member of HM Forces. 'Never again,' he said and I accepted the admonishment. Later in the morning the CO, Lt Graham Farrell, popped his head around my door and with a twinkle in his eye said, 'Give Tanya my regards! Well done.'

Trudy, our younger daughter was also to parachute with The Red Devils but **NEVER** from the RAF Balloon.

176

The Visit of His Royal Highness Prince Charles, Colonel-in-Chief to The Regiment

During 1977 His Royal Highness had completed a basic course at RAF Abingdon in Oxfordshire and at his request afterwards, became the Regiment's Colonel-in-Chief. This visit to The Depot was to be a formal one and our Regimental Colonel had it coincide with the Regiment's 'Airborne Forces Day'. We had a morning parade at which one of the Depot Recruit Platoons marched off the Square, followed by the Old Comrades March Past. As the Senior RSM I was very involved with the visit from the parade point of view. As head of the Sergeants Mess into which he was to be made welcome, I saw him in.

All my Mess Members and their wives, the Mess staff and Christine and I were presented within the Mess anti-room. Welcoming HRH into the Mess on his arrival after the formal parade and before lunch in the Officers Mess, I asked him to sign our visitor's book. It was his first formal visit as Colonel-in-Chief.

We found Prince Charles to have a remarkable memory. Whilst introducing my Mess Members in the anti-room informally, though standing, and with drinks I introduced Colour Sgt Frank Pye. As he was about to shake hands he said to Frank, 'Colour Sergeant we have met before. Now where?'

Frank an unforgettable character in his own right said, 'You should remember me Sir, as on my Instructors APJI Course at Abingdon, I dispatched you from the Balloon on your second descent!'

The Prince said, 'No wonder I remember.'

Before all members and their wives enjoyed a buffet lunch and afterwards Airborne Parties on the lawns, Regimental Bands, Beer Tents, Arena Displays and Parachute Exhibitions from The Red Devils, and we were honoured as a Mess photograph was taken, with all members of the Mess and their Colonel-in-Chief seated and outside the Mess. In the photograph also featured was Lt Gen Farrar-Hockley GOC South East District and PARA. Colonel Mullins, Lt Col Farrell and The Regimental Adjutant Major Norman Nicholls.

The sun shone, the bands played and what a day!

177

One of our Mess Members C/Sgt Lenny Sara left the Service after 22 years and on to retirement on the day of this visit by HRH. He was presented to Prince Charles on the Parade of Old Comrades. With the help of Larry Signey, 'The Aldershot News' reporter, and Jeff, his camera-man, I obtained a super 10 x 8 photo of Lenny shaking hands with Prince Charles. Bill Surman our Depot Pioneer Sergeant framed the photo and that evening Chris and I visited Lenny's retirement pub, where he was now 'Mine Host', and handed him the photo for all to see.

Within seconds it was mounted on the pub wall, behind the bar.

Her Majesty the Queen's Jubilee Medal 1977

1977 was the 25th Jubilee year of HM Queen Elizabeth the Second's, ascension to the Throne, a Silver Medal was struck to mark the occasion.

Serving at the time it was rather believed that all serving members of Her Majesty's Forces would receive the Medal as a token of their service. If the Government could not make such funds available to provide all, it was proposed that Service Personnel be allowed to purchase the Commemorative Medal. Such a proposal was made at Depot Para 1976, Headquarters at The Regimental Sergeants Majors Conference, at which I as the Senior RSM, was the Chair. Our written proposal was submitted to Regimental Headquarters through our Regimental Colonel. Many other Service Units proposed the same minute to their conferences.

Come the day of the Jubilee only FIVE Medals were on issue to The Parachute Regimental Headquarters and the Depot. This was the allocation from South East District Headquarters. The strength of our Para Depot at that time was about 270 strong. After the Regimental Colonel and Depot Lt Colonel in Command had received theirs, CO Depot was ordered to award one to a WO2, one to a Sgt and one to a Cpl. Taking up our allocation.

I, as the Senior Regimental Sgt Major did not receive one and, what was worse, neither did the Senior Quartermaster Lt Col Jack Hobbs with over 30 years' service. This almost caused his resignation. In 1992 at the next Jubilee Celebration **ALL** members of HM Forces were allowed to purchase the Commemorative Medal.

By this time I had left the Service. This sticks in my craw, even today.

A laugh over a pair of Briefs

Christopher, my brother, whilst living in Vine Close, loved a challenge! After all, he did shoot rapid and centre fire pistol for Great Britain. He tried his damnedest to beat me his brother at badminton. Having been honed during lunch-time breaks for four years within TA drill halls I was unbeatable. We played usually at either his or my depot gym as a ritual each Thursday evening.

Followed by games of darts at 'The Windmill' pub and sometimes golf matches, the outcome was much the same. He never played cricket! Going for the smoother events in life, he took up sailing and became an Ocean Skipper. Cars were another passion and he was forever heading through windscreens.

I had an MGB Roadster 1800 with overdrive and in very good condition, courtesy of the MT REME Fitters. Christopher had a mini-cooper.

It had to be, that one day, taking a visit to the pottery at Rowlands Castle and on the way to Southsea with one of our children each, all became competitive.

We had to meet on Buster Hill, a long winding double carriageway of about two miles. He had previously passed me and from a single into this dual, somehow was trapped behind a bus. I in overdrive shot past and we never saw him again until he walked into the pottery miles away.

Pop-eyed, he said, 'You're mad!'
Chris bought an MGB GT the week after from a main dealer at Staines. Chicken-shit yellow in colour, he thought that he had, 'The Daddy'. It did not prove to be. Although we never raced MGBs he got to understand that the MGB GT was a slower vehicle because of heavier weight!

We as brothers were always winding each other up as well as doing favours for each other. An ideal chance of a wind-up came as Christine and I were walking the tow-path of the Fleet Canal one Saturday morning with the dog. I saw a pair of sexy black lace briefs on the canal iced surface. Moving them toward me by use of a

179

broken branch I retrieved them, squeezed them dry and put them into my Barbour jacket pocket. Christine was most indignant! 'I don't want those dirty things,' she said, 'throw them back.'

'No' said I, 'Cunning Plan.'

Coming back home and into Vine Close passing brother Christopher's car door, the car a big old Rover being parked outside his house, I quietly opened the front passenger door and threw the knickers up the well on the passenger side as far as they could go. There was no effect for a few days. Then one mid-morning, could have been the following Saturday, I had a most irate brother knock on my door.

'It's you,' he said, 'It's you. Put some knickers in my car.'

I protested my innocence and asked how such a thing could be. He said that he and his wife Annie had been shopping in Aldershot then back at home on leaving the car they had found a pair of lacy briefs wrapped around the heel of her shoe.

They were not hers and she was not amused ... accusations flew! Divorce was threatened, other painful punishment. Well, I have to say, though awful of me, I did wind him up. After two years or so and after his lovely posting to the Far East, I did confess to being the 'Knicker Shifter'.

Depot Mess Night: 'The League of Gentlemen'

The PMC of The Sergeants Mess was approached by the Secretary of 'The League of Gentlemen' to host a social evening within the Mess, the proceeds of a raffle and/or donations to go to show-biz charities.

The Mess would have to field a team of eight players to take part in a darts competition. The League would field two teams. We were asked to do the same, and so asked for a team from our local branch of The Regimental Old Comrades to make up our second team.

On the night the first of the two teams of the League of Gentlemen had the ever popular actor Kenneth Beckinsale as their captain of show-biz personalities. The second eight was made up from The Scotland Yard Fraud Squad! Two Superintendents included to keep order. The Show Biz Team came in style – Black Tie with the darts presented to each player on a velvet cushion, before each throw. It was, of course, a buffet evening with our ladies present and a most super night until after midnight was had by all. We had a return match later in a Thames side pub at Kingston.

I have two fond memories of these parties in addition to the camaraderie. The first, being presented with a fraud squad tie. The second? Swimming the Thames, after midnight! (Well, I was once Middle East Champion).

DEPOT THE PARACHUTE REGIMENT 1978
Receiving The Queens Commission and Posting Out

Mid 1978 I was called to Lt Col Farrell's office to be given the excellent news that I had been selected for a Commission into The Parachute Regiment in the appointment as Quartermaster. I was to leave my present post as Senior Regimental Sergeant Major in September and would be joining my old Battalion the 1st Battalion as its Motor Transport Officer. The Post I had held years previous as a Warrant Officer! This would see me settling into Commissioned Battalion life before attending a six week All Arms Quartermaster Course at the RAOC Depot Blackdown in 1979. My future in the Regiment and as a member of an All Arms QM Commission should see me progress into a further army career until aged 55.

In September 1978 The Depot Sergeants Mess gave Christine and me a terrific Dining Out within the Mess, with a congratulatory menu and handsome leaving presents and kind words. I handed over the Office and Duties of RSM to WO1 Jackie Henderson, a fellow Warrant Officer whom I had known for many years.

The day after I was called on interview by the GOC South East District, a 200 yards walk away, to meet General Tony Farrar-Hockley, my one time Brigade Commander. General Tony congratulated me on Commissioning, wished me well and confirmed my posting to 1 Para.

Having been granted a week's leave between appointments I made the most of it: changing uniforms, Mess dress accoutrements and badges of rank.

I was very fortunate in one respect; when leaving the previous 2nd Battalion in 1977 and on being dined out, the Mess members had presented me with a sword.

I reported into the 1st Battalion to take up post as the MTO in late

181

September. Lt/Colonel David Charles made me most welcome as he introduced me to the officers in the Mess mid-morning. Many Officers were of course well known to me. In particular Captains Barry Andrews, John Williams DCM and David Woods. The Adjutant Adrian Freer, John Easton and Majors Brian Wilde the 2 i/c and John Crosland. All had served in Aden.

I was to see the Brigade Commander during the afternoon, Brigadier Mike Gray. He had been my CO in Northern Ireland 69/70 and years previously in 1955 we had attended the same course at RAF Abingdon. We knew each other well.

This probably accounted for the most informal interview ever. I never saw him in his office. Whilst walking from Battalion Headquarters and bound for the MT Yard, Brigadier Mike passed me on the roadway coming out of Brigade Headquarters. Stopping his Staff Car and having wound the window down he called me over and said: 'Tom, I'm supposed to see you this afternoon but don't have to now. Congratulations, well done, I see you are a Lieutenant. That will not do, you are much too old and wise! You are now a Captain. Go home and tell Chris to sew another Pip on or buy a new rank slide. I have, by the way, told your CO David Charles and he was to tell you after our interview! See you!'

What an excellent way of being promoted, I thought.

Of the two other Quartermasters in the Battalion, Captains Banks Middleton the Technical Stores QM and John 'Patch' Williams DCM, the Regimental and Senior Quartermaster, I came to hold John as my mentor. He had earned his DCM in a fierce fight in Borneo when, as the Company Sergeant Major, he had saved the Company being overrun by his skilful use of a machine gun. The Company at the time were being attacked on a feature by a Battalion of Indonesians. In the attack John lost an eye. Hence the nickname 'Patch'.

I was to work with him for six months or so taking Battalion advance parties to Denmark, to accommodation on Salisbury Plain and exercising on range work at Lyde and Hythe. He had two memories for me. One as a cricketer whilst at Hythe, the Sgts challenged the officers to an evening match of 20 overs each.

We, the officers scored 74, the Sgts were skittled out for 35, with John bowling at one end, me at the other. 'I never knew you could

182

bowl so well!' I said.

'Like you,' he said, 'Ex-Grammar School Boy. Not bad for two old duffers.'

His other memory, or mine of him, having seen him perform in the Mess Bar, when arguing always stand on his 'blind side', as in a heated exchange of words he was likely to throw a punch. Those I saw were rarely effective, nor meant to be!

When John left the Battalion in '79 and was relieved by Major Arthur Channon he took up the post of The Senior Quartermaster to the Army's Staff College, in the rank of Lt Colonel. There, in addition to his Quartermaster duties, he was able to lecture the future military leaders on leadership.

USA: Fort Campbell. Kentucky/Tennessee 1979

March 1979 saw the Battalion training with the 101st Airborne, in and around Fort Campbell. The Camp covered a vast area, some said of 25 miles and was split between training areas in Kentucky and Tennessee. Before the Exercise I reported to UKLF Headquarters for briefing as this was to be a costed Exercise and I was given a budget for vehicle hire, fuels, cleaning materials and camp stores. A part of my remit was the taking over of soldiers' accommodation, double decker wooden hutted in the National Guard area of the camp.

The Battalion soon settled in and took advantage of the vast training areas. Once when delivering ammunition to a selected range area I asked for a range template for the constraints left and right and distance. The American Safety Officer told me to tell the Company, 'No constraints! Further than your eye can see! Do what you want.'

We had the joy of working with helicopters on call. Once on delivering the whole Battalion in fighting order as the MTO and in hired transport to an LZ. we saw the Battalion disappear within 20 minutes, when all I was left with was vehicles and drivers, to return to camp.

We were also able for the first time to parachute from a massive jet aircraft, the American 'Skymaster'. Ninety parachutists each side port and starboard. Amazing.

Of course during our six weeks or so, life was not all work day

183

and night and we were able as a Battalion to use all of the on post facilities. Cinemas, theatre, bars, recreational clubs and Messes and the on post golf course and pools. Off post, and all ranks had four days off, one could tour the battlefields of the wars between North and South in the 1800s. Visit 'The Grande Old Oprey' at Nashville or visit the off post villages, towns and markets in rural Tennessee.

'Netting With Arthur'

The Battalion's Regimental Quartermaster (clothing, equipment, Messing and PRI) on this Exercise was Major Arthur Channon MBE. Having taken over from 'Patch' Williams, most of Arthur's Service had been with 3 Para and so we had never served together.

Arthur was a keen bird watcher of the feathered variety, one of the few soldiers to be licensed by authority to capture, ring, record and release birds. Within his field kit and even on exercise Arthur carried 'Mist Nets' and telescopic poles. He was fascinating to watch. He would set up before nightfall and before roosting time. I helped him set up on a number of occasions. His favourite and mine was the Red Cardinal, somewhat like a super-sized British Robin Redbreast, but with much more striking colours.

Back in the UK and on an invitation to Arthur's bungalow in Farnborough, we found that he had an extensive aviary around the back, with dozens of different birds. A pet owl flew indoors which would perch on Arthur's shoulders. At this time Christine and I owned a keet we named 'Elvis' because of the crop that came over its eyes. The bird could not talk but was an outstanding mimic whistler. I taught it to whistle, 'Three Blind Mice', 'Half a Pound of Twopenny Rice', and 'Reveille' all the way through.

When leaving the Battalion later in 1979 and posted as Quartermaster to Ulster for a while I asked Arthur to look after our bird. He agreed and we saw him into the aviary with about another half dozen parrot types. On meeting Arthur at a Regimental conference a year or so later in the UK, he said, 'That bloody bird of yours has taught my lot to whistle 'Reveille', they are driving me mad!' Elvis lived a few more years and Arthur kept him! Elvis loved the birdy company.

184

USA: The Tennessee 'Walking Horse'

Whilst at Fort Campbell and one afternoon off, a pal and I were invited to a nearby ranch, the home of the Tennessee Walking Horse.

Massive great beasts the equivalent of a British Shire Horse, they were trained to high step on parade, and walk or waltz on street carnivals.

On the day we arrived, they were let out to grass, the first time for weeks, having wintered indoors. We were asked to ride one. No blooming fear, they came into the paddocks like tanks and mad as hatters. The owner had a pair set up in their finery and to music we were shown their peculiar gait. They picked their front feet up almost vertically from the hock to chest height, seemed to place each hoof down with little forward progress whilst the back end of the horse seemed to waltz from side to side. Uncanny yet beautiful to watch.

Hopkinsville, Tennessee: Mayoral Invite

The surrounding camp area of Fort Lewis had two nearby villages: Clarkesville, where many 101st Airborne retirees lived and Hopkinsville, where up to 3000 chickens per day were spit roasted.

The Officers Mess Members were kindly invited to lunch one weekend by His Worship the Mayor.

The town was out in the sticks of Tennessee and the Town Hall was a large veranda'd wooden build with porches, solidly built in the 1890s. Within the Mayor's parlour was a massive table taking up most of the room, where poker was played after business was done. There were old six-shooters and Indian relics on the walls and a few scalps but not of the tourist type. The whole building could have graced any movie and the people we met, our hosts could have taken part. Outside, there were horses tied up to hitching rails.

Within sight of the verandas there was a dirt road network where truck after truck went to covered but working charcoal pits where hundreds of chickens were being spit roasted, slid off skewers when cooked and packed hot into grease-proofed containers. Evidently the product of the pits supplied most of the county. On any one shift we were told, 3000 birds were moved.

185

We had a cracking afternoon on roast chicken, spuds and beer. These charcoal pits were something though. Just the place to hide a troublesome neighbour?

The 101st Airborne Veterans, Clarksville

Most Airborne Retirees in this area of America lived off Post but a few miles away, in the local town of Clarkesville, the local Mayor was an ex-101st Airborne Colonel. It was super to see the Military Post and local town as one. Unlike the British Army, whose officers and soldiers are shunned once having left the service, the American serviceman retains full on Post or on Camp rights, once he or she has served a full career.

There are excellent facilities: shopping within the PX, medical facilities and admittance to Hospitals, the use of all Mess facilities, Officers, Sgts and Soldiers Canteens, leisure facilities, gymnasia, swimming pools, golf courses etc. there are also Education facilities.

The British Counterpart gets a six week 'Demob Course', a minimum pension then, 'Out of sight, out of mind! Try your luck with the National Health Service!'

Whilst at Fort Campbell we attended a couple of retiree parties, played pool, quoits, darts, had drinks in the Messes and some played golf. We met WWII Airborne Vets and 'Bands of Brothers'. One notable, Master Sergeant 'Skully' Macullough, was a good golfer and a wartime hero, holder of the American 'Silver Star' and Purple Heart etc. His best pal had a backside full of plastic having been shot up. They called him 'Ping Pong Balls'. Don't ask why.

The ULSTER DEFENCE REGIMENT
Armagh 1979 – 81

On the roll of All Arms Quartermasters, I could of course be posted anywhere. Principally Airborne and trained, the Regiment had first call.

During the 'Troubles' in Northern Ireland the Parachute Regiment had an obligation to support one of the ten Ulster Defence Regiments. Our obligation was to support the 2nd Battalion the

186

Ulster Defence Regiment in and around Armagh: Loughgall, Newry, Newtonards. Places to the border really south of Armagh. The Battalion had both Catholic and Protestant members who endeavoured to keep the peace on the streets, and at nights in patrolling and setting up road check points.

Most soldiers were part time and there was a small permanent Cadre. The principal threat to peace of course was the IRA in the area with their on-going fight against The Crown and the threat and murder of police and Protestants.

The Parachute Regiment or Airborne Forces provided much of the permanent Regular Army Staff of a Commanding Officer: Training Major, Quartermaster (Major or Captain), WO1 RSM, a Signals SNCO and one or two other weapons training instructors. I was to take up post in November 1979.

The Posts were accompanied and Christine and I took up residence in Armagh on what proved to be a secure estate. Many senior police lived there as did a local MEP. It was impossible though for our 12 year old daughter Trudy to attend the local school, and so Trudy went off beforehand to boarding school at Lillingstone Dayrell in Buckinghamshire.

Charmandean: The Boarding School 1979 – 84
Younger Daughter Trudy

Having been warned of the posting to Armagh it fell to Christine and I to find a suitable boarding school in England for Trudy, our 12 year old daughter.

Living as we were, still in Vine Close, we were most fortunate as WO1 Ralph Weaville on the close had a daughter already attending boarding school in Buckingham.

Not to complicate things our elder daughter Tanya aged 19, a trainee hospital pharmacist, lived in at Farnham Hospital then, somewhat later, at a very nice flat in Bournemouth.

Trudy from home in Vine Close was able to visit the boarding school hosted by Alison, Ralph Weaville's daughter, and without much fuss, once Christine and I had attended interviews with the School Principals Mr & Mrs Askew, our daughter moved to the school as a full time boarder.

She was there for five years and at least received a continuity of education; although not popular with her throughout, it proved to be in later life a sound period of her life. It enabled her to be the manager of a hotel and now an independent Post Mistress at one of the few thriving post offices in rural Wales. Whilst there, in addition to receiving a sound education she obtained a Gold award in Elocution and DRAMA!

The school was an 'all-girls school' at Lillingstone Dayrell in Buckinghamshire, not too far from Aldershot as it was to prove in due course. I had the Red Devils drop in on one sports day! A training drop as the team leader, Captain Micky Munn, called it. On the line-up after the drop, which took place on the sports field opposite the school entrance, the teaml leader presented Mrs Askew, the Head, with a bouquet of flowers produced from within the Red Devil jumpsuit. The girls were impressed and in particular when the 'Red Devils' stayed for tea. There was one delightful teacher at the school with a most marvellous name, Mrs Twelvetree.

Life with 2 UDR in Armagh

The Battalion was a hard working one, with a small permanent Cadre of Regulars during the day commanded by a Captain, with the normal Headquarters to call on for Operations, training and administration. The Battalion came into its own out of hours, with Platoons of part timers working from Company bases at Glenanne, Loughgall and Drummad Barracks in Armagh.

Trying to keep the Peace in this so called 'Bandit Country' of Armagh, and so near to the border with Eire, was a thankless task. This area was full of hard liners, both warring tribes of Catholics and Protestants. The Company Base of Loughgall where 'C' Company operated from, commanded by Major Alfie Briggs, was to hit the National Press when eight hoods were taken out by the SAS during a failed attempt to blow up the base with a 40 gallon drum of explosive in transport immediately to the base by Digger Bucket.

During my tour with the Battalion we had vehicles caught by IEDs. The Battalion Second in Command Charles Armstrong lost his life being killed outside his office in Armagh, the result of a car bomb. A lady 'Greenfinch' soldier was murdered, as was one of our

Sergeants at his daytime customs post on the border. One of my staff took his own life, the pressure of constant threat getting to him.

As the Quartermaster, I endeavoured to keep these lads armed, equipped and fed. Messing was a problem, in particular during the winter months. I had an allowance to feed the permanent staff and, before patrols, made sure that they had a substantial meal as they were often out for hours.

Believe it or not there was no messing allowance for the part-timers when out on the ground. I broke all the rules and had container meals prepared and delivered. When I left the Battalion after two years I had racked up a messing debt of a considerable sum. I left a reasonable written explanation for the Bean Counters and Auditors as to why and when the men had been fed. Having not been called back nor court martialled, the powers that be in Ordnance Headquarters must have been embarrassed enough to write off my debt.

Without attempting to appear in the Superman mould I was expected, as the duty officer, to visit the UDR check points and vehicle patrol points at night. Driving at night down country lanes in and around Armagh was not for the faint hearted. On my own and in my civilian 'Q' car, changed each month for security reasons I used to before leaving surround myself with flak jackets to afford some protection in the event of being caught in ambush. I had a Stirling Sub Machine Gun with me and sat on a pistol. (Having won the individual Champion Walther PPK Pistol Cup at the Battalion Skill at Arms Meeting I must have thought myself invincible!)

The Lighter Side of Ulster

Whilst in Armagh, Christine and I had tucked away in the garage an MGB in British racing green. We used to leave our protected quarter on weekends and explore the beauty of Northern Ireland as tourists.

What a most beautiful country, from the Mountains of Mourne in the south to the Antrim Coast, the Giants Causeway, Port Rush and Port Stewart in the north. The beaches were excellent but the sea so cold. When the girls came out on holiday we used to go to Benbane Head and Carrick-a-Rede where there is a rope bridge 70 metres over to an island. Newcastle Beaches in the south were our favourites and the dog was quite fazed out when the grey seals off shore popped up for a look.

My CO. Lt Colonel Sandy Ogilvie was a keen golfer and together we managed to play eleven different courses, only a couple more notable in Scotland when the Battalion, part-time and full-timers went on Summer Camp for a well-earned break. We played St Andrews, Troon and Dundee. I once played Belfast and had the honour of meeting Fred Daly, a past British Open Champion. He had the smallest hands that I had seen on any man.

'Bushmills' the Whisky Distillery is off the North Antrim Coast Road and one summer Philip my brother-in-law and pal David Lamb came over from England via the Stranraer – Larne Ferry, to take up with me a six-berth caravan, on a secure site and owned by a policeman. We had a long weekend as tourists visiting the breweries, pubs, playing golf and sampling the triple distilled whisky at 'Bushmills'.

The Carrick-a-Rede Rope Bridge

Not far from the Giants Causeway and off the North Antrim Coast Road there lies an island only one hundred yards or so from the mainland. This small island of Carrick-a-Rede is connected to the mainland by a slatted walkway or 'Rope Bridge'. Looking down through the slats when crossing the turbulent swelling sea below seems to be more like 100 feet or so when it is actually no more than 70.

The Bridge was fashioned to enable local salmon fishermen to have access to the island small shore to work nets, to net the salmon in season when migrating. A track leads down to a stone built fishing shed more or less at the waterline. If the conditions were favourable it would be possible to work a small boat from there.

The island in area is no larger than an acre. A small charge is made to cross over to the island using the bridge, as seats and picnic areas are provided, as one discovers once across. We crossed one lovely afternoon as I carried the dog less it should fall through the slats of the bridge. Having had a super picnic and spent an hour or so looking round the Island, it was time to leave to return to the car.

Christine, who must have been brooding about the return journey flatly refused to move! Vertigo! Going over the Bridge with daughter Trudy and the dog and picnic basket I then returned for Chris. I walked backwards, we were nose to nose! Chris did not look down. Pity but we never went over again!

The Officers Mess 2 UDR Armagh

The members met whenever possible, once a month, Ladies Dinner Night, Black Tie, at Drummad Barracks on the outskirts of Armagh.

The Irish are convivial hosts and the 'Crack' is always good. At times the Ladies provided a potato dish themselves, with skins on! They had a way with the humble 'spud' that Chris and I had never experienced.

There were some real characters within the Mess and none more so than Captain Tommy Moffet an Ulsterman through and through but with the most cultivated 'Oxford Accent'! His Grandfather had been a surgeon general to the British Forces in India. Tommy worked for the Milk Marketing Board during the day and for the UDR at night. On a visit to his home once for supper Chris and I, up in the hills, saw the Grandfather's accoutrements, Sam Browne, Sword, Cockade Hat. All laid out on a sideboard.

Tommy, though an Officer in the UDR, was a rugby fanatic. He had played it at county level and now, although a spectator, was always, through contacts, over the border and off to the Internationals. He and I became good drinking partners in the Mess and it's fair to say that he weaned me off beer onto the Ulster 'Bushmills Whisky', the Orange label though, NOT the Black Label 'Blackbush'.

He had one peculiar but endearing trait. Looking you straight in the eye, he would in this cut glass Oxford accent say, 'Excuse me old boy!' Place his glass, half full or otherwise on the bar and thereupon collapse onto the carpet in front of the bar.

In a moment, seconds! he would regain his feet, reclaim his glass and say, 'Sorry about that old boy,' and carry on drinking.

After a couple of collapses, Bea, his good lady, who always kept an eye on him from the ante-room, would excuse herself from the girls, collect Tommy and drive him home.

191

Why not take some Exercise, Sir?

The seconded Training Major to the UDR Battalion during my tenure as Quartermaster was Major Philip Butterworth. I knew him of 1 Para as OC Support Company. Philip was a confirmed bachelor, enjoyed the ladies company in small doses but was more into classical music, tea in Armagh with the Bishop. Cigars, stocks and shares and fine wines.

A dark horse was Philip and not many other than I knew that as a Subaltern he parachuted into Suez with 3 Para in 1956 and the good shot that he was, dropped an Egyptian Sniper holding up the Battalion advance. Soldier of Fortune and into his forties he, when he left 2UDR, was appointed as Military Attaché in Korea and Garrison Adjutant in The Falklands, on a later secondment.

The Regimental Sergeant Major, WO1 Frank Newbould, remarked to me one day in passing, 'I don't see Major Butterworth taking much exercise, Sir. He doesn't use the gym, doesn't play squash or golf. We never see him do anything!'

I said, jokingly, 'Have a word with him RSM. As a Para!'

This was on a Thursday. The following Monday the RSM popped into my office, after information. The story went like this!

'I spoke with Major Butterworth about taking some exercise and he agreed. He asked me to meet him at the Camp Gate at 0830 Saturday morning and he and I would go for a walk in the safe areas up to Tandragee and around the country lanes. A UDR patrol vehicle would keep an eye on us occasionally so it would be better if we wore boots, puttees, lightweight green trousers and a sweat top! He said that he would enjoy a walk. I met Major Butterworth at the Camp Gates at 0830 he said, "Good morning, Mr Newbould. Right! Let's go!" They were the only words that he said. Seventeen miles and two hours later when we arrived back at Camp, Major Butterworth said, "Thank you, RSM. We must do it again sometime." Then he left me and went off for a shower. It's fair to say I was shattered. What do you think of that?'

I said to Frank, the RSM, 'Didn't you know?'

'Know what?' he said, having never ever served in the same Units as the Major.

192

'Major Butterworth was at one time, not that long ago, the officer commanding 'P' Company, the dreaded PARA SELECTION COMPANY. He is one of the fittest men on two legs!'

Frank was enlightened and never approached the fitness subject again. I saw Philip during the day and he remarked that the RSM had seen fit to ask him to take some exercise.

'Cheeky Young Pup,' he said.

'Four Screws and a Barrel'

In the office at Drummad Barracks mid-morning, whilst chatting with 'Joe' my able RQMS, Gloria my lady clerk, and Sgt Steenson one of my stores staff, the conversations were interrupted by an elderly UDR corporal who had been told to, 'Report to the Quartermaster'. The Corporal in question was in uniform and so having taken him into my office, the inner sanctum so to speak, he stood before me and attempted to salute.

The UDR salute was a salute like no other, usually two fingers (the right way round) but more of a tap of the forehead than what is shown on the 'movies'. Anyway, having got over that hurdle, he held out his left hand and in the palm were four stainless steel screws and a barrel of, as I recognised, a WALTHER PPK PISTOL. (Now all members of the UDR whether on or off duty carried such, having been issued with this, as a personal protection weapon).

The Cpl said, 'This was all was left, Sir!'

I asked him to explain and he said that whilst at work he had decided to clean the pistol. Having removed the magazine and ammo he then stripped it into its component parts and placed it on the tray. To get rid of the grease on the bits he then lowered it into the liquid below. He worked in a wet battery manufacturing plant. All the base metal and the plastic grip disappeared to mush. We then saw the CO. I retained the bits, the Corporal paid for the PISTOL!!

LEAVING THE UDR and Posted to
2 Para as Quartermaster, 1981

Christine and I were dined out in style. I remained in Armagh to hand over the appointment to Captain George Bell. A fellow Para.

193

Then a couple of weeks later I joined Christine who had returned to Aldershot to take over a married quarter, once again in Vine Close, off the Farnborough Road. The same barracks accountant saw us in, dear old Topper Brown (ex-Para).

He was to do us a super favour four months later when a detached quarter became available at Knollys Road, the best quarters in Aldershot at the time and he gave us the nod. This was to be our last married quarter in England. Two more only would follow, one in Wales, the last in Berlin.

I reported into Albuhera Barracks to 2 Para to take over the appointment as Quartermaster from Major Peter Bing MBE, to find that he, and the Battalion were on Exercise in Kenya. Nevertheless, settling in, I found my way around past familiar territory and made myself known to the Battalion's rear party.

The rear party Chief Clerk Sgt Magill did ask me one day if I would be agreeable to a task not usually asked of Quartermasters, who would rather 'Hang 'em, than forgive 'em'. He asked me to speak up for a soldier in detention who in the Battalion Cells was awaiting a District Courts Martial for Desertion.

The soldier in question was expected to have an officer speak up for him from the Regiment and as the only other on the Battalion Rear Party was a Subaltern, I was asked as the one, with probably more clout.

I interviewed Pte Thomas Meechan in the cells and must say that I was impressed with his attitude to want to 'Soldier On!' Though not with his reasons for going 'Absent Without Leave' in the first place and thereby being classed as a Deserter after ten days. In his words he was happy soldiering in 'A' Company, a rifle Company, with all his mates when suddenly and without prior warning he was posted to 'Support' Company. He didn't get on with these much older soldiers, didn't want to be in the Mortar Platoon, asked to return to 'A' Company and to his mates but was refused. He then went absent.

The good thing in his favour, after a month at home in Scotland his mother persuaded him to give himself up to the local Military Police. He was brought back to Aldershot and placed within 2 Para cells.

I attended the Courts Martial in Aldershot, stood in front of the

Board of three Officers, the President, a full Colonel and spoke up for Pte Meechan, explained his reasons for absence and desire to remain in 2 Para. I also produced previous written reports. I was thanked by the President and asked to wait whilst the Board delivered its verdict. (Beforehand, the Chief Clerk had guessed three months detention and dishonourable discharge!)

Well, my testimonial must have had some clout as the verdict given was: 'One month's detention in the Unit Guard Room and Soldier On!' The Chief Clerk back in Barracks was amazed.

Pte Thomas Meechan continued to soldier with 2 Para. He was deployed to The Falklands on 26 April 1982 and lost his life gallantly at Goose Green in 'The Falklands War'.

Prince Charles attended the Memorial Gathering late June 1982 within 2 Para main kitchen anti-room and spoke with the bereaved families. His Mother and Uncle who attended spoke with me as the Officer who had saved their son at the Courts Martial.

His Uncle said to me, 'No regrets, Sir, our Tommy died a soldier!'

Belize, Central America 1982
Recce for the six months Tour

In February 1982 a small advance party from 2 Para took off for Belize to see what would be required of the Battalion Operationally and in men and materials to effect a six month tour May to October of this year. The Battalion would be deployed in company groups in both North and South Belize to the borders with Guatemala, to stop this country being a military threat to Belize, which had recently become independent.

On arrival in Belize and at The Military Headquarters at Airport Camp the Battalion Advance Party of The CO. Lt Col 'H' Jones, The 2 i/c, Training Major, OC HQ Company, Paymaster and I took up with our counterparts of the existing Battalion, The Royal Anglian Regiment and over three days went our separate ways to learn what was required.

I was taken under the wing of the Anglian Quartermaster and was briefed of the Company locations and how the system of supply worked for the provision of food, water, rations, ammunitions, equipment and other supplies and the upkeep of generators, refrigeration. Fresh food supplies. Transportation of all by air, helicopter, road and even by sea.

The Battalion split in half would have two Companies south and a Headquarters, and three Companies north and a Headquarters. Quite a complex situation! Some 180 miles apart.

After four days and with all our Brains having been in overdrive the CO called a 'Mop Up' meeting for the Recce Party within the Brigade Officers Mess at Airport Camp. We were at the table for hours, with plans, maps, charts and logs. Not only was the patrol and secured Company positions covered but parachute training, field firing with heavy weapons, an inter Service Exercise and even leave facilities for the 'Toms'.

The CO gave his outline on which company would be where. After which we all spoke our piece on how it would all work. The last being training.

Things did get a little heated in particular during the 'Training' package. Colonel 'H' Jones who was quite forceful in manner and never suffered fools gladly was really pushing the point when he said, 'No matter what the Operational Commitments are, 'TRAINING' will go on and each Company in turn will go through a set package whereby they can fire off their heavy weapons i.e. Mortars, Anti-Tank Guns and Heavy Machine Guns.'

He looked across the table direct at me and said, 'Tom, when I want this ammunition pre-positioned, I Fucking Well Want It There!!'

I said, 'Colonel, don't you swear at me! You will get what you want, when you want it!'

There was a deadly silence then peals of laughter, then 'H' said, 'Sorry, Tom. Gentlemen, let us all retire to the bar, we have done far too much today!' That is exactly what we did.

I had never served with Lt Col 'H' Jones previously in any appointment, but from that day he was, my man. He never suffered fools, was impetuous, but what a leader.

He and I, in his short life remaining, got on like a house on fire. He was to lose his life commanding at Goose Green during the Falklands War against Argentina.

Contrary to rumour he would listen and I have first-hand knowledge of this. There was a time on the MV Norland, and during the voyage south to the Falklands, 2 Para had on board a Warrant Officer who was found not to be pulling his weight. Getting everyone's back up and in particular the Seniors, so much so that the Second-in-Command wanted this Warrant Officer to remain on board the Norland when the Battalion went ashore.

The Colonel, who had not travelled with the Battalion on the Norland but by RN Fearless, with Operational Headquarters, joined the Battalion within San Carlos Sound. Briefed by the Second-in-Command on our readiness for war and to go ashore. He was asked to decide on the Warrant Officer. Colonel 'H Jones sent for the Padre, David Cooper and I, and in private conversation he took our advice that the Warrant Officer be taken ashore. There it was proven that in battles to come and in particular in the saving of Welsh Guardsman's lives at Fitzroy after the bombing of Sir Galahad he did sterling work.

BELIZE NO! – No 2 Para Falklands – YES!

'A Quartermaster's life is not an easy one'.
Warned for Belize, prepared and packed for Belize. Thirteen containers full of kit and spares to support the Battalion deployment from May to October 1982 was on the high seas. The Battalion relaxed and was sent on two weeks leave before fly out.

Early May 1982, one lovely morning with Chris and I at Knollys Road, Aldershot there was a knock on the door and there stood Lt Col 'H' Jones. Pullover, unshaven, car behind him.

'Tom, can you meet me in the office at 2 o'clock this afternoon and tell me what we have on the high seas to Belize? We will have to change tack, we are off to The Falklands.' Arctic instead of Jungle.

Within the next ten days, officers and soldiers were recalled from leave. Much midnight oil was burned by the Quartermaster's Staff and in particular by the Battalions Technical Equipment Quartermaster Capt Banks Middleton. We were preparing for war. Warned by Col 'H' that we as a Battalion would probably end up as

Garrison Troops for three months after the taking back of the Island, we had to think of more than just combat supplies i.e. fighting order, boxed rations and ammunition.

We had to take the stores on board the MV Norland at Hull to sustain the Battalion in that environment for three months. As a result and to coin a modern phrase, 'Thinking outside the box'.

I was the ONLY Quartermaster of seven on the Falklands who took paraffin HEATERS! Free standing, boxed, 600 of them and spare WICKS! The 'Toms' even took parade uniforms and packed green army suitcases. I had these stored on the Norland.

Our sister Battalion who had already been warned for the Falklands were under the mantle of The Royal Marines and their Headquarters, and travelled in light scales. Theirs was a proven supply chain provided through the Royal Marines Administrative Headquarters. They were to travel on the Canberra and RN Fearless.

On the 24 April 1982, together with thirteen 4 tonners of kit and equipment and with a party of all the Company Quartermaster Sergeants and my own Quartermaster's Staff I arrived at the King George Dock at Hull in Yorkshire to board the MV Norland. The Pride of the Fleet of North Sea Ferries.

In the next 24 hours we were to load all stores into the Norland, in addition the 'War Pack' of ammunition and explosives. I was able to meet the Master 'Capt Don Ellerby' and his crew and able to formulate a plan for the arrival of the Battalion Group. The storage of all stores, ammo and weapons in secure areas and the accommodation for all, in cabins for the long journey south. The two pursers on board John Crowther and John Grinham were paramount in their willing help and assistance.

Messing could have been a problem but we agreed to a two shifts system, with all being fed from the main kitchen. Officers and seniors 30 minutes after the 'Toms'. My cooks were to supplement the Norland cooks.

2 Para group were to join the MV Norland at Hull but this was changed at the eleventh hour to Southampton. I was informed that the Battalion would be taken on board the Norland on the 26 April at **Portsmouth.** So the Norland sailed from Hull with helicopter decks being welded on, up top whilst we were on the move.

Docking on the morning of the 26th I was able to leave the ship, to report back to 2 Para and to brief the Second-in-Command Chris Keeble and the Adjutant David Woods on reception, weapons storage, security, accommodation and messing arrangements whilst on board. Seeing the Tech QM. Banks Middleton, he had been able to procure extra machine guns to take south with us so a secure berth was nominated for them.

We set sail through Portsmouth Harbour the evening of the 26 April bound for Sierra Leone and the Ascension Islands: The Battalion lining the ship's rails and with all Company and Battalion Flag flying from the Halyards. A tremendous send off. Thousands of spectators.

The Quartermaster Staff at Sea

During the journey south from Portsmouth the Tech QM and our staffs had the nightmare of sorting out what had literally been stuffed on board in boxes, crates and pallets at Hull to get the ship away within 24 hours. It took TEN days to sort out the ammunition and explosives. We were to cross deck men and equipment at a Port at Sierra Leone to our sister ship the Europic Ferry. On this were our small combat vehicle fleet and artillery.

The MV Norland anchored offshore at the Ascension Islands ten days or so after leaving Portsmouth and the Battalion trained together with the Royal Marines on boat drills for going ashore.

During the journey to the Ascensions, meetings were held with the Second-in-Command as to what weapons and equipment, arms, and ammunition would be issued to the soldiers before the assault onto the beaches. We even did trial weight packs. The weight that each man would have to carry ranged from 80 to over 100 lbs, horrific.

Leaving the Ascensions, things took a serious note. Some of the crew left, having been given the option of not progressing into the War Zone. Most stayed on board and were invaluable in helping us move all stores and ammunition into little boats, even while under air attack in the Falklands Sound, in what was termed 'Bomb Alley'. The Norland civilian crew were fantastic.

199

The Battalion at War Falklands May – June '82

From the Ascension Islands, south to the Falklands, hard training took place. Running the decks to keep fit, shooting and zeroing weapons, briefings on shore drills, first aid practicals, and exchanges and packing of equipment. The ship was blacked out at night and noise kept to a minimum. We travelled in convoy, under air and sea cover by the Royal Navy.

On arrival offshore it was decided by the CO, Lt Colonel 'H' Jones, who had joined us from HMS Fearless the High Command Vessel and before we anchored within the Falklands Sound, that the supply to the Battalion would be carried out in two places:

'One, the A Echelon under the Tech, Quartermaster Capt Middleton, would go ashore with the Battalion's Combat Supplies i.e. ration packs, ammunition, signals spares!!

Two, the bulk of the remaining stores and heavy ammunition i.e. mortar, anti-tank rounds, would remain on Norland, in the anchorage, as long as possible. Netted loads of heavy ammunition, pre-planned would be sent – on call to the Battalion on Sussex Mountain once the Battalion had gone firm. This would be under the arrangements of Captain Godwin and the Quartermaster Staff remaining.

The soldiers' suitcases would remain on board throughout for when, and if, we became garrison troops.' All the 700 or so suitcases of all ranks were collected under Company arrangements and I had them secured on a car deck within the Norland that was locked and raised to give security, thanks to the Purser John Crowther. Even when the whole Battalion group had left the Norland, Quartermasters Staff included, and the ship left, commissioned on other tasks i.e. running Argentine Prisoners back to Argentina, those suitcases remained secure.

They were to be reclaimed when 2 and 3 Para eventually joined ship for the return voyage to return to the Ascensions and back home.

Friday 21st May under cover of darkness and toward the dawn the Battalion went ashore in RM assault craft. Our last task was to issue most soldiers with primed grenades to take ashore and for most, 3 inch mortar bombs to take to the beach. We saw the Echelon off

200

with the combat supplies. The Norland Crew mucked in and was a fantastic help to us for hours. The first supply base ashore was set up by Capt Middleton and his team at 'Blue Beach', San Carlos, within a set of empty pig sheds some 800 yards from the beach, courtesy of the local farmer. The whole area on arrival was under guard and patrols of 40 Royal Marine Commando who were to guard Blue Beach throughout and lost Marines under air attack within The Sound, at San Carlos.

Once all troops were off, going ashore, and this included Para Medic Surgical Teams, 9 Squadron (Para) Royal Engineers and Ground Forward Air Controllers, the Norland put out to sea as the threat of air attack within the Falklands Sound and San Carlos was imminent.

The following day 22 May saw the Norland return to San Carlos offshore, and with the Battalion firm on Sussex Mountain overlooking the Sound, my team sent off 18 loads of netted ammunition by helicopter from the aft LZ.

The Argentinian Airforce, now alert to the landings, became a constant threat, and all ships within the Sound came under attack. More so the Naval ships as block ships at either end. HMS Ardent and Antrim were bombed and sunk.

All hell was let loose within the anchorage and anti-aircraft guns and missiles were prolific. On deck and within the air alert klaxon at short notice, my lads were netting loads when an Argentinian 'Skyhawk' came jinking down the Sound just a couple of hundred feet above the waves. We could clearly see his face. His mission completed he was clearly trying to get to hell out of the place.

We had some of my staff up top manning machine guns, behind 40 gallon oil drums of water and they were credited with 'The Kill', as the Argentinian Skyhawk exploded off the aft deck and showered us with 'confetti'.

I, on deck and speaking with the Adjutant on the radio set, as to what netted load was coming his way, saw the Aircraft, heard the explosion and being on my knees at the time facing the Education Officer, Captain Mike Beaumont, heard him shout, 'I'm hit, I'm hit.' Showered with debris and light metal and, smouldering between us in the gloom, was what looked like a part of a missile cover. I stood up and stamped on it! The piece broke in two. Having patted Mike down and discovering no holes in either him or his kit I gave him a half of what had hit him! (We have the pieces to this day).

On recovering and the air around clearing I heard the Adjutant on the radio say, 'God that was a close one, Tom.' (They must have had a grand-stand view from Sussex Mountain).

Well, we did get all the netted loads of ammunition off as ordered. It was said that a 1000 lb bomb had missed the Norland off the port deck. Off we went out to sea again. Safe haven.

The Norland returned the next morning to anchor under Naval Escort and I was taken off to attend a 'Q' conference at Red Beach, San Carlos, chaired by the Q staff of the Royal Marines. At this conference we, the Quartermasters, gave our holdings of combat supplies.

On return to the Norland by lighter we passed HMS Antelope, smouldering and burning. She was to explode later that evening and break her back. Many of the Crew of the Antelope came aboard the Norland, the Antelope Captain having given the order to abandon ship. My stores were able to fit them up with warm arctic clothing.

Monday 24 May, anchored within San Carlos Bay, saw my Quartermaster Staff with the cooks and clerks that I had been left with, load 2 x LCU (Marine Flat Bottom Boats) with the remaining ammunition left on board and combat supplies. Splitting my existing QM Staff and with the TQMS, WO2 Del Amos, I sent off 18 staff and some soldiers under command of Capt Mike Beaumont, the Education Officer, to deliver all stores to the Technical Quartermaster, and for them to remain ashore at the Echelon at San Carlos to assist Capt Middleton and his team.

All the time we were harassed by Argentinian aircraft and kept having to pause loading between Air Alerts (klaxon) being sounded. We were scheduled to have three additional LCUs come alongside the Norland lower cargo entrance to take off all other stores. Clothing, weapons and signals spares and Units spares of all description, including our 600 HEATERS. This process was cancelled because of this high constant threat of air attack.

So together with my remaining 'B' Echelon Quartermaster Staff and the Engineers on board working the Fresh Water Osmosis Plant once again, the Norland left the Sound and put out to SEA. It was felt with the naval cover being sunk on an almost daily basis that there was not sufficient cover within the Sound for the MV Norland nor the other large troop ship The Canberra.

That was why despite all the ballyhoo to the contrary, the QE2 never came near to the Falklands but transferred troops from a safe berth at South Georgia, which was by now safely in British hands 800 miles away. That is why safely at sea, the Norland went off to South Georgia two days sailing away to pick up the Gurkha Battalion of 5 Infantry Brigade and 5 Infantry Brigade Headquarters.

During the voyage back to San Carlos where they were to disembark I was able to brief the Commanding Officer and staff of the procedures on board, and I made my staff available as guides for their disembarkation at Blue Beach, by RM LCU.

During the days at sea the Echelon was kept fully aware by ship's radio of the battle on land to take Goose Green. I was confident that the Battalion had the ammunition and weapons for success. The sad news hit all on board that in the battle, the Battalion had lost Colonel 'H', the CO, the Adjutant David Woods, two other of my fellow officers and seventeen NCOs and Toms, most of whom I knew by sight and many by name, having been not only their Quartermaster but to some, their RSM some five years previously.

It was a sickening blow.

Tuesday 1 June back in San Carlos Waters

At 0900 hrs the Norland anchored offshore with Royal Marine small boats at our disposal, the remainder of the Battalion's stores and equipment were taken ashore to the jetty at San Carlos.

This Operation took all of 18 hours to unload and the whole Norland crew was invaluable. We had no mechanical handling devices. Every store item boxed or otherwise was moved by hand. I cannot praise the Norland crew enough.

All stores now being at the Tech QMs firm base, in and around the 'Pig Sheds' and outbuildings and under canvas cover, the whole of the Quartermaster's Staffs of about 32, including cooks and drivers were together for the first time ashore.

Once again, the team was split and Capt Middleton and the RQMS and the A Echelon NCOs and soldiers took off by helicopter with ration packs to join the Battalion at, by now, Bluff Cove having left Goose Green.

1st to 14th June

The Echelon at San Carlos continued to send netted loads of ammunition and boxed ten-man ration packs forward to the Battalion wherever they were. By helicopter sometimes by scout, (Teeny weeny airways). Whenever I sent the TQMS forward with supplies, he was shot at and had to take cover. At least three times he was chased. On his return he usually said to me, 'Had to go to ground yet AGAIN.' Often, on guesswork it was 60 boxes of ten-man rations forward by any means. We were 90% out of radio contact.

The Unit mail came through me from ships at sea and it was my proud boast that no-one in 2 Para went without cigarettes as I had taken thousands off the Norland.

The Echelon whilst at San Carlos did sterling work, netting ammunition loads under air threat. We saw an Argentinian Vulcan taken out by the Naval Ship's Missile, pass overhead, lose a wing at about 30,000 feet, and plummet into the sea some two miles away.

The week before on a similar sortie, two Royal Marines had been killed in our area and a number wounded. The cooks made ovens out of oil drums and there was always a hot meal laid on for passing SAS Patrols coming out of the hills. We even formulated a hot shower system.

A work party was sent to Fitzroy and Bluff Cove to follow the Battalion on its move forwards towards Port Stanley. I had heard of the move from the San Carlos Jetty of the Welsh Guards and so tacked onto the Sir Galahad, an echelon small party of the Education Officer Capt Mike Beaumont and my TQMS WO2, Del Amos, to deliver another 60 boxes of ten man ration packs.

I remember distinctly saying to both Mike and Del, 'When that ship docks, get off the bloody thing as soon as you get there!' They did, to a man. Thank God for common sense.

The Welsh Guards did not, with tragic consequences.

The Battalion had one other major battle, and this was on the outskirts of Port Stanley before 2 Para became the 'Van', the first Unit to enter the Port as Victors. The Battle was for Wireless Ridge. Up to the assault, one of the Company Quartermaster Sergeants I had originally taken with me to Hull to load his company stores, Colour Sgt 'Doc' Halliday, was killed by an artillery or mortar shell, after the 14 June and the surrender of the Argentine Forces.

We, the Quartermaster's staff handed over much of the ammunition, stores, equipment and rations to 5 Brigade Headquarters, in location at Blue Beach and, together with our personal kit, were taken by helicopter to join up with the A Echelon and the Battalion in Port Stanley.

We were accommodated within the local school. After a few days we were given the glorious news that the Battalion was not to be garrison troops and to remain on the Island but that we and our sister Battalion 3 were to return home. The Prime Minister wanted a Victory Parade and who better than 2 and 3 Para.

Homeward Bound Post War Falklands. The MV Norland

My God, what a welcome sight. The Norland, offshore at Port Stanley at anchor. I was given the news that the Battalion and our sister Battalion 3 Para were to board the Norland en route to the Ascension Islands in mid Atlantic, there to be taken ashore and then flown from the Ascensions to land at Lyneham in Wiltshire.

So with the Quartermasters of 3 Para, captains Norman Menzies and George Brown, we boarded the Norland; for me back on familiar territory, to work out with John the Purser the 2 Battalion's reception and storage of arms. Officers and all ranks were soon on board, settled in, were able to make phone calls to the UK though limited, and life became one of de-brief, sorting kit and equipment out and preparing for home. The Medics were busy treating trench foot and injuries.

It is fair to say that we had one hell of a party on board to celebrate Airborne Forces Day. Gifts were exchanged, The Master, Don Ellerby got to keep the Helmet that he always wore on the Bridge and in particular when the Norland had been in the Falklands Sound.

We were of course mindful of our losses and the Padre David Cooper once again came into his own. As Quartermaster, on board I had one onerous task. When a soldier dies whilst serving, in barracks or on the battlefield, his personal effects are collected, documented and returned to his next of kin. Usually boxed and through the MOD arrangements. This process is called 'A

205

Committee of Adjustment'. So, on the Norland I had the officers' and soldiers' suitcases identified by the Company Quartermaster Sergeants and delivered to me and placed under lock and key.

I asked the paymaster Captain Harry Quinn to be a member of the Committee and he and I took the suitcases one by one to a quiet deck aft on the Norland where we documented and boxed all personal effects. The military uniform items were retained by me and were brought to account, to be 'returned to stock'.

We found the odd item within the suitcases that we felt sure the families would have no interest in i.e. a girlie magazine, so both Harry and I, with a nod of agreement, tossed the item into the South Atlantic. The occasional note was found leaving an item to a named person, these went to the Adjutant.

The task completed, the sealed Next of Kin boxes were then treated as secure stores and were taken from the Norland onto the Aircraft at Ascension, then by road from Lyneham to Aldershot and into a secure lock-up. With the CO's approval, Lt Col David Chaundler agreed that the personal effects would be delivered not to the MOD, but taken by Battalion Officers and handed over direct to the next of kin. Our eighteen bereaved families appreciated this compassionate token as it took place.

As I remember, and things like this one never forgets, we had two Casio watches returned in effects from the Burial Documentation Unit at San Carlos. One an officer's, one a corporal's. I had put them in the wrong boxes! One of the Widows, Capt Chris Dent's wife, had noticed the difference! The Casio watchstrap was a different colour! Soon sorted on a telephone call and the swap made. Everyone was happy. In the UK it meant so much to all relatives to receive their loved ones effects and so quickly. 'Family is Family', and a personal visit meant so much more.

Back on the Norland and a hell of a party, the first to let our hair down. In the ship's lounge, sparse though it was, 'Wendy', the ship's Gay Guy, played the piano and the beer came out from the ship's stocks.

Leaving the Captain's cabin, where I and a dozen others had been celebrating until after midnight, I lurched my way back to Cabin No 1007 to find Capt Harry Quinn (the Pay) and my fellow QM, Banks

Middleton, already on their bunks. Opening the cabin door, the light going on automatically, I forgot to step up over the metal door-step. I fell into the cabin and full length 'Kissed the Sink'. Someone shouted 'You OK?' I mumbled a reply then crawled into the bottom bunk squeezing my nose. I must have done a reasonable job because later in the morning after much cold compress, the nose was as one but I had two black eyes.

This got me much sympathy when landing eventually by Brittania Aircraft at Lyneham. People really thought that I had been in the Wars.

Return to Aldershot June 1982

On return from Lyneham and The Falklands War, we still had a job to do. Marvellous though it would have been to 'Bomburst' on leave from the Battalion Lines. I did convince the CO that we should remain within Barracks for four clear days to sort out our kit and equipment losses, re-demand to bring us up to scale and sort out all the weaponry and our own kit and equipment. This lull proved to be invaluable. We all then had a couple of weeks well deserved Leave.

Post war parades were held in London. I was able to attend the Remembrance Service in St Paul's Cathedral and in our Battalion Lines, Prince Charles our Colonel-in-Chief came for lunch and to meet and speak with our bereaved families.

The MP, Roy Mason, visited the Battalion for lunch and made presentations to the Battalion on behalf of The Houses of Parliament. I had the honour of sitting with him as a fellow Yorkshireman! At the top table! I don't think the CO, being a Southerner, would have understood him.

Don Ellerby, The Master of the Norland, visited the Battalion and at an Officers' Lunch presented the Battalion with 'The Norland Trophy', a replica of the ship in silver, on a plinth presented to the Battalion by North Sea Ferries.

At last, on leave after the Falklands I went north to see sister June and family, and to stay with Christine's Mother, Lois, in Shafton. Christine's elder brother Keith, a live wire, was running a bar complex on a caravan holiday site near to Scarboro'. We were invited to a six-berth private caravan on site and an evening's

207

entertainment within the large theatre on site. Christine elected to stay with Mum, which opened the door for 'The Pennine Way Pals' of yesteryear to have a night out.

Phil Smith, brother-in-law, David Lamb, top man and Tetley's Beer Fan and I, rolled up at the large caravan park late on Friday afternoon, there for the night! Settling into the six-berth/TV installed caravan, we got suited and booted at 8pm hit the noisy, live music, lounge bar.

During the evening of stage show and compere, there were tributes given to Falklands Veterans on holiday and all were called to the stage to collect 'awards'. Bottles of Scotch etc. My two companions said 'Get up there', when brother-in-law Keith let it be known that 'Captain Tom Godwin' of 2 Para was in the audience! Although wearing my Para Tie, I declined to go up on stage. Enough was done for the three of us with regards to free booze and we left a private bar after midnight bound for our caravan, less David, who in the bar purely by chance, had met a previous wedding bridesmaid of many years ago.

Philip and I, in finding our beds within the van and half off to sleep, were awakened by banging on the caravan door to find David there dishevelled, torn shirt and covered in mud and grass marks. He groaned his way into his berth and there I checked him over, nothing but a couple of sprung ribs. When asked what had happened he said that he was escorting the lady home to her caravan when in the moonlight he looked at the sea and it seemed so close from the lawn that they were walking on that he suggested a walk along the sandy seashore below. He stepped out, and fell 30 feet! Down the bank and onto the beach. His walking companion fled.

The next morning, Saturday, as we were in David's car he drove, but couldn't change gear owing to the pain from his cracked ribs. On cue, I changed gear. Whilst Phil, in the back of the car getting over a mammoth hangover, was due to play cricket for College Grove at Wakefield at 2pm where he was the fast bowler. We dropped Phil off at 2pm.

Later that evening in 'The Crown' at Ossett, Father's old Pub, Philip said that when bowling he did not remember anything of the first three overs, not even being thrown the ball. However, he took seven wickets to win the match.

Return to Armagh 1982: Post War Lectures

With the close association that 2 UDR had with The Parachute Regiment, the CO asked our CO Colonel David Chaundler if the Battalion would send someone over on a Mess night to give a presentation on The Falklands War as 2 Para had witnessed it.

The Battalion Officers at that time were of course in great demand, in particular the CO. 2 i/c, Ops Officer and the Company Commanders, to lecture to all and sundry: the P.M., Army Staff College, Sandhurst, Imperial Museum etc. etc.

Quartermaster of 2 UDR, CO 2 sent me to give the build-up and the Q side of life and Capt Colin Connor MC to give the combat side of life and in particular the Battle for Goose Green, he being the Patrols Commander. The evening, within the main drill hall and to officers and all ranks not on duty, went down really well and it was marvellous to see so many of my own friends.

I was also called upon, together with the CO to give lectures on 'Leadership' at The All Arms Tactics Wing at Warminster. The audience? Captains on promotion. Had to smile, one student was the 2 Para Adjutant!

BELIZE CENTRAL AMERICA 1983

At last, the Battalion was on its way to warmer climes, one year later than expected! Where we should have been prior to the Falklands War intervention.

Two excellent happenings though: one, we had already carried out the recce and with the same Royal Anglian Unit in situ; two, the kit containers sent by sea months ago with Sports equipment and much of tropical and jungle green clothing had arrived.

An out of the blue presentation was made to 2 Para by the City Fathers of Beverley in Yorkshire, on the East Coast. The CO asked me to attend and to present Town Chambers with a Battalion Plaque and Unit Flag.

I saw the Chief Clerk and asked him to look through the Battalion roll to find any soldier who came from the area. By pure luck he came up with one of the 'Toms', from the town. Pte Blee. Of all things, the lad's father had served with me in Aden and I had been his Platoon Sergeant. Steven Blee.

The reception, held at lunchtime within the County Council Offices, was an informal gathering and County Councillor Don Rose handed over a cheque to the Battalion for £1000. To be spent, they asked, on sports kit. As another co-incidence I had known the Councillor years previous when we were both senior ranks within 12/13 Para Battalion.

Belize Six Months March – August 1983

British Forces have continued to serve and Exercise in Belize since its independence at the invitation of the country's Premier. This helps to maintain sovereignty against the intimidation of an incursion by the neighbouring country of Guatemala which faces its eastern seaboard. Officially, British troops are stationed there for the purpose of jungle training, also field firing at the open range complex at Baldy Beacon.

As far as 2 Para were concerned the Companies were positioned at four distinct and separate locations, the OCs having virtually an independent Command. Two of the Companies were located in the South, some 180 miles from Force and Battalion Headquarters. Replenishment to these Companies in the south was by Air and Sea. There was hardly a road or track to run the distance from Belize City to San Pedro in the south.

The 'Toms' were tasked with Jungle Patrols as well as patrolling some open lands and river courses. Guatemalan patrols were often seen at their border and during our Tour, soccer matches were played with them! (Shhh, Who plays Who!).

Belize has its own small defence force but fair to say, would be no match for a Guatemalan incursion. A small number of British army instructors were serving a Tour attached to this Defence Force. In fact, one of my pals was on such an accompanied Tour of two years. Major Barry Andrews and his wife Ada. In addition to the soldiering aspects of the tour there was much scope for adventurous training in the hills and offshore at the Cays.

Belize has the second largest barrier reef offshore outside

Australia, and a 'Blue Hole' for diving, the envy of the world. The Battalion set up a Leave and Water Sports Centre for the 'Toms', where they could fish, water ski, scuba dive and even hire small craft.

Two companies were based in the north; one, some 40 miles north west of our main Headquarters at Airport Camp. The other at, in and around Airport Camp providing area security, escorts and local jungle and village patrols. This secure base was a 20 minute drive from Belize City, Ten from the airport.

As the Unit Headquarters Quartermaster, my staff and I were responsible for all stores provisions, combat supplies, fuels etc. to ALL locations, by land, sea and air. When possible we did provide fresh meats, fruits and vegetables to all, in sealed chilled polar packs.

I had two able assistants on whom I relied explicitly. The Tech Quartermaster, Banks Middleton, who did the distribution once stores had arrived at the jetty at Punta Gorda in the south. The other was the invaluable WO2 Mick Cotton, the Support Company CSM, who worked direct for me during the Tour, as liaison with the RCT skipper of the boat running all fresh supplies and fuels.

Who Swam Alligator Creek?

With Christine coming out on holiday from the UK by RAF indulgence aircraft for the Battalion's families I, during a weekend off, carried out a recce to the Ambergris Caye, a 20 minute flight by 'White Knuckle Airways' from Belize City Airport.

Staying at 'The Hideaway Hotel' on San Pedro I decided that, although a lovely hotel, somewhere more private would be better, where I would not run into everyday PARAS on leave. So, out came the local map, which showed a hotel across the river inlet to the inland lake, from the sea. Walking north toward it, I did of course find my way blocked by a fairly wide and muddy looking sluggish river. Not to be deterred and being the swimmer that I was, it was off with the sand boots and shirt, these onto the shoulder with the wallet, and I swam the creek. I then walked the Mangroves line for a mile and ended up at the reception desk of this rather nice hotel, amidst palms, on the coast and with a small marina.

The lady receptionist gave me a drink and the ten-day tariff, and I thanked her and walked outside. Walking down the steps outside I met the hotel's manager who had just greeted two guests from a boat in the marina. Not having seen me before he asked me where my boat was moored ... and what assistance could he offer? I replied that I did not have a boat and that I had received all the information that I required from his receptionist.

He seemed quite put out as he said, 'You must have a boat, Sir, the only way to this hotel is by sea!'

I then told him that I had swum the river across from San Pedro.

He said, 'You can't! That is Alligator Creek, I have been here 20 years and have never, ever known anyone swim it. I am taking you back, Sir, to the fishing harbour at San Pedro by the Hotel Launch.'

Back in Belize City I had a T-shirt made:

'I swam Alligator Creek
and survived'

Sometimes I get flashbacks, those critters must not be hungry at 10.30am. My own staff were the unsung heroes as the whole set-up was a hell of a supply chain, and in particular when the heavy weapons firing took place and pallets of ammunition were required.

Most of my time was spent out of Headquarters and each week I would visit all locations, everywhere including border observation posts, usually by Wessex Helicopter in the south, scout and vehicle in the north.

Travel by road and air was always exciting. Secondary jungle, Mayan ruins, exotic birds, butterflies galore. My Airport Camp 'Oppo', Captain Terry White, the Paymaster, used to set out with me on the odd Sunday afternoon to visit the local villages, have a beer and play the local darts. The mainly Carib villagers were a happy lot, plump, well fed and always smiling.

Major Barry Andrews, an old chum of mine now serving as an instructor with the Belize Defence Force, had a married quarter not far from our Camp accommodation, and he and his wife Ada would give Terry and me the occasional invite.

Indoors he was found to have a pet Cote-Monde, called 'Squiffy', which would usually be draped over the back of the settee. They said these squirrel type animals could not be tamed! Barry's was and

212

he only ever caged it when he and Ada went out. Its party piece was to lie on its back and suck an egg dry without losing the shell. It also used to tear the legs off the ground crabs as a delicacy.

All off duty soldiers were allowed into Belize City and the Unit Transport ran a shuttle for those in Headquarters and at Airport Camp. All were advised to travel in and around the City in parties of four. We were unarmed of course and most bars were 'Low Life'.

A weekend off, 'on the Cayes', the small offshore Islands, was a different experience: small with well-appointed hotels, super eating places, excellent bars. Music, Music, Music, Carib Rum and Coke. San Pedro was the Battalion officers and seniors favourite. The Hideaway Hotel, The Paradise Resort Hotel and Captain Locos Bar.

The 'Toms' on their excursions, saved up their days off. All took leave whilst we were on the six months tour. Cancun was the favourite and for some by air to Mexico City.

Some of our wives travelled out to Belize on RAF indulgence flights. My wife Christine made such a trip for a ten day holiday and, although threatened by the medics at the time to send me back on the same aircraft that she had come out on, due to concussion that day, after a training descent, I persuaded the RAF Surgeon that I should stay, having been offered a safe haven for us both at Barry and Ada's married quarter. I layed low for a week then Chris and I flew off by Teeny Weeny Airways to San Pedro and The Paradise Hotel.

Having returned from our super holiday at the Paradise Hotel where we had a Cabana on stilts, ten paces from the sea, we had a night out with Barry and Ada in Belize City. A four star set up, for lobster in black bean sauce.

Quite decorative cockroaches were crawling up some of the dining room walls but the Food and drink was absolutely Al nevertheless!

We had an eventful drive to get there. From Barry's quarter the drive into Belize City to find the hotel took about a half hour. We had to drive the riverbank road for most of the way and it was Blue Crab migrating time. Thousands upon thousands of Blue Crabs leave the river, cross the road and move inshore to mate. We just could not miss this carpet of crabs and had to crunch through for hundreds of yards. Into the outskirts of Belize City and still not

213

within street lights, we had to run the gauntlet of popped up locals trying to stop cars to sell the occupants drugs or to get a lift into town.

Suddenly and without warning a group of males from beneath the trees jumped into the road and Barry swerved but kept on driving, shouting to us, 'Daren't stop, must keep going.'

At the same time the wing mirror on my side shattered and something or someone hit my arm resting on the open window ledge, my elbow being outside. The blow was quite severe and made me pull my arm in and swear, to hold my arm against my chest. We headed towards the city street lights, pulling up under one. Barry came around and I straightened my arm. No obvious damage but a painful elbow.

Barry looking at me said, 'You have blood on your shirt and on your pocket.'

I patted my pocket, felt inside and there to our amazement was a mangled FINGER!

One weekend in Camp we were host to a small Naval Party visiting the Headquarters. I was asked and took them to the Orange Walk Golf Course, a facility that had been made within the sugar factory grounds, owned by a Brit, an hour's drive away. The roadway for most of the drive was absolutely straight and, whilst travelling in the small mini-bus we saw in the distance a light-aircraft land, and, as we got near we saw we saw a group of men pulling the aircraft backwards into a clearing to clear our road.

I asked our Belizean driver to stop whilst I took a photograph. He said, 'No, these are Drugs.' And kept on driving! I managed covertly as we passed to photograph the aircraft and more important the number on the tail. Back at the Int Section at Brigade Headquarters I handed in the film with an explanation. Later I was told that the aircraft belonged to a Government Minister!

Some Reflections of Life on Belize

In Airport Camp, the Force and Battalion Headquarters Officers Mess held a films night on the Patio once a month. Stand-up projector, suspended white sheets as a screen. The films came through SSVC the Army Kinema set up library. We were to see 'The Poltergeist', this having done the rounds in the UK.

All seated on the patio, power on, the projector lamp blew. Power on again, the lamp blew again. Power on again. The main fuse blew. End of night – no film, back to the bar.

The film was taken to Punta Gorda in the south to be shown to Headquarters and one of the companys. I had a phone call from the Tech QM, Banks Middleton, who said the film projector was set up in the men's canteen. Open sided but with a large Attap Roof. The projector was running as was the film when a hell of a wind blew up and blew off the Attap Roof. Some soldiers received minor injuries – one soldier, a broken leg! End of night – no film.To my knowledge this film: 'The Poltergeist', was never shown in Belize.

Battalion training and the firing of the Support Company heavier weapons was to take place within a large hilly waste area of Belize, called 'Baldy Beacon'. There we were to fire mortars, anti-tank rounds and the heavier machine guns. Each company would be withdrawn from its normal patrol duties and would attend a morning to view from a hillside stand the capabilities of these support weapons as they were fired off into the target areas up to 2000 yards away. The Royal Air Force would also take part as an inter-service exercise and show what their strike aircraft could do.

My staff over four days, together with the MT drivers, slogged up and down hardly drivable tracks to deliver the heavy ammunition required. The CO asked me to provide something on the hillsides for the RAF to destroy! Or to shoot at. For three days I, and a party of scroungers, visited the city's dumps and waste areas and moved old cars that had been dumped onto a flat-bed and up to Baldy Beacon. There we positioned these scrap cars on eight separate hill-tops. On the very first day of viewing from the stand, and on the very first run in, the bloody RAF destroyed the lot! To vapour! These cars we had hoped would have been sufficient for the four days. Wrong! No more cars.

215

Raol's Rose Garden

Half a mile from the main Airport Camp, off the main road to Belize was 'Raol's Rose Garden'. Not a garden, but a well-appointed bar and brothel. Put out of bounds to the Battalion but fair to say used by force troops, it was known to be patrolled by the Military Police who did apprehend the odd sneaky .

The 'Toms' when off duty used to go into Belize City in groups of four, usually to a bar called the 'Big C', where the girls lined the bar rails and you would not have taken your Aunty. 'Toms' being Toms, they were often split from 'The Rule of Four' and ended up alone and after a taxi back to Camp. The odd Tom, meeting with the locals, got bottled, i.e. usually belted over the head with a coke bottle and robbed.

After much lobbying by officers and senior ranks to the CO it was felt better to bring all nights out nearer to home and, if so, Why not use 'Raol's Rose Garden'? Hear, hear.

The CO, David Chaundler, being a sporty type, set up an inspection committee of himself, the Padre, OC D Company Phil Neame. OC HQ Coy Tom Smith and myself, the Quartermaster, to look to the soft furnishings.

We were met by Mr Raols. Drinks. Bar. Public Rooms. Bedroom inspections. We left before midnight.

The CO still put the place, 'Out of Bounds'. Much to our amazement!

Fort Lewis: Washington State, USA

Belize well behind us it was back to conventional training but this time at FORT LEWIS, USA, and exercising with The American Rangers, 'The Green Berets'. Once again I took over the accommodation but, this time, with arctic clothing and stores as we were to exercise in snow covered hills and in Company groups, all to go through a survival package for four days, living off the land.

The area was not that far from the Canadian Border, though we were at TACOMA and were to Exercise and Adventure Train on the foothills of MT Ranier some 12,000 ft high.

Each Company group of 100 took to the hills under control of the

American Rangers. I visited each as they were briefed at the mountain base before going native. Capt Terry White, the Paymaster, provided the funds whilst I, with a $^3/_4$ ton vehicle, procured 100 live rabbits and the travelling cages from a local livestock farm for each company group. At the base we handed over the rabbits to the soldiers. One rabbit each! Four days food.

The Old Tom never ceased to amaze me. The first three groups of 100 soldiers could not get the bunnies quick enough to kill and make into portions. The last group of support and HQ Company soldiers, mainly old sweats, tucked the rabbits in their smocks, kept them warm and let them go in the forests.

We were at Lewis for almost a month and carried out helicopter drills and even parachuting from their mammoth sized jet powered Starlifter Aircraft. What an experience.

Down town Tacoma was something: girlie bars, porn shops and off base stores where you could buy weaponry, even assault rifles, but out of bounds to Brits.

Harry the Pay and Banks the Tech QM and I visited Seattle one afternoon, travelled on the overland rail system, above the street, cars below. We went to the Seattle revolving tower and restaurant and at 1000 ft. up had a very pleasant meal. The restaurant revolved in exactly one hour and it was amazing to see below sea-planes landing in the sound.

We were also able to visit the Washington State Parliament where I actually sat in the Speaker's Chair.

A pleasant visit was made to the Olympic Brewery where, on this day of all days, three new beers were being tested and the booths were open 10am until 4pm. When we handed our questionnaire papers in, the Brewery Rep said, 'OMG. Brits! They know all about beer.'

In the Officers' Mess in Fort Lewis and within the large lecture hall our CO gave a talk on the Battalions' exploits on the Falklands. Their Post Commander gave a mop up of their Green Beret exploits on GRENADA. Theirs was embarrassing and they had the guts to say so.

POSTED TO BRECON IN WALES
The All Arms Tactics Wing, School of Infantry

Having served for almost three years as Captain Quartermaster 2 Para, I was dined out in style by the Sergeants Mess at Albuhera Barracks, Aldershot. The CO Lt Col David Chaundler, also being dined out was leaving too. 'Proud to say that as 2 Paras' QM I had seen the Battalion through 16 major moves, including the Falklands War.'

The Officers Mess saw Chris and me dined out, during a Vicars and Tarts Night. I borrowed a surplice from 2 Para Vicar.

So we left Knollys Road in Aldershot, Trudy was still at Charmandean Boarding School, now finishing off her education at seventeen years of age. Tanya had taken off for America on a student exchange for the second year and was in the process of working at Bedford, NY for Mrs Laura Remsen as Nanny to her two daughters tutored at Summer Camps.

I was to take over as Quartermaster from Major Tom Smith, Para, who was retiring. We took over a detached three bedroomed quarter just outside the Camp's rear gate, named Warren House. Our next door neighbour worked at Headquarters Wales, also a Para but RAOC. Major Bob Manners the SO2.

Deering Lines was situated just on the outskirts of Brecon Town and immediately off the main A40 road through mid-Wales east to west. Deering Lines, The School of Infantry, All Arms Tactics Wing, had been years ago 'The Battle School'. It was set up in the early 60s to give Para recruits, and later NCO courses, a rude awakening as to the rigours of hard and physical soldiering over the Sennybridge Training Area and the hard and harsh Brecon Beacons. The Powers that be had cast envious eyes over this estate and had it taken over as a wing of The School of Infantry. The Parachute Regiment still had an accommodation block, its own resident Captain OC, and a small staff of drivers and instructors. During my three years' appointment and whilst there for the next three years, almost all arms courses had a strong Para instructor influence.

The main thrust of training now was to provide field training in tactics for all junior and senior NCOs of the Infantry. In fact in my Regiment if you hadn't completed 'Junior Brecon' as a Corporal or

218

'Senior Brecon' as a Sergeant you would never be promoted and your days within the Paras were numbered. The Courses were physically demanding, always on the ground wearing a minimum of 35lbs of kit, students AND instructors.

Initially, I had a one and only boss, Lt Col George Smythe MBE (for gallantry in NI) - a wonderful man, hard as nails, fit, humorous and out on the training area every day, or up and over the Brecon Beacons. George being a 'Green jacket' RGJ, I used to pull his leg and tell him that he should have been a Para. His reply? 'Tom, I am not doing bad as I am.'

George had been Commissioned from The Ranks, but from an early age as a Warrant Officer, not to go on, within the Quartermaster Appointments, but as Command Appointments and he had completed the Regular Army Majors Staff Promotion Course. He was to have a sound influence at *this* Tactics Wing and, although I only saw him in my first year, I was delighted to see him being awarded the OBE for his efforts. He was to go on to another Command as full Colonel.

He is one of the very few who can wear both the MBE and OBE together, as one usually replaces the other. The MBE for George though bore the Silver Cross for Gallant action. So the two could be worn together.

Chris and I settled into 'School' life as the courses ran six and eight weeks in duration with a ten-day break in-between. My hardest mental task was to realise that I was actually 'at home' for seven days a week for 30 days in the month. Although visiting the courses out on the ground, often container meals at night, it wasn't the same as packing the old suitcase and being off for three weeks, six weeks! Three months! Six months!

However, we soon got over it as 'Sam' the Labrador came into our lives. Trudy finished boarding school and Tanya came on holiday from USA with a boyfriend.

I was to inherit a super staff. My RQMS was an ex-2 Para Warrant Officer, 'Big' Fred MacFarlane; my accommodation Storeman was Cpl Elliot, another ex-Para, with Scottie an ace civilian Storeman. WO2 Bill Hearne was the MTO and a Para that I had known for years. The RSM was WO1 Edwards.

In the Officers Mess, Capt Howard Vaughan had been a Colour

Sgt when I had been the RSM of 2 Para in 1976. He was now OC Platoon. Major John Easton ex-1 Para , as I knew, was OC Junior Division.

My lady clerk was Mrs Dawn Wyatt and her elder son Mark played rugger for Wales at No 15 during the three years that we were to be at Brecon. Her husband, Tony, was a local School Headmaster. Christine and I, on a day out to Crickhowell, often used to drop into their beautiful hillside Barn House at Bwlch (a Welsh name that I could never pronounce, they pronounced it as BOOK!).

We had some laughs as Dawn was always interested in what Christine and I had been up to at the weekend, and went into hysterics when she found out that we had been to Carmarthen in the south instead of CAERNARFON in the north, looking for the Castle where Charles, the Prince of Wales, had been crowned. I told her that the Council Offices at Carmarthen didn't seem to live up to it.

In the office one day, Dawn informed me that a wife of one of the ACC Cook Corporals wished to see me. I had, on the Monday, banned the Corporal from attending the Cpls Club for a month, because of his conduct within the Mess on the previous Saturday. He and his wife had been fighting, late in the evening. As Quartermaster, the cooks came under my remit. I asked Dawn to show the lady into my office. Dawn did so and announced her name. The lady stepped into my office, seemed to take one look at me and fainted on the office carpet. Gracefully, I might add, rather like a dying swan.

I said to Dawn, 'Water please', and she dashed off, coming back quickly, she looked at me and as I hadn't moved from behind the desk stood there, water in hand, not knowing really what to do.

I said, 'Throw it on her Face!' The lady on the carpet opened an eye and I asked her to take the adjacent seat. Dawn retired, still with water in hand.

'The Dying Swan', the lady in question on the previous Saturday night's fight, had come to plea on behalf of her hubby, that they be allowed to use the Cpls Mess on the coming Saturday. I said, 'No, the ban stands - one month.' She swore at me. Dawn kicked her out.

One morning Dawn came into my office and informed me that there was a lady on the telephone, 'from down the Valleys.' She had asked to speak with the Quartermaster!

On the telephone the lady asked, 'Do the army take DOGS?' I replied that they did under certain circumstances. She said that they ran a public house; the dog, an eighteen-month Labrador/Retriever, was getting too much for them and the husband wanted it out of the place and into a good home. Now the dog was with his brother a couple of hundred yards away.

'Sam' of Brecnock. Labrador/Retriever

Christine and I visited the Pub in South Wales one early evening in March 1985 and were handed over an eighteen-month, almost white Labrador/Retriever. The family would not sell the dog but just wanted to know that 'Sam' had a secure home through the army. On meeting him for the first time, I called his name, walked him up and back the nearside lane, opened the car boot and in he jumped! We took Sam home to Warren House, Brecon, where we had him at home for a week. I made calls to the veterinary services in Aldershot but they did not seem at all enthusiastic to take him on. Having had him a week at the office with me during the day and with a couple of long walks up the Beacons, it rather seemed that we were taking to each other. Daughter Trudy was home from 'Charmandean' Boarding School, so on the first Sunday afternoon we decided to have a vote, 'Should we keep him?'

The vote was a unanimous, 'Yes.' Looking at him I swear *he* even put his paw up. On the Monday I telephoned the owner, asked her if she minded if we kept him, she agreed that we should and just asked that she could see him after six months. I readily agreed and we eventually did just that. Sam the Lab was now ours.

During our three years at Brecon Sam became my constant companion. We had a routine whereby he came to work with me in the office and around the Camp domain during the day. Christine would take him from me at mid-day and then walk the canal bank for a couple of hours; he would swim in the River Usk. In the evening we would often walk the Talybont Resevoir area or the seven mile disused railway track.

Sam was an awesome student; within the year I taught him to walk to heel, to go out to a whistle and what was more important, to return and to walk the hills without bothering the sheep. To sit and

221

stay, no matter how long and to regard his basket indoors as his safe haven and the car boot the same when travelling. I trained him to the gun as I owned a 12 bore. Never to get in front of me and whenever I stopped, he sat and looked upwards. Retrieving game: ducks, rabbit, pigeons, he had such a soft mouth and would carry the game back, sitting and waiting to drop the game to your hand.

He had one trait that we could not break him from however. If he saw a squirrel on the ground before we did, he would kill it. Also, rats in the garden under the bird table. He was often uncanny and used to surprise me. One morning Colonel George and I were walking in Camp to visit the new build. I had Sam to heel when he suddenly shot off into a roadside bush and within seconds had returned to me with a live blackbird in his mouth. Christine took him a walk one afternoon at the side of the River Usk, he ran into a rocky pool and brought out a salmon. She came back to my office to tell me that there was this salmon now on the bank. You can guess what I said? When she returned to the river bank it had gone!

The dog really had, 'Duck Mania'. No duck was safe, either in the river, in the bushes hiding or best of all shot in flight coming in, on the reservoir. Fellow officers out on shoots used to call to borrow Sam for the day. Out early morning on a reservoir waiting for the ducks to come in, we had a split party on the banks. Major Nick Gaskell had a young dog on the opposite side to where we were and on the first shot, his very young dog, 'Poacher' took off. Nick, having searched the woods for an hour, came back to the vehicle park. We sent Sam off to find 'Poacher'. He brought him back.

A powerful swimmer, once on Llangorse Lake in winter, he with Duck Mania, ran onto the ice, and went through it. I could never have rescued him. With encouragement, shouting and the whistle call, somehow his webbed feet had him back on the ice to return to us.

He had a party piece both in Brecon and in Berlin, where I was to serve my last three years before retirement. During the day I would visit the soldier's dining room and the kitchens, speak with the Master Chef and see that the food was as it should be. Sam usually being with me, I would leave him outside the dining facility at the main kitchen entrance. I would tell him to, 'Sit and Stay.' Be it for ten minutes or 40, he would be there on my return. Sometimes

222

sitting with a sausage in his mouth! The cooks could never get over this one! I had taught him to eat nothing outside his bowl at home unless I broke it in my hands and gave it to him.

When in Berlin sometime later, I was in a secured area, bars on the windows etc. The Naafi vehicle used to roll up outside; the driver blew the horn, then the Headquarters personnel would troop out for Kit Kats, me and Sam included through the revolving door. We got into the routine that Sam would hear the horn, go to the door and wait for one of the office girls to let him out, join the Naafi queue, then return with the Kit Kat that someone had bought him. Half for Sam, half for me!

Whilst in Berlin, we entered the Commander's 10 km fun run. Sam and I walked it within the two hours. There was also a raffle and a party on the green at the end. I bought 'Sam' a strip of raffle tickets. The dog won a case of beer.

Walking the Berlin Forests in West Berlin on weekend we surprised a party of about 30 wild pigs within a clearing. Sam dived in as they were scattering and before I could shout 'Stay' he brought back to me, in his mouth, a live piglet, squealing its head off. I looked around for 'Big Daddy', as these pigs were large, 15 stones and more with 4" tusks. However, not to be seen. So I took piglet to the edge of the clearing and off it ran.

Whilst in Berlin, Christine and I joined a German Weekend Walking Club. The Berliners really took to Sam and always looked out for him. Prior to this, he was a well-travelled dog.

Leaving Brecon in 1987 after three years we drove to Berlin from the UK. Sam travelled the journey in the car. Whilst in Berlin on Posting, we, with him, visited Bavaria, Switzerland, Liechtenstein and the Harz Mountains, as well as the whole of Berlin's Forests.

On leaving Berlin we had, as the rules were then, to put him into quarantine for six months at kennels in Somerset.

When I retired from the Regiment and came home from Berlin in 1990 we picked him up from kennels and he spent a year or so with Trudy in Brecon, whilst Christine and I took up a Rental in Cyprus, until we bought a small village house in 1991 in a mountain village.

In 1992 Sam joined us in Kalo Chorio in Cyprus as I had returned briefly to the UK to fly Sam out to Larnaca from Heathrow. A costly exercise of £598. He was to remain in Cyprus for the rest of his life,

223

walking the hills with us, swimming in the reservoirs in the Troodos Hills, walking the beaches or lazing on the patio. In winter he loved the snow on Troodos, in summer, a canny dog in the shade.

I didn't hunt with him, and Chris and I regarded him as being in retirement. John and Renate Lawton, ex-pats and John, having known Sam whilst in Berlin when as a CQMS on my staff, loved him. They had a house with a large garden in the village of Anoyria, they used to, borrow Sam in particular as he aged and wanted trees and shade, it was at their house that Sam died at 14 years of age. John said that Sam made a move to go outdoors, laid under a tree and with John holding him, he passed away.

We buried him above the village on a hill known as 'Top of the World', under a stone named 'SAM'.

Snowdonia – Beddgelert – The Watkin Path

Christine and I were very fortunate in that at HQ Wales there was a retired ex-Para Officer, John Mitchell. Ex-Quartermaster, 7 RHA and thoroughly good egg. He and his wife Joyce had been in Bahrain during our accompanied Tour and in the same Battalion Group in 1965. Now settled in Wales and in a lovely bungalow on the outskirts of Brecon he let it be known to us that he had the use of a Bothy or weekend cottage on the lower slopes of Snowdonia, a couple of miles from Beddgelert. Hafod y Llan Farm at Nantgwynant. He offered us the key for one weekend and up we drove.

Adventurous though we were and having driven down the farmer's track we were surprised to see what met our gaze on parking. A broken down tractor parked outside a dilapidated farm outbuilding. A creaking double door leading into an earth floored tool room led us into one room with stove and 3/4 bed with sagging mattress. No piped water, outside chemical loo and water, by bucket from the adjacent stream. One electric light bulb hanging from the ceiling of the one room. Having looked in first on opening the door, I sent Sam the Lab in to chase any rats.

Well, we had come prepared: Sleeping bags, cutlery, crockery, tins of curry, rice and beans. We did however go helter-skelter into Beddgelert three miles away for a decent meal and a loo job. We did sleep well! Shock and booze, and were up to feed Sam and off on our planned walk up Snowdon about 9am. 3,561 ft. to the summit.

I had planned for us to take the longer Southern Route to the summit known as the 'Watkin Path'. We passed on the way the 'Gladstone Rock' upon which he was supposed to have spoken to the slate miners years ago. Onto the lower slopes of the mountain and then past the slate miners' old broken down, former stone built lodgings. After a good three hours of uphill walking we were 400 yards or so from the summit and now had to zig-zag up a scree slope, by this time enveloped in cloud. I kept having to leave Chris with Sam the Lab, whilst I found the way.

At last we had reached the summit, the café and the mountain railway terminus. I had promised Chris a return down the mountain by train and then the bus to Beddgelert and a short walk home. We found the café was closed for repairs. The Rail service was cancelled for the day!

The ONE day of the year and we were not to know. What an awful shock after 12 miles. I gave Chris the option. Go back on the path we had come up on, or a shorter, steeper route to the YMCA Café on the roadside that we could see somewhere below and judging by the vehicles in the park it was open. Chris opted for the YMCA. Good Girl. There we did have hot chocolate and Kendal Cake. My idea was then to hitch a lift on the main road to Beddgelert and to return to the café to collect Chris and Sam in our own car.

Chris said, 'No! You are not leaving me here, we are all walking home.'

I said, 'That's about seven miles around the reservoir.'

Chris said, 'Let's go.'

Some three hours later we were back in our 'Cottage'.

A shower, with heated water from the stove, pumped through a garden spray setup whilst standing within a child's pump up garden pool. I made the curry and rice. We slurped the bottles of red wine and then knew nothing 'till the morning.

I reckoned, all in all on our 'Watkin Walk' we had done 18 miles and climbed up and down over 3,000 ft.

What a Weekend Adventure!

On a couple of other weekends we took in The Llwedd Horseshoe, and the slopes at Tryfan. The Sygum old copper mine and the river walks in Beddgelert village. We travelled on one of Wales' little railways from Porthmadog on the estuary, inland some miles to the old slate mines at Tan y Bwlch passing through Tanygrisiau and Dduallt. A wonderful scenic morning out with a lesson at the terminus quarry on how to split the slate into tiles.

The small railway carriages were well appointed with comfortable seating, with at the front and rear observation cars, large panoramic windows. Having reached our destination of the old slate mines we had a break of about an hour before boarding the train once again to return on the single line track, this time to Porthmadog.

I had just settled Chris into the observation car, when on hearing the guard's whistle and feeling a slight movement of the train I saw an open carriage door. I slammed it shut and the train picked up speed. The next thing I saw was a crab-like figure in uniform clawing at our carriage windows. It then disappeared along the platform we were about to leave behind.

Sometime later and whilst we were on our return journey, the guard appeared. He announced in a loud voice to all in our observation car that someone had shut the carriage door on him before he could board. Once the train was in motion the closed doors locked! Thank God he had been able to hop on board at the very last carriage. He said that such a lock out had never happened before in the 12 years he had been doing the job.

Christine said to me, 'Trust You!'

The Portmeirion Peninsula and Village

A must for all who visit North Wales, this village is well known for its Portmeirion Pottery displayed in quantity at the village shop: The pottery distinctive in its own right having decorative plants and flowers on its design.

The Peninsula of mixed woodland, azaleas, rhododendrons, camellias and other exotic shrubs is set out off pathways leading to the beach of White Sands Bay. There is an hotel within the peninsula, view points from it and the famous Look-out Lighthouse.

The whole village, once within the confines, is set up to an Italian design with terraces, a central piazza, a pantheon or dome all to enhance the various highly decorated dwellings of a Gate House, Bridge House, Toll House, Battery, Watch House, Chantry, Government House and other Italian style buildings. One really does think one is in Italy when walking the streets. It is uncanny and beautiful.

The television series 'THE PRISONER' was filmed entirely here. A mind-bending series starring Patrick Magoohan. The Penny Farthing bike is still against the wall. Christine and I had more than one visit here.

Family happenings whilst at Brecon '84 – '87 and Brecon Friends

Trudy having left Charmandean School secured a flat in Brecon, and a boyfriend and employment at 'The Castle Hotel' in Brecon where she was to become the undermanager.

Tanya, now living in America and employed as a Nanny to a family at Bedford, New York, came home to Brecon to introduce us to Tony Chateauvert, a PGA professional, and the love of her life. Whilst here I tried to have them marry within Llangorse Church when they had set the date. To no avail. They were to be married at the home of Tanya's employer, Mr & Mrs Ted Remsen. He had made the whole wedding celebration, reception and service in the grounds of his beautiful home at Bedford. A present in its entirety as he said, 'To Tanya, his third daughter' in appreciation of the way that she was bringing up his two, below teens daughters.

Tony's parents Betty and Wally Chateauvert, who were touring Europe during this time, spent some time with us at Warren House and we were able to take them in and around Brecon and to Llanthony Abbey. Betty, a celebrated artist in her own right was never without her sketchbook. She sketched, then in time completed, a painting in oils of Sam our Labrador.

Brother-in-laws Albert Kendrick and Phil Smith, together with David Lamb and two other golfers, came to Brecon for a golfing week at Craddock Golf Course, just outside the town. I was able to put them all up within the Camp accommodation during the student's break between courses. Chris and I were out with them for lunch at the Golf Club. I managed a round of 18 holes a couple of times in the week and was able to show the lads in the evening a selection of Brecon's Pubs.

Whilst in Brecon and in our second year we took in The Brecon Jazz Festival: Music in the streets under canopy sponsored by Ford Cars. What a delight. With Trad Jazz Bands from as far away as Holland, all coming into the town. The pubs were open and some were selling steak sandwiches through open windows.

At this time the bandstands were in open spaces in the town; outside Lloyds Bank on the High Street, on the Green opposite The Black Bull Pub,in the Griffin Car Park and on the municipal car park – all for free.

Now the whole venue has gone too commercial, Jazz mainly indoors and fees to pay. My old RSM of 1 Para of yesteryear, Bucket Lawrence and his wife Liz came to visit on a long weekend from Guildford, together with their black Labrador.

So Sam had a friend for the weekend.

Brecon, having been and even now a Para orientated town, held many retirees as residents, The GOC Wales Major General Peter Chiswell, shortly to retire, was dined out within the Officers Mess at Deering Lines, our Battle School. Christine and I were guests at his retirement Welsh Farmhouse and supported his charity walk up 'Cockett Hill' overlooking Llangorse Lake.

We often used to meet him and his wife Felicity at the home of Colonel Roger and Freda Miller who lived at Llangynidr, complete with house side stream and duckhouse. Roger, the ex-2 i/c of 2 Para, who of course I knew like a brother, used to bring beers and wines up from his cellar to his usual, quarterly dinners! We were to reciprocate years later in Cyprus. Dave Fenwick, Rogers S/Major on The Falklands and within the Regiment, was also a frequent visitor with me, to quaff ale on a Saturday afternoon, if not in the 'Red Lion', the village pub.

Lt Colonel Jack Crane and Ursula used to meet us in town, often at the Brecon Market. Jack had been my OC at one time, then I his RQMS in Belfast when he was Quartermaster 1 Para. Jack was now retired, aged 55, and 'Camp Commandant' at The Barracks in Brecon, HQ Wales. The staff was in for a shock when he was appointed, for with the agreement of General Peter (ex-Para), Jack held a weekly five mile fitness run. Boots, green trousers, sweat top!! The drivers, clerks, administrators were not much amused when they found out they could not keep up with Jack!

In Town lived Andy Anderson, ex-C/Sgt 1 Para, now retired. His wife Anne used to work in the local jewellers. We had served and had known each other for years, in particular in Patrol Company. Colin Butcher ex-C/Sgt and another retiree had an art decorative and mural shop in the Brecon Town Centre. In fact, in and around Brecon Town I could have listed many more, if called on a nominal role.

The All Arms Tactics Wing had about one hundred Gurkha Officers, NCOs and soldiers on Strength, mainly to act as enemy in all phases of war for the students out on training at Sennybridge Ranges or on The Beacons. I was responsible as Quartermaster for their welfare. Christine and I were always invited to their DWALI weekend celebrations and what a joy these were. They were marvellous hosts. Their Gurkha OC. 'Bugs Thapa' wasn't a bad golfer either.

Their staff and cooks did me a great favour when the officers and permanent staff dined out Lt Colonel George Smythe during his handover LUNCH to Lt Colonel John Hunt. The Gurkhas carried hot curry in containers and tables, chairs, Regimental silver, candelabra for the CO handover celebration to the summit of **Peny-Ffan** at almost 3000 feet. Wines and beers also!

Within the All Arms Deering Lines Tactics Wing, we were a hard working staff, the All Arms Instructors, in particular, working day and night when the courses were on. There was much night training.

I was given another further task as the Planning and Liaison Officer for the Deering Lines Rebuild Phase I and II. This came about through the retirement of a major at Wales Headquarters, who was not to be replaced. He was the present go-between the contractors and military requirements. He worked closely with the PSA architect David Hullah.

The PLO input was most important and, although surprised to be 'lumbered' with the job, it was of course in our interest. The wooden accommodation huts for students were to be replaced for all time with substantial brick barracks blocks, with slate roofs.

I took to this task with relish and David Hullah the architect was more than helpful in meeting our requirements and having 'Monks', the contractors, carry out the work.

My request included a 'wet area' for students to de-gunge within the accommodation block basement before moving into their living quarters, the provision of industrial washing machines, the preservation and drainage of the soccer pitch and the design of the weapons cleaning rooms, in particular for use at night. I even squeezed a double squash court out of the budget. Seeing the contractors most days and the architect at least twice a week it proved to be a harmonious task. During my three years I saw all the student and permanent staff accommodation replaced and the new build of the Sergeants' Mess and MT complex.

One addition caused much laughter! With Colonel George being in on the act, and through Unit funds, I purchased and had installed near to the guardroom entrance/exit, an old fashioned GPO telephone box. George with a wicked sense of humour, said that the tactics wing could never have a bright RED box so he had it painted 'deep bronze, green and black' rather like the army camouflage vehicles but the students could never find the bloody box in the dark.

Within 'The Officers Patch' in Camp I had one particular pal, Major Jimmy Read, OC HQ Company, and an elderly established member of The Queen's Regiment. He and I were to be found walking our labradors, late evening around the perimeter of Deering Lines. The dogs got on so well, his black, mine white, that each Thursday evening we would end up between 9 and 10pm having a dram, or three, within the Officers' Mess Bar.

He, being slightly older than me, missed the annual fitness tests. A team from the Army Physical Training Corps could visit any military unit at any time to carry out a personal fitness test. All ranks were chosen from the Unit's Nominal Roll at random. Up to 50 years of age! I was the ONLY one in the bracket 45 to 50. Major Read was older, the Commanding Officer, younger! I caught the test two years running!

The test was a run of one mile and a half out from Camp under supervision within 15 minutes. Then return at best speed to be clocked within 15 mins – age related! I hated running! I could leg or 'Tab' it anywhere, with or without kit. Running gave me the willies. Of course I completed it as I was still very active and fit, and still parachuting. Swimming was and still is my passion. At that time I used to go to the Brecon Baths, twice a week 8am – 9am and swim lengths in the company of my doctor, a fine swimmer and good for 100 lengths. Dr Dymyon is still using the pool, like me, into his seventies.

'Godwin's Walks in Wales'

During our three years at Brecon and with time off on most weekends on summer nights with the Black Mountains, the Ffans, the river, canal and waterfalls all within easy reach, it was a walker's paradise and we logged over 20 separate walks.

I did put together a Walker's Guide, complete with Ordnance Survey Maps and photographs taken on each walk. Some of short duration, just over a couple of hours. One walk, Hay-on-Wye to take in all the high ground over the Beacons to end at Peny-Ffan and 'The Storey Arms', took a couple of days. Sam and I had a night in the heather (pub lunch at Bwlch).

We also walked the whole tow-path from Brecon to Monmouth along the canal in the Usk Valley, much of it having disappeared to be channelled into the river below Abergavenny. Housing estates block what was the original waterway. The canal does not now run through to Monmouth.

Our favourite walk was one of twelve miles - five hours from 'The Storey Arms' below Peny-Ffan, to take in the 'Tommy Jones Memorial', the Ffan, The Cribin, Big Ffan, and The Horseshoe, the two miles circular ridge overlooking the village of **Llanfrynach,** to end up at the pub, 'The White Swan'.

We were so taken up with this that we took my QM Staff and the Gurkha Headquarters Staff over the route. Christine led the way and we finished up having drinks and a Gurkha Curry in the pub car park. Major 'Bugs' Thapa, the Gurkha OC, was most impressed, in particular, with Christine our Guide.

231

Holiday in America Christmas 1986

By Virgin Atlantic from Gatwick, for the Princely Sum of £182 return. Daughter Tanya and Hubby Tony had set up home at 13 Washington Avenue, Pleasantville, New York. Tanya had an office job and worked for General Foods, whilst Tony was the Assistant Golf Pro at the Bedford Golf and Tennis Club. A private club going back into the previous century.

It was our first opportunity, on this holiday, to meet the whole of Tony's family and what a joy it was. Tony's father Wally was an absolutely super host and made Chris and I feel at home within their nearby house. As members of 'The Shore Club' he and Betty laid on a party in our honour at which we met Amy and Julie their two daughters. Paul, his son, Tony's brother, was there, with his charming wife Sue. We were all seated at a large round table, balloons flying, tinsel everywhere, as in America! What a meal.

Tony took me golfing during the week at Bedford where I learned a salutary lesson: 'If the golf ball goes into the woods – leave it!'

'Drop out' at no penalty. No-one goes off course into the woods because of Lyme's disease or Snake Bite!

Whilst there we visited Mohawk Lake and the beautiful New York apartment of Tony's sisters Amy and Julie on Madison Avenue NY, where they laid on a super Christmas dinner and drinks. The luxury apartment even had a coal fire!

Into New York we had dinner in China-Town, authentic, with the Chinese. Not tourists, but us! We took in all the tourist sites of Times Square, the Twin towers, (God forbid), the Empire State Building, the Chrysler Building, the World Trade Fair and the East Side.

Tanya had an English friend, Mandy, whom she had known from her pharmacy days in England. Mandy was working as a nanny in Pleasantville where she kindly invited us all to dinner. All in all we had ten days or so of absolute over indulgence amidst lovely family friends. What a Christmas and with New Year in China-Town to follow.

Before we left, we had dinner with Ted and Laura Remson, Tanya's former employers, whose girls Tanya had tutored and had brought up so well during their early and teen years. They are all still so close and as I now speak, in the year 2013, both girls are married and have children of their own.

On this holiday at Christmas in 1986 Ted and Laura pushed the boat out for the four of us. The house and surroundings that befit an oil stockbroker made me most envious of the one thing I could not get my head around. Ted had his own drive-in, petrol pump dispenser on his house drive.

FAREWELL TO BRECON - POSTED TO BERLIN

In my last six months at Brecon I was called to the MOD Postings Branch near London to be interviewed by a Lt Colonel as to where my ultimate Quartermaster Post was to be.

As my parent Regiment was to continue as the Parachute Regiment, I was still required to carry out four descents a year and to retain pay; in the event of a war situation the Regiment would have first call on me as a Quartermaster. Now of course in my fiftieth year this would be unlikely.

I was in effect in my last years of Service and the Postings Branch was to offer me a senior post. I was actually asked where I would like to serve. I remember asking for CYPRUS as a first choice and Germany as a second, having never served there but to exercise. An accompanied Tour of three years was on the cards.

Where I was to go though depended on an in-post Major Quartermaster coming to the end of his present Tour. (One out, one in!) I Returned to Brecon and, within the month, I was notified that my next posting would be to Headquarters Berlin and the Signal Regiment, in effect the Berlin Garrison Quartermaster, a Post since the Second World War held by an All Arms Quartermaster Lt. Colonel. Christine and I were delighted: what a three-year posting and, to me, the chance of promotion to higher rank.

In our final six months in Brecon before Posting, whilst at the All Arms Tactics Wing and still an ex-Officio Member of the Sergeants Mess, I was lucky to be invited into 'The Guards' enclosure tent at the Derby. What a day out with immaculate hosting by one of our instructors being a Guards Warrant Officer! Brecon to Derby by coach and return. Pub stop on the way back. I didn't have a winner but did see the jockeys and horses at the Winning Post. The Officers

233

Mess held a farewell luncheon for us both and Sam the Lab, where we were presented with a painting and hand crafted wool mural of Pen-y-Ffan from Nicky Gaskell, Major Gaskell's wife.

Later in the afternoon, suited and booted, I was picked up by chauffeur and transported to the Sergeants Mess by DUMPER TRUCK for drinks and the presentation of an ornate walking stick complete with Labrador head.

I sold our car to the Gurkha Headquarters after much persuasion, for £750. We had taken up the purchase of a new Peugeot 205 Rocket, duty free, for our next and last posting. Had to laugh when, within the month, the Gurkha Sergeant Major asked me for a refund, for a new clutch! I told him to bugger off. The car had 'L' plates front and rear and within the month since purchase I had seen at least seven Gurkha learners driving the car.

Christine and I, at the end of three years, were so sorry to leave Brecon. We had made so many friends from Viv the Camp landscape gardener to Arthur Bowley the Brecon Mayor. Officers and soldiers of different Regiments as well as our own Para pals. Wonderful tradespeople, Paddy Sweeney, the super butcher, Major (Retd) Stan Smith, the Curator of the 24th of Foot Military Museum at Headquarters Wales and my own super, both military and civilian, staff.

The Regimental icing on the cake so to speak was being invited to an 'Airborne Night', a dinner at the New GOCs House 'Penbrin' in the company of Major General Sir Peter de la Billiere and an Airborne guest who had once been my Company Commander and Regimental Colonel, Brigadier Joe Starling. The night wasn't all 'shop talk' either. I had just completed a bee keeping course at the Brecon College and General Peter was an accomplished bee keeper with hives in the garden!

Christine said, 'Well, that conversation was a change!'

Berlin Headquarters, The Olympic Stadium

Into a world of opulence, and Berlin was just that. No real financial constraints as back in service life in the UK. We worked within the parameters of what was known as, 'The Berlin Budget'. Each Sector was expected to show to the East Berlin, Communist and DDR sector

234

what we were about. The French, American and British Sectors as well as being the defenders of Berlin, competed against each other in Military Showcases.

Ours in the British Sector was the Annual Queen's Birthday Parade within the grounds of the Olympic Stadium. A parade of the Infantry Battalions followed by a luncheon for 1500 under a white marquee in the presence always of Royalty.

The French had a similar, 'St Michael's Day'. The Americans, lavish Change of Command ceremonies. All within their own Sectors of Berlin, West. Cross Sector invites were always given, to include the Russians from their Sector in East Berlin ruled by the German Democratic Republic, the DDR. We, as British officers and soldiers were allowed into East Berlin in uniform and through an armed and manned checkpoint. Even by private car. One could always take personal friends in too.

The East was impoverished by our standards of shopping and display goods. Their showpiece was one of culture, museums, the lavish opera houses and ballet performances, which Christine and I were privileged to attend.

The city had a ring of steel around it. Mine fields, tank traps, dog runs, all controlled from watchtowers day and night. The city internally was divided East from West by The Berlin Wall, manned by the DDR state police and soldiers. This divide covered bridges, roads, rivers, internal lakes and canals.

Lives were lost by Berlin citizens living in the East attempting to cross these demarcation lines into the West of the city. When we arrived in 1987 the Wall had been in existence for over 20 years. Even if an East citizen did tunnel into West Berlin, free access to the west of Europe could not be gained, as to leave Berlin into Europe one had to drive a corridor with checkpoints manned by the DDR and the Russians. Transport by rail was possible but only on the one line and the engines were changed at Magdeburg and all passports had to be produced and the rolling stock searched underneath. Even we, when driving the corridor by road were subject to stop and search, and a stamped reason for travel beforehand had to be obtained from one's sector headquarters.

This Berlin Sector carve-up had been formulated immediately after WWII at the Yalta conference to give access to Berlin to **all**

235

victors. even though the Russians actually took Berlin, and the allies, the Americans and Brits were over 100 miles away and therefore all within belonged to or was under Russian occupation, but Churchill, Stalin and Roosevelt divided the city. Churchill afterwards gave De-Gaulle a part of the British Sector.

This really was the set-up when Christine and I drove the corridor, having travelled by ferry from Hull to Rotterdam then by road through Belgium, Venlo, into West Germany and so to Braunschweig, the start of our journey east.

We had a week to settle into our super quarter on the officers' patch of Headquarters Berlin, at 56 Waldschulallee, Berlin. My work headquarters was two miles from the Olympic Stadium, one mile from the officer's hotel named Edinburgh House and Pool and four miles from the centre of West Berlin. Beyond the quarter's perimeter were woods and lakes unlimited for miles until one hit the ring of steel, the manned and wired border.

After a week or so I took up appointment as Quartermaster to Headquarters Berlin and the Signal Regiment. I inherited a super staff as all Quartermasters' Staffs are. (Otherwise we get rid of them!). In all, I had 53 military and civilians to keep all of the administrative responsibilities viable. WO2 John Taylor my RQMS and Coldstream Guardsman, to boot, was invaluable when it came to Royal Visits and the layout for the luncheon for 1500 guests. My other two serving Warrant Officers, George Rawlings and the Stadium Master Chef, Bill Marr, were seasoned unflappable professionals. My lady clerk Veronica was an absolute gem. Any letter draft written would be on the desk and typed up within the hour.

John Bartlet the rations expert was a computer wizard and Oscar, 'A Yorky', kept the Crockery Store and Royal Pack for 1500 guests as if it was his own.

All of the Stadium day-to-day requirements came under my remit. For the soldiers the norm of rationing in peace and war: Arms, ammunition, accommodation, clothing requirements, equipment and spares. For the Berlin Headquarters, major and minor works services, grounds maintenance and freight delivery.

Other appointments that I inherited were, Chairman of The Allied Airborne Association; on the Board of The Edinburgh House

Military Hotel and Officers Club; a member of the Committee of the Military School and PLO of the new Spandau Military Shopping Complex.

I came under Command of the Lt Col of the Signals Regiment for administrative purposes but really worked for Berlin Brigade and British Sector Headquarters. My office was within the secure keep of the old Olympic Stadium administrative buildings and I was a very proud member of The British Officers Club, Berlin.

Although the post I was in had been of Lt Colonel rank, I was to be denied this, as the CO I came under was asked, in my first three months, if the appointment could be carried out at Major Rank as opposed to Lt Col rank. The CO, Lt Col John Munnery agreed that it could, thus pleasing the Bean Counters at the MOD. At this time in 1988 ranks were being downgraded everywhere to save the treasury money. For instance GOC Wales had been downgraded from Major General Rank to full Colonel Rank. Of course I could do the job in the rank of Major otherwise I would not have been here in the first place. Lt Colonel (Quartermaster) would have been a super finale to my career. However, it was not to be.

In hindsight though it would cost me about £3000 a year pension. Lt Col Munnery had never thought that one through, probably as he had already secured his pension pot.

Even within Sector Government Headquarters, Brigade Headquarters and other Allied Headquarters I never found that the lack of a higher rank in this well-established Post was any drawback. I did my job, ran the show and worked for private soldier to general, within their entitlements.

If it ever came to an argument and to rank pulling as it did once, with a full Colonel, I dug in my heels and told him 'NO'. He saw my CO about my refusal. I saw his, General Corbetts, Chief of Staff. My mentor and holder of the Berlin Budget purse strings. The answer was still, 'No' and the full Colonel went off having displeased the powers that be. One new Civil Servant of Brigadier Rank did try to pull rank at the supposed handover/takeover after the costly refurbishment of Edinburgh House, The Officers Hotel and Club in 1990. The accommodation rooms, suites and main kitchen areas had been closed under refit for many months and were due for completion, to be handed back to the Military Board the first week in the New Year. Given the task by Sector Headquarters to Chair the Board, I enlisted the help of the other Major Unit Quartermasters in Berlin to carry out, with me, the takeover/inspection program. As I recall, they did a floor each of rooms, suites, corridors, safety equipment. I inspected the refurbished kitchen and the hotel ground floor. The verdict, on our mid-morning meeting, after each spending a couple of hours inspection – 'Not ready for occupation.' In my inspection of the kitchen, for instance, the 'cook's hand basin' had not been fitted, nor had all the fire doors.

A Bolshie Civil Servant at the time attending the handover/takeover washup, on hearing my verdict, 'Not fit for occupation', told me that these outstanding works would be completed, but in the meanwhile the hotel would open in three days time to occupants. He emphasized that, 'Major, you cannot refuse!'

Having an interest and around at the time though not on the Board was my mentor. We had a Word. He asked the Unit Quartermasters if they could return on call after a week or so. All agreed that they could.

The SO1 Sector Headquarters then gave his deliberation and told the Civil Servant, 'You have heard what Major Godwin, The Chairman of the Board, had to say, The hotel remains closed. The Board will reconvene in ten days time and we will take it from there! By that time all the work must be complete.' At the second time of asking, It was!

I thereafter had no disagreements with Civil Servants or the Property Services Agency for the rest of my Tour. Not even when I chaired the large rebuild takeover of The Naafi complex on the old site of Spandau Prison that had been demolished when HESS, the one remaining NAZI prisoner, had died.

The offices, living quarters for officers and senior ranks within the Olympic Stadium and the amenities were first class. The Officer's Mess was a substantial building formerly used by Hitler as a Mess when using the nearby tennis courts. The Olympic Swimming Pool was available to all during the day and there were unlimited sports pitches and even a well tended cricket ground.

The well decorated soldiers dining hall, with wall murals, was formerly the Olympic Fencing Hall. The Sergeants' Mess was a new build and built to German standards. The actual 1936 Olympic

238

Stadium, open to visitors, was only a couple of hundred yards away under the control of The Berlin Authorities' Civil Department and secured by them. We had the use of the parade ground for the Queen's Annual Birthday Parade.

I occasionally met the site manager and caretaker of the Olympic Stadium and they were agreeable to showing our military guest parties around. I hosted a Gurkha visit for about 30 at one time with accommodation and messing and they were shown the Stadium. All were most impressed, German building, as no other.

The Stadium was host, once whilst we were there, to an athletics meeting, attracting the top athletes throughout the world in competition. A guest in, 'The Tribune Block', I was able to see Carl Lewis, the USA champion breast the tape and win the 100 metres just below me. He also, at this Championships, won the long jump.

The Waldbuna, an amphitheatre bordering the Olympic Stadium, hosted such stars as Tina Turner and The Stones whilst we were there, and Chris and I were privileged to see the shows.

On one's time off in Berlin, there was much to see. We attended the Ice Festival or Dancing on Ice, the October Fest in our British sector, the French and American theme nights in their sectors, band concerts, the theatre and such productions as 'Cabaret' in German. Nights in East Berlin really were outstanding; the Opera, 'Swan Lake' the Ballet, all put on in lavish theatre and opera houses, with hundred piece orchestras and full ballet ensemble from The Russian Ballet Company.

Chris and I made use of the Officers' Club pool, a half mile from our house, and we swam 30 lengths a couple of times a week before I went off to work for 9am. Weekends saw us, with the dog, with friends on walks within the Berlin Forests.

What many visitors did not realize was that West Berlin was made up of 2/3 water, lake, canal and forest.

We joined the German Spandau Walking Club. There were sponsored walks in selected areas of 10, 15 or 25 kilometre walks, most weekends of the month. There would be recognized stopping places along the route where the walkers could take a beer, have soup and sometimes a physical, blood pressure tests etc. All under the club walks' arrangements. At the end of the walk, where the walkers usually ended up in a school hall, there would be substantial food laid on. Often, and outdoors if the weather was kind, brass band music would be played. Small souvenirs like medallions were given to each walker completing a walk.

Christine's Mother Lois, on being on holiday did a couple of walks, one of 15 kms when well into her seventies, to secure a medallion.

As mentioned previously, we had in Berlin 'The Allied Airborne Forces Club', of which I was appointed 'Chairman'.

At the time by pure coincidence all three Generals of the British, American and French Sectors were ex-Airborne. (Paras). Our General, Corbett, had been the Commander of The Guards (Pathfinder) Company when a Major some years ago at Pirbright near Aldershot. General Francis Cann of The French Sector had dropped at Suez as a young officer in 1956. Whenever he and I met he would always remind me that we were the only two Officers in Berlin who were in Suez and held the Medal bar. The American General was still an airborne serving general. In addition the Berlin Brigade Commander, Brigadier Oliver was also ex-Para, having been CO of 9 Para Squadron Royal Engineers some years back.

Henri on our Committee was ex-French Foreign Legion. Major Mick Priestly on the committee was ex- RAOC. as was Major Roger Walls. Ex-Warrant Officer Brummie Walsh, the Bursar of the Allied Military School was ex-1 Para and an old chum of mine. In fact in Bahrain in 1962 I was his Platoon Sergeant and he the L/Cpl Signaller. He had been in Berlin some time with Mary, his wife, who was on my staff in the Stadium as my sports stores storewoman.

Our Committee met monthly within the Civil Service Club on the Heerstrasse, and we would plan for our usual six monthly event, always a buffet in convivial surroundings, always with our ladies. The membership? Airborne or retired airborne.

We held the get together parties whilst I was Chairman in the American Sector at their Golf Club, in the French Sector in a large canal craft and in the British Sector in the Olympic Stadium Sergeants' Mess.

Our Secretary was Mrs Mavis Pickin, an English lady employed in a British Military Office during the day. Mavis was the fixer and kept the minutes of the meeting. Our President was an Airborne, American full Colonel, Jerry Dillon.

We agreed to host German ex-Para who were living in Berlin and this worked well. They came to all our events with their wives where possible but through their Chairman I did limit their attendance to 30 at any one event.

A member of the Committee and one of my closest Airborne buddies was Barry Airth. Ex-ROAC but now the Chief Fire Officer within Berlin Brigade. Barry and I met often within sector and brigade responsibilities and travelled together once a year to inspect the accommodation at the Berlin Ski School and Mountain Outdoor Centre in Bavaria. We also used to travel together to Arnhem and to the Memorial Ceremony once a year for Arnhem Day.

With all of this rosy picture of parties, shopping, time off and visits to the East it would be hard to realize that The Allied Forces in Berlin were actually under threat. The Russians had done it once and had isolated Berlin City within the Soviet Block. It took the sustained, 'Berlin Airlift' to break it, when everything required to maintain life for both military defenders and civilians living in the city was flown in. It lasted for months until Russia agreed to lift the Blockade.

As defenders and, in particular with the Infantry Units, we were trained to fight any ground occupation. On a particular Code Word, given out day or night by telephone, radio or siren troops, at short notice, we would take to the woods, manned check and crossing points and broke open ammunition. The Headquarters and The Signal Regiment had a part to play and I too was dug out of a nice warm bed in Waldschulallee to motivate and exercise as a Defender.

I left Christine at home, with Sam the Labrador. Usually after a couple of days the Exercise seeming to have satisfied those in Command, life returned to normal. Status quo prevailing.

A real perk of life whilst a posting to or from Berlin was to travel into or from by military train, one like no other, 'The Berliner'. It ran the corridor through East Germany to the eventual haven, Berlin.

'The Berliner' - The British Military Train

During our time in Berlin it was the only British Military Train in regular service throughout the world. It ran every day of the year except Christmas Day.

241

The Berliner normally took about four hours to travel from Berlin, through the Soviet Block Corridor to Braunschweig in the West. It carried officials, military and their families and guests of families. All required to have in date passports as of air travel, plus sector headquarters travel movement documents.

From Berlin the train starts from Charlottenberg Station in West Berlin. It then stops at **Potsdam** where the engine is inspected by East German officials before its passage through East Germany. On this journey the train is halted at **Marienborn** station. At this station OC train, normally a major from The Berlin Brigade headquarters together with an RCT Warrant Officer alight from the train, march along the platform, meet, greet and salute their Russian counterparts, go into an office and produce all the passports and travel documents for inspection. In the meanwhile the train is once again inspected by East German officials.

The documents and passports of travellers having been checked, OC train and the WO bid farewell to the Russian Officer and re-board their train. The train then passes into the **German Federal Republic** and stops at **Helmstedt** where a West German engine takes over from the East German engine. It terminates at **Braunschweig** main station where it is prepared for its return journey to **Berlin** mid-afternoon.

The train's operation and administration was carried out by 62 Transport and Movement Squadron RCT (Berlin) with the co-operation of both East and West German railways. The dining car staff and some who have served for years was provided by Compagnie Internationale des Wagons-Lits. The dining cars were victualled by Supply Ordnance and NAAFI, Berlin. It was expressly forbidden to take photographs during the journey or indeed use binoculars.

Brigade Headquarters were caught out a couple of times and had to find OC train at short notice. I was asked and jumped at the task. Taking Christine with me for the day she had three hours shopping in Braunschweig before we returned to Berlin pm. Silver service breakfast on the way out of Berlin. Silver service four-course dinner on the way back.

All OCs train were presented with a 'Berliner Train' bottle of Potsdam Port at Potsdam on the return journey, usually to be drunk before reaching Berlin, with guests within the half hour.

An honour and tradition that I was able to receive twice, during my

242

time in Berlin: I was able to arrange for mum-in-law and her travelling companion, Mrs Kaye, to take the trip whilst on holiday with us in Berlin. They were looked after like royalty and even were presented with the 'Port'. I know because I met them at Charlottenburg Station, giggling like schoolgirls. All of seventy!

Whilst at the halt at Marienborn, and producing all travel documents to my Russian Counterpart, his interest as a Para on this occasion was in my parachute wings. A member of the Russian Airborne he was familiar with the normal blue British wings but had never before seen the blue/green/gold APJI lettered wings. I was able to inform him that it was an instructors' wing presented after a two weeks course at the School.

I asked him to attend our next party in Berlin as a guest. Russian military guests were invited to attend the celebrations of Our Queen's Birthday Parade etc. He had to decline as he said that he was not sufficiently high in rank. Pity! It would have been a first.

I was to do another couple of journeys on 'The Berliner'. The signals regiment officers and seniors took a day off, arranged by the CO and Christine and I had another shopping day. Pity now that those wonderful days are bygone once the Wall came down and Berlin East and West was reunited. Troops dispersed and out of Berlin in the early 90s 'The Berliner' was to be no more!

What wonderful memories.

HM The Queen Birthday Parade Berlin

The Parade Spectacular of the year as far as British Forces Berlin were concerned.

The parade, review and march-past was held within the Berlin Olympic Stadium grounds, on the 'Maifeld', a lawned area of some acres with the Olympic Twin Towers as a backdrop.

The Infantry Battalions of Berlin Brigade would be dressed in best parade dress and would be reviewed from a parade vehicle and from a rostrum as they marched past the reviewing stand in slow and quick time. At the reviewing stand would be the general officer commanding, host to royalty on this occasion.

Whilst Christine and I were in Berlin, the Princess Marina, the

243

Duchess of York and the Princess Anne, represented Her Majesty the Queen at this annual parade in celebration of HM Queen Elizabeth's Birthday.

A suite was made available for their convenience within Berlin Brigade Officers Mess.

After the parade and within our stadium enclosures marquees were set up with large circular tables to hold a luncheon and drinks for 1500 senior guests from the Berlin, German, French, American, British and Russian civilian and military headquarters.

My stores held this 'Royal Pack' and my staff and catering platoon were responsible for the execution of this lavish reception.

Afterwards the 'reviewing royalty' would, after a suitable break and change of attire, be escorted to other venues within Berlin Brigade to meet soldiers, their wives and children. The Harvel Military School was a favourite.

As I had quite a part to play in these proceedings year on year, Christine and I before the luncheon were fortunate to be presented to HMs representatives: The Princess Marina, the Duchess of York and the Princess Anne. The official photographer being on hand we are fortunate to have the photographs as lovely memories.

We were to meet and greet Princess Anne on one other occasion within Berlin Headquarters as she was, 'The Colonel in Chief' of The Royal Signals Regiment. On this occasion a less formal affair. 'Pullover Order', I wore a maroon '' Pullover.

Christine sported, 'Sunglasses'!

Outside of Berlin and our Visitors In

During our three years, Chris and I together with Sam the Labrador used to travel the Berlin Corridor by private car to The Harz Mountains. A journey of just over 100 miles to take up a weekend caravan on the wooded outskirts of Bad Harzburg: A lovely little 'Spa' Town of cobbled square, lovely food and usually on weekends a brass band playing within the village square. There was a cable car that took two persons at a time to the summit of a hill overlooking the town.

The caravan site had a lovely bar/restaurant and I swear that after the drive from Berlin the best Bratwurst and beers were had within this establishment. On site was also a five star hotel. The nearest 'Tourist' town was Goslar. Well worth a visit for stunning buildings, pristine clean pathways, (even in winter) and roads. Goslar was home to the famous 'Harz Roller', the Canary! My Uncle Stanley back in Wimbledon UK, enthused about this bird.

During our second year Chris and I hired a motor caravan for ten days and took off by German autobahn to travel to southern Germany, into Bavaria, The Algau and Steibis. We travelled the so called, 'Romantic Route', had a boat trip on the Plansee, took the cable car to the summit of 'The **Hochrat**' at Steibis, 2 m. where the Labrador, Sam, loved looking at the cows below. The Church at **Weiss**, was unforgettable.

We viewed castles, churches and the most stunning scenery and of the Stubetal Valley.

On the route back to Berlin we looked in at Heidelberg the university town, the castle, grounds and famous brewery.

We were privileged whilst at Steibis to walk the hills down to the parade ground together with dozens of dressed 'COWS' to be paraded in the afternoon, judged and awarded the accolade of best individual, herd, milker, breed, class etc.

The presentations of 'Bavarian Cow Bells' were given to individuals on stage and within the largest marquee that I had ever seen.

One side complete with Hogsheads of beer, large ladies with ample girth, serving four or six beersteins to thirsty farmers from out the farms. The food, pig roasts, wild boar with all the trimmings. How we got home to the caravan afterwards I barely remember, taxi I think! Within the beer tent as I recall, table after table of large ruddy cheeked cowmen and farmers and their sons and ladies. The men in Leden Hosen and Tyrole. Hats of all sizes, decorated with spring flowers. The Ladies, pigtails, Durndle skirts and flower embroidered tops.

What an annual festival! Fantastic.

We made the road trip back to the UK a couple of times, through West Germany, Belgium and France, ten-hour trip but easy driving on the autobahns. We usually came in at Dover or Ramsgate. One visit was a Parachute Regiment dinner held in London at the guildhall. The other when Sam the Labrador on return to the UK in

245

1990 had to go into kennels for six months and we had to give him up in Dover for kennels in Somerset.

Chris and I took two main holidays within our three-year Tour. To New York, Pleasantville on the outskirts, and to see our elder daughter Tanya and son-in-law Tony Chateauvert who was by now the head professional golfer at the Bedford Golf Club, Westchester County. Ten days to Cyprus to set up our retirement let in Limassol and to stay with for a short while Terry & Carole White, he an old pal of mine, having been the paymaster of 2 Para.

We had many visitors to stay with us at 56 Waldschulallee, our home and one or two at The Edinburgh House Military Hotel when I was able to secure a room. All, without fear or favour, loved Berlin at that time.

We hosted family, both our daughters, Tanya from New York with hubby Tony and Trudy from Brecon, Wales with Sue her friend; Christine's Mother, Lois, with her travelling companion Mrs Kaye; My sister June from Ossett, Yorkshire with Albert our brother-in-law; Christine's brother Phil and his wife Linda; My sister June's son, Brendan, and his Student Uni pal. In fact I gave up our house basement to them: Bedroom/games room to come and go as they pleased.

Para pals were always dropping in. 'Queen's Messengers' who carried diplomatic mail into Berlin. All now retired from military service but still active but now on the civil list. One was my ex-CO. 2, one the ex-2 i/c 4 Para and one a serving major with me at one time. Curry supper was the order of the day.

To remind me of those great days at Depot The Parachute Regiment when RSM. Lt Colonel Jack Hobbs the Regiment's Senior Quartermaster telephoned me at work and I was able to book he and his wife Pat into The Officers Club for a week whilst Jack now retired was able to visit the opera houses in East Berlin. We greeted them in, off 'The Berliner', and that evening had a super dinner at the club. Jack was good company but always told of his hate for ROSES.

'Filthy things,' he said, 'They drop their petals everywhere!'

So, to pull his leg in 2013 I put a rose on his Grave within Aldershot Military Cemetery. Jack would chuckle at that!

246

The Berlin Wall 1961 – 1989

This Barrier between East and West was constructed by the GDR East Germany (The German Democratic Republic), in August 1961. The Wall served to prevent the massive emigration and defection of peoples in the GDR East into West Berlin. Prior to this two and a half million people had escaped. It cut off, by land, West Berlin from the surrounding East Germany and East Berlin.

From this day there was a ring of steel with concrete barriers, tank traps and minefields looked over by watchtowers, surrounding the whole of the city.

This barrier, or 'Wall', split the city to divide East from West, except for a crossing point under arms, and alarmed barriers at 'Checkpoint Charlie'.

In 1989, after civil unrest with East Berlin, triggered off by political changes within the Eastern Bloc, mainly in Poland and Hungary, an end to Communist Rule saw the following: the mayor in East Berlin changes. The Mayor in East Berlin stood down and the Mayor Elect asked for free and fair elections. This led to the East Berlin/German Government announcing that free travel East to West, and West to East be allowed for all citizens from 9 November 1989.

People flocked to the Wall adjoining the divide next to the old parliament building, The Reichstag, that evening. Citizens on both sides climbed and stood on the Wall. The GDR Guards stood idly by not knowing what to do. 24 hours previously, people would have been shot. Within 24 hours the Wall was breached. Massive holes were knocked through, whereby people could come and go as they pleased, the first time in 28 years. Many came through or over the Wall to see relatives then returned home, back to East or West that night.

Christine and I drove to the Wall to witness the sights of people clambering over, dancing on the Wall top. Candlelit venues were being set up, fireworks being let off. TV Crews were in evidence from West Germany and even UK outside broadcasts. Citizens were at the Wall with hammers, chisels and axes. We joined in and secured chips and small pieces of the Wall, to be mounted later on a wood plinth as souvenirs.

I was soon to be involved in, 'Operation Resettler', in the work capacity as the Brigade Quartermaster. The Mayor of Wilmersdorf asked for assistance and my team set up a feeding station of hot soups, bratwurst, bread and drinks.

The Mayor had the financial team give the Eastern Refugees 100 DM each over two nights against their identity cards. Berliners whom we saw in the square adjacent to the Wilmersdorf Town Hall were extremely grateful for this kindness shown to them. We did see families actually meeting who had not seen each other for so long. It was heart-breaking. Many people cried.

It was a great privilege to be there at this time. Christine and I witnessed history in the making on 9 November 1989.

The Berlin Adventure Training Centre Bavaria

The Berlin Budget financed an Adventure and Ski Centre in Southern Germany, some ten hours drive from Berlin. This last outpost was in the Algau region not far from the main 'Kur' Town of Oberstaufen. (The Cure or Kur being a regime of health fasting and dieting, taken up in this region by tourist film stars).

The Adventure Training Lodge was a large wooden building, Alpine Style, built over three floors and with all amenities to house classrooms, stores, showers, messing and offices and providing sleeping dorms for up to 100 students and bunk rooms for a Captain OC and a dozen or so Senior NCO Instructors. There were outdoor stores for canoes, sledges, skis and other outdoor equipment. The Lodge was sited off the village road to Steibis and on the lower slopes of the HOCHRAT Mountain at 1832 metres.

A cable car some two miles away would take four person cars to the summit of the mountain in about 20 minutes. There was then the choice of descent by Ski, Glider or Shanks' Pony, about a two-hour walk if one chose the descending zig-zag path.

Wintertime saw the students ski, sledge or practice cold climate survival. Summertime - ridge or mountain walking, climbing or canoeing. The students came for two-week courses, mainly from Berlin although, where there were vacancies, from other soldiers/units stationed within West Germany.

As Quartermaster Berlin it was my delightful job to visit the Lodge once a year, to meet the OC and instructors and to see what

248

was to be done for the upkeep of this facility.

I would then arrange exchanges of accommodation, stores, mattresses, duvets etc, provision of a cleaning pack, works services to repair broken items, plumbing, pathways etc. Monday to Friday was the work schedule. Saturday to Sunday inclusive was time away from Berlin. Ample time to get to know the surrounding area, take a trip up on the cable car and usually walk down, once in the snow, helped by Sam my Labrador. I used to ask my old pal, Barry Airth, to join me for the week, in his capacity as Chief Fire Officer, Berlin Brigade.

Barry did have much to inspect and to make absolutely safe. The whole Lodge apart from the roof was wood. Fire doors within had to be working and of sound construction, fire and smoke alarms were critical.

There was an absolute NO SMOKING BAN except for within the Mess hall and bars.

Work completed for the day we had a most enjoyable stay. Out and about with a Taxi on the odd occasion to the Piano Bar in Oberstaufen, and off the mountain or 1/3 down from the summit we would meet 'Scottie' – 'Mine Host' at his mountain bar and restaurant. There he would get us away from the 'Hoi Polloi', leave his wife and girls to run the place and then retreat to the back of the restaurant to his private quarters and view. We would be invited to sit at what I believe he called 'The Stemple', a special table, kingsize with ample chairs, with a balcony with a most wonderful view 1000 ft below where the cable car was to be seen. There we would drink and eat like kings, chew the fat and spend a couple of hours. We would then make our way down the winding wide pathway and safe route to join the minor road back to the Lodge.

Always a super break from Berlin and its flat landscape, I was able to visit the Adventure Training Centre three times in three years! Well, someone had to do it! The dog loved it.

**Charity Marathon Swim: From *The Berlin Bulletin* **

"Friday 12 October 1990 sees Major Tom Godwin and Father Tim Forbes Taylor go for Gold within the newly refurbished Olympic 50 metre swimming pool within the grounds of the Olympic Stadium. The swim of 5000 metres will be completed within two hours.

This is in aid of Airborne Forces Charities in this the 50th year since Airborne Forces was formed. Please give your support, visit the Pool and throw your DM into the buckets provided. Or just come along between 1200 and 1400 to give 'ORCA and FLIPPER' a cheer."

'Housefrau' at 56 Waldschulallee

Whilst we were in Berlin within married quarters, Chris was allowed help in the house with regards to cleaning, laundry and housework as a 'Housefrau' or cleaning assistant was allowed from the Berlin budget.

We were very lucky to have the help of Linda Paterson and, indeed, that of hubby Ian as they were both students of the Berlin Philharmonic Orchestra. Both played the 'French Horn'. They worked for us part-time, grew to love our Labrador Sam and so 'Dog Sat.' on many occasions whilst we attended officers' mess nights. They had a small flat a mile or so away but much preferred nights in at our house! Our cellar was ideal also for practice on the French Horn.

Chris and I became firm friends until it was time for them to return home – to Australia. We had farewell parties and in their honour I planted a Eucalyptus Tree within the garden. We still keep in touch. Ian became a teacher, Linda - a civil servant.

Although students over two years of the French Horn they were not of such a high standard as to be invited to join The Berlin Orchestra.

The Gurkha Visit to The Berlin Stadium
The Famed 'Kukri Dance'

Within the UK during the 80s, Gurkhas continued to serve in the British Army at Brecon in Wales at The All Arms Tactics Wing, and at Crookham near Aldershot where there was a Gurkha Infantry Battalion with its Headquarters. Through their own arrangements a party of about 30 was to visit the Berlin Music Festival to be held over two days within the famed Deutschland-Halle indoor stadium.

They had booked the party in, under sector headquarters arrangements, contact with the German Berlin authority being through the government/sector liaison lady, Frau Helga Gallier.

Most of the Gurkhas were musicians and had brought with them bagpipes, woodwind instruments and drums. They had traditional dance dress with them and were expected to perform a village dance, to their own music, within the festival hall, a spot of about a ten minutes performance.

This was where I got in on the act!

Berlin Brigade Headquarters had asked me to host the party, to arrange accommodation within our lines, meals and transportation. In addition, during their five-day stay I arranged a tour of Berlin for them and a guided visit of the complete Olympic Stadium.

Frau Helga Gallier was much in evidence within the city visits as interpreter. She was at sector headquarters, the lady who had access to all shows, concerts and sporting venues, and was usually liberal and quite fair in doling out free tickets to all British Battalions and minor units. I had a great liaison with her when it came to brewery and golf venue visits.

Anyway, on this visit of the Gurkhas, as I was their sponsor so to speak, she asked me if the Gurkhas in their village dance would display the famed Kukri Knife. I said that I would see what could be done. On seeing their band warrant officer he said that there was not such a Dance!

I said, 'There is now.'

Within a couple of hours he and I had devised as a part of the dance to music, a set of slashing, wheeling and blood curdling cries that in effect had the Berlin audience mesmerized during the two night performances. For the first, last and only time the Gurkha Kukri

Dance was seen to be alive. Frau Gallier was inspired!

The Diary of our final year in Berlin 1990
Farewell and to Pension and Resettlement

Chris and I used to keep a wall chart in the kitchen at home in 56 Waldschulallee. Coming across it in the year 2013 I could not believe that we got up to so much. I record it now, or at least the main events, month by month.

January 1990
1 Rest Day, after New Year's Party
3 to 5 inclusive – Walking in Harz Mountains, 25km walk, met old friend Colonel George Smythe from Heidelberg, came up for walk.
6 Cinema Berlin, Garlic Pizza. Theodore Haus Platz
8 Edinburgh House, Cocktails
12 RMP Party
14 Ice Hockey Team Preussen Home
17 Visit into East Berlin
21 Ice Hockey
24 Christine to Brecon by air to see Trudy
25 Ice Hockey
26 Signals, Black Tie Dinner Party
27 Brigade Staff Duty Officer
28 'Joe' my Clothing Storeman, farewell party Stadium
30 OC. Train, 'The Berliner'

February 1990
1 Edinburgh House Committee, lunch
2 Mayors Invite Wilmersdorf
3 Soccer, Olympic Stadium
4 Ice Hockey
5 Champagne 'O' Gp.
6 Irish Guards, Cocktails – Suit
10 Ice Speedway
12 Dentist (2 teeth)
13 Edinburgh House, Glenfarclas Whisky Club Meeting
15 Drive to UK

16 Officers' Dinner, Guildhall, London
18 Meet Christine at Brecon, drive back to Berlin 19th
FRI 23 QM Staff Informal Party Stadium Club. Buffet
25 Visit East. Sector Mission House Invite.
Lakeside. Over Glinnekar Bridge. Diplomatic Exit

March 1990
2 Ice Hockey. Preussen Stadium
5 SSVC Party Edinburgh House
9 Sigs Regt Major 'Craig' Dining Out, Stadium Mess
10 Berlin Brigade Duty Staff Officer
15-20 Visit Adventure/Ski Lodge Bavaria, South Germany
21 Berlin Circus, Deutschhalle
25 Curry Lunch Stadium
31 German Invite. Club in Spandau

April 1990
1 Walking Club 20 km Walk, Lichtenrade Area
4 Golf Gatow. David Phipps and Baz
6 OC Train. 'The Berliner'
8 Stag Night, Sigs Offrs. Charlottenburg! Cultural Evening
10 Whisky Meet Edin House. Glenfarclas Club
11 Host at Home. Sylvia & Terry White. Ex-2 Para
12 Tegal Airport. George Smythe. Ruth & Charlie
Mess BBQ in Evening
13 Stadium Officers Club – Chinese
15 Edinburgh House Dinner
16 Tiergarten Fair
18 Brigade Golf Gatow – David Phipps
20 Black Tie Offrs Mess
22 Mess, Curry Lunch
27 Airborne Party USA Golf Club
29 Fun Walk RAF Gatow
30 Mess Jazz Night

May 1990
1 To UK driving Harz – Zeebrugge – Dover, with Chris
3, 4, 5 UK. Brecon. Golf Brecon Town Course. See Trudy

6 Return to Berlin
8 Glenfarclas Fusiliers Edin House –Jungle Kit
9 Royal Engineers Invite – Suit
11 Offrs Mess, 'Plantation Night'
14 Meet Colonel Jack and Pat Hobbs, Edinburgh House
16 Meet Quartermaster Designate Major John Leighton
Blues & Royals. (To take over Oct 90)
19 HM the Queen Birthday Celebration. DE.
Reception. Intro to The Princess Anne.
22 Lunch Officers Club
24 Golf Gatow, Barry Airth
26 GOCs Residence. The Villa Lemm Ball
27 Brigade Duty Officer – Stadium
30 Meet Daughter Trudy Tegal Airport
31 See Tina Turner live at Waldbuna Stadium. BBQ in Mess after

June 1990
1 Gatow Golf Club – Cocktails
2 Walking Club Spandau 20 km
3 Leave for CYPRUS 0300. Until 17th
22 Golf Gatow against PSA
23 Bill & 2 i/c Dinner Heerstrasse
24 Fun Walk RAF Gatow Perimeter
25 Dinner Edinburgh House
27 Brigade Duty Staff Officer
29 Mess BBQ RAOC
30 Mess Cocktails

July 1990
1 French Sector Wandertag, Wooden Walkways. Marshland
4 USA Sector. Lunch. Change of Command Parade
7 Sigs Regt: In Stadium BBQ Host CO. Lt Col Mike Collins
9 Party @ Lt Col (RE) John & Sheila Geany
10 Edin House Hotel. Glenfarclas Whisky Club
14 Devon House, Summer Ball. Teachers. PSA. Civil Servants.
15 John Lawtons 10 km Fun Run. Sam and I walked it with Hans.
Police Inspector. RAFFLE. Sam won the beer.
16 WRAC Party. Devon House. Suits

17 Berlin Brigade Duty Staff Officer
18 Takeover New Build, 'Brittania Centre', Spandau
On behalf of Sector Headquarters.
20 Farewell Party for C/Sgt John Lawton and Renate, retiring to Cyprus.
27 Lt Col. John Geany 50th Birthday Party
28 Philip and Linda into Berlin. Officers Club

August 1990
1 Attend Fair US Sector & Phil & Linda. BMWS Tour
2 Phil & Linda Funkturm Tower. Tour West Berlin & Stadium
3 Allied Airborne Party. Boat Trip Berlin Canals.
Super or supper? Buffet and Drinks inc German Fallschirmjager
4 Phil and Linda return UK
11 Olympic Stadium. USA Services V Los Angeles Soccer Match
12 Ice Hockey Berlin Stadium
13 Major John Crosland ex-2 Para & Fam into Berlin
Fix Caravan Site at RAF Gatow
15 Attend American Fest with JC & Family
19 Harz Mountains 20 km Walk
21 Host General Geoffrey Howlett ex-Para, drive to
POTSDAM. San Succi Castle. Morning out.
23 Brigade Duty Staff Officer
24/25 Host Wilmersdorf Mayoral Weekend Fair.
Sigs Regt involved running bars and food stalls QM staff included.
Fair and Music on Streets
26 Walking Club. Tegal Forests. 20 km, Chris & Sam
30 Attend Ice Hockey. After, drinks at Waldschulallee Bar in Woods with Barry Airth. HANS, mine host.
31 Drive to Caravan Bad Harzburg. HARZ Mountains

September 1990
1 and 2 Walking in Harz Mountains, Forests
7 Champagne Reception Brigade Mess
Band Spectacular. Sigs Farewell to Chris and I
8 Brigade Duty Staff Officer
9 With Chris & Sam 20 km Walk in Wanderfreunde
10 'Berliner', Military Train. Trip out with Chris

13 Southern Germany to Berlin Adventure Training Centre. attended Cow Festival @ Steibis.
Cheese Factory until 17th. Return through Heidelberg.
18 Brittania Centre. Official Opening. Shops etc. Regimental Bands. Eats. There as Guests of Brigade Headquarters
19 Moscow State Circus Deutschland Halle Berlin
21 Queens Messenger for dinner at home
22 'Mon Cherie' in Wilmersdorf with Sigs Officers
24 Colonel George & Ruth call 8pm
27 To Brigadier Oliver's for dinner 8pm
28 Dined out by Quartermaster Staff within Stadium Club.
    Presented with Super Berlin Prints.
30 Lt Col John and Jean Geany gave Chris and me super, 'at home', Farewell Lunch.

October 1990
1 Into Brigade Mess Pre Handover of Married Quarter 56 Waldschulallee. Chris and I Room in Mess.
2 Handover of Married Quarter to Ordnance Services Berlin.
3 Chris off to UK and Mothers from Gatow.
Thomas to follow after Appointment Handover.
7 American Sector Walk. Farewell to Club Walkers.
Super souvenir Badge 'Global USA'.
18 Farewell Dinner at Edinburgh House Hotel and Officers Club. Hosted by President and Committee of The Allied Airborne Association. Handed over duties of Chairman to Major Roger Walls. Super Presentation from Sec Mavis Pickin of chutist in Glass.
22 to **26** Handover Quartermaster Appointment and duties to Major John Leighton, Life Guards.
27 Leave Berlin by Road through Berlin Corridor, West Germany, Belgium and Rotterdam to Hull, North Yorkshire and to join Christine at 3 High Street, SHAFTON. Yorkshire, West Riding (Into Retirement).

RE-SETTLEMENT AND INTO RETIREMENT 1990 – 1991

I actually retired from The Army and The Parachute Regiment in my 53rd year, the date, the 7th Jan 1991, when I attended at The Depot

Browning Barracks for a release medical. From that date I was placed on 'reserve', but my days with regular forces were over.

Whilst in Berlin and in my last six months of service my regimental colonel, Jeffrey Mullins, had offered me one further appointment to take me up to my 55th year. I was offered Officer Commanding of the Parachute Course Administrative Unit at RAF Brize Norton, a post that I would, in normal circumstances, have given my eyeteeth for.

However, the Colonel was only able to offer this appointment for just over one year. This would have been most unfair on Christine, as from Berlin we would have to set up house in Oxfordshire, yet within the year we would be on the move again looking for a house to live in retirement. I declined the post and asked to be granted early release knowing full well that I had qualified for retirement pay in the retired rank as Major. My release was agreed.

From November I had qualified for an army resettlement course. This absolutely useless six weeks is all that the government is prepared to offer any serviceman, officer or otherwise, supposed to prepare them for civilian life and employment.

The British Army, Ministry of Defence, Government Bean Counters and the like, offer the very worst resettlement package known to man.

Most officers I knew attended the Aldershot Military Resettlement Course on bricklaying and plastering to enable themselves to carry out small jobs around the house! That was just about the worth of the course.

The American Forces Resettlement is completely different. University two-year Degree Courses. Membership to existing office clubs, medical and shopping facilities whilst the British answer seems to be, 'Once out of sight, out of mind'. The now so-called 'Forces Covenant' is not worth the paper that it is written on.

I took up my six weeks' resettlement course with brother-in-law Ian Smith, Christine's brother. He worked at that time for Yorkshire Television on outside broadcasts, working from a contract base situated just outside Pontefract in Yorkshire. The memory of the little I recall is that I had a ball. Never in one's wildest dreams though would it give me training toward a future career.

During the early morning I drove from Mum-in-law's house at

257

Shafton, a half hour drive or so to work, to meet Ian from the outskirts of York where he lived. I recall two large box type vehicles in the yard that were driven to various sporting venues and outside broadcast topical villages, where the sport or news of the day would be transmitted from these vehicles by their controllers, through telescopic and retractable dishes onwards to relay points such as the Emley Moor Mast, at 1000 ft plus, on the lower Pennines. This was long before digital signals in the early 90s. Signal by relay was the name of the game.

I remember one afternoon following Ian as the cameraman on the touchline of a soccer match at Sheffield, trying to keep as close to him as possible carrying a hand held circular dish, to transmit the signal to a larger one at the side of a gap in the Stand. Doncaster Races was another venue that I attended, this time over three transmission days. A programme from Coventry Cathedral was another venue, when the Queen Mum re-opened the newly restored cathedral to its former glory after destruction during the Second World War, by German bombers.

When and if things were quiet during the week brother-in-law Ian and I used to visit dwellings on the Yorkshire Television extreme areas to prove if they could receive a TV signal or not. Or would it be Cumbria? For this Operation I drove a very sophisticated Top of the Range 'Rangerover', whilst Ian carried out inboard tests to the 20ft powered telescopic and retractable dish on a pole. I was often amazed when we found ourselves miles from anywhere! Farmhouses, isolated houses etc., the owners having purchased TV sets in wonder at who COULD provide such a service: Sometimes Yorkshire, sometimes not. During the six weeks that I was with the Outside Broadcast Unit, the regular week-day sporting venue was professional wrestling from Sheffield recorded during a Wednesday early evening, but actually shown for transmission during Saturday afternoons. There I met week after week the Irish sporting commentator Kent Walton. What a Pro!

The system followed the same pattern week by week: Into Sheffield for 3 pm. Set up cameras, transmission vehicles in car park. Prove all systems working to black and white boards in wrestling ring. Switch off all power, retire to pub 5 pm. Kent Walton into pub 7 pm, by taxi, train from London. Kent a couple of pints, be given programme on who would be wrestling on the Bill. 7.20 leave pub, power on. Kent Walton take up commentary seat and commentate for following hour. Leave wrestling hall 8.30 pm. Power off. Two pints in pub with Kent. All well! Kent taxi, train back to London 9.30. 10 pm vehicles and equipment pack up. 10.30 drive back to base one hour to Pontefract. Late start Thursday mornings – for noon.

That was my release, resettlement from the regular army. Nothing toward a career but thoroughly enjoyable and quite well paid too for the out of normal hours working arrangements.

Christine and I, at this time, had set our hearts on living in Cyprus for the foreseeable future, so I had not considered employment within the UK, although it is fair to say that not only through the regimental net had I been offered OC the courses administrative unit at Brize Norton, I had been offered a travelling vetting officers' post for future officers by the MOD, on my retirement and after Berlin. The die was cast – Off we were to go to Cyprus during February 1991. Farewell Winter.

Journey to Cyprus February 1991 by Road and Ship

The 7 January 1991 saw me attend a final release medical at The Depot The Parachute Regiment, Browning Barracks, Aldershot. Also on release by pure coincidence was my old CO The Depot Colonel, Graham Farrell MBE, during my former years as RSM. 1977 -1978. We had much to talk about as he had just given up Commander of The Sovereign Base at Episkopi, Cyprus after three eventful years. I told him of our plans to settle in Cyprus on retirement and he said although continuing to work within the UK, he and his wife Gloria were looking forward during 1991 to purchasing a holiday property on the Island. Therefore we would no doubt meet, in the future in Cyprus!

Leaving the Regiment for the last time on the 7 January left me with no regrets. I had without a doubt completed over 36 years of service, with behind us, the most marvellous memories. Now, for retirement and into the future.

We planned to leave Christine's Mother's house at High Street, Shafton in South Yorkshire during early February and travel to

259

Cyprus by car. Our VW Passat Estate would take us to Hull to board the Ferry to Rotterdam then drive through Germany to stay with friends at Heidelberg; on to Innsbruck, through the Brenner Pass into Italy, drive through Italy to the Mediterranean Port of Ancona, take the ship 'The Mediterranean Sea' to Athens, then board another ship 'The Paloma' to Cyprus and the Port of Limassol. I had purchased the sea crossing tickets during January through an old Airborne pal of ours. Captain Terry White, who was already living in Cyprus. At Christine's Mum's we packed into the car what was dear to us, leaving the rest of our stuff boxed, ready to follow us by sea.

The second week in February saw us drive to the King George Dock at Hull to board a North Sea Ferry for an overnight berth and to disembark at Rotterdam the next day. We were absolutely amazed and delighted to find that the ferry was 'The NORLAND', the ship that I had boarded in 1982 to take my Quartermaster Staff and 2 Para to and from The War in The Falklands! Not only that, the Purser now on board, John Graham, had also been on our epic journey.

Once it was known that Christine and I were on board for the night's crossing, we were treated like Royalty. Champagne dinner, super cabin and on board old shipmates making themselves known. We had to curtail the hospitality somewhat as on for the following day we had a seven hour drive or so from Rotterdam to Heidelberg. The road journey thereafter was uneventful as much of the route was familiar to us as having been part of the route in the past to Berlin. It was a joy to drive the German autobahns.

On arriving in Heidelberg we were the guests of Colonel George and his wife Ruth. George, now serving as Liaison Officer with American Forces, had been my past CO at The All Arms Tactics Wing Brecon, in Wales 1974/75. Colonel George Smythe, a former 'Green Jacket' and super Commander had been awarded with the OBE on leaving Brecon. We stayed only one night as we were on a tight schedule to drive to Innsbruck the very next day but we had time late afternoon and early evening to visit the castle grounds, take a horse taxi and visit Heidelberg Brewery.

Colonel George having booked us into a hotel in Innsbruck, we drove off the following morning making the hotel before nightfall. The weather was cold at that time of the year and so we did not see much of the town, except for a rather nice Italian restaurant. The following morning saw us off through the Bremmer Pass, without any snow or ice holdups, to drive hours into the long flat plains of Italy to board the ship 'The Mediterranean Sea' at Ancona before nightfall. We docked the next day, before mid-day at Patra on the west side of Greece and then had an hour and a half drive to the Port in Athens, over the Corinth Canal.

We were due to board our cruise liner, 'The Paloma', the very next day. Knowing that Chris and I had to find a hotel to stay the night in Athens we were lucky enough to get into conversation with an ex-pat in the bar of 'The Mediterranean Sea', and he told us to look out for 'The Alfa Hotel' as we neared the Athens port. He said that it was easily spotted from the elevated motorway into Athens and for this he was proved to be spot on.

We came off the motorway, booked into the hotel for one night, left the car and took a taxi to the shipping office within the Athens port. On the way, we saw the cruise ship 'The Paloma' at berth in the harbour.

The clerk at the shipping office then gave us the bad news! What a shock! 'The Paloma' would **NOT** be sailing the next day, nor any day! The War in the Gulf States had cancelled any cruises through the Suez Canal, a destination through Limassol, Cyprus and beyond.

The shipping clerk asked us to attend the office the following afternoon and said that it was likely that he could get us to Cyprus but within the WEEK, but not as scheduled.

The Alfa Hotel, Athens

So from the shipping office at the port, late afternoon, we re-visited the Alfa Hotel where I had left the car. We saw the manager and changed our stay from that of one night to the possibility of a week. He was happy and so were we with the deal offered on a bed and breakfast tariff, though lunch could be taken any time. We were then shown to our room on the ground floor as I had requested. To keep an eye on the car and on the small storeroom allocated for keeping the contents of our car.

What a room we were shown into: King-sized bed, stereo headboard with port and starboard red and green lights flashing to

261

ordergreen and red lights, flashing to order, mirrored walls and mirrored ceiling! Chris asked if we had been given the honeymoon suite! Or were we in a house of ill repute? At breakfast the next morning we were the only clients in the restaurant.

We were out in the car during the morning, visiting the old Olympic Stadium before we went to the shipping office once again.

This time we were lucky to be given the good news that we would be found a berth on a cargo/passenger ship, leaving Athens in five days time, bound for LIMASSOL.

The second morning at the Alfa Hotel after breakfast saw us meet our lady room cleaner. She told us that she changed all linen every day! All towels, all bathmats. She asked us, how long was our stay? When I replied a week, she seemed amazed! She hinted that no-one stayed for more than two nights. I did however explain our circumstances.

After a couple of days it did seem to be a most peculiar hotel. Few ate in the restaurant at any time, yet the bars in the evening were busy. During our five days we never saw one child, nor indeed any elderly pensioners! All of the rooms that I saw when shown by the lady cleaner had mirrored walls and ceilings. Clients seemed to visit in shifts as we saw from our ground floor entrance room! Taxis with business people during the afternoon and private vehicles with couples, all well-dressed. The 30s/40s crowd came in the early evening and into bars and rooms. Late night - older men, younger girls, expensive cars late evening. The clip-clop of high heels on floors late every night. Even police cars one evening! Chris and I could not fault the hotel and we had a lovely stay, even to packed lunches.

During our Athens stay we did visit most of the tourist attractions and even the high banks of the waterway of the famous **Corinth Canal**. We saw what was left of the Elgin Marbles and the Pom Pom Sentries outside the seat of Government.

Our farewells to the Alfa Hotel were said on the sixth day and we set sail early evening from Athens, having watched large freight lorries being reversed into the ship through the large stern doors. The passengers seemed to be no more than 30 in number and of these most were vehicle drivers. A lady called 'Kay', a Lebanese, seemed to latch onto us as company. We were due to dock at Limassol Port the very next day but this was not to be.

During the first night, having slept very well, I awoke as I thought that without movement the ship was too quiet. I dressed and went on deck in the early morning light to find the ship at anchor. On asking one of the ship's officers what was going on, he said that the sea was too rough to travel with the freight and that we were at anchor, sheltering behind the Island of Amorgos, off the Greek Coast, and would be here for some hours.

Christine and I ate a hearty breakfast, no one else seemed to bother much. Our fellow passenger, Kay, had toast then a lie down.

The very next morning we docked at Limassol Harbour and I well remember running over material sacks to make up the gap between the ship's ramp and the port quayside, the Porsche driver behind us looking on with interest.

Into Cyprus and Settling in

Once through the Cypriot Port Authority with just one minor hitch (the car engine block number was out one digit, with that of the paperwork), we were on our way to the rental property agents to pick up the keys for our three month let on the sea front in Limassol. A three bedroomed, fourth floor flat on Spirou Arousos Street, a half-mile from the port and the same distance from the town centre. The sitting room, complete with ornate bar had a walk on balcony that faced the sea. Pleasant though it was the street below was a main sea front thoroughfare, busy until 2 am or so, and after six weeks or so we decided that it was not the Cyprus that we had sought after and so we gave up the rental.

In the meanwhile, as our knowledge of Cyprus was well informed, we decided to look at rentals to the east of the Island. Ayia Napa, Protaras, Dyrenia. We were both swimmers and walkers, and the sea at the east is crystal clear, and there were walks along the coastline Protaras – Ayia Napa was a National Park area and so we aimed toward this area.

At a property office in Ayia Napa we were most fortunate to meet Lucy, an English ex-pat, settled in Cyprus, a one-time member of the WRAC now working for the property company. She took time out to show us rentals.

263

We visited two in the Protaras area. One was a terraced house, four hundred yards or so from the sea, but with no shops within sight. The other was a detached 'Villa' in its own grounds within an estate of four similar small two bedroomed houses, half a mile from the Tourist Crescent of Protaras and a mile or so from Fig Tree Bay. The quiet hillside road past the house led to the shopping supermarkets of Paralimini, some three miles away. After a good drive around the area and a visit to the owners of the property, we decided on a one-year rental.

The owners were the bank manager of the Paralimini Co-operative and his charming wife, who also ran a travel agency. (This proved to be handy for flights back to UK!) The property was to be a dowry house for their daughter and, as she was only four, our rental, should we wish, was safe for years to come.

We settled into the house at Protaras. It had no street or house number but a visit to the main post office in Paralimini gave us a box number for mail. We did not have a telephone! There were no mobiles in those days and so we used the tourist phones and phone cards.

We soon made friends. Adam and Nicky, both London Cypriots, ran the 'Rocks Restaurant' at Protaras and he introduced me to a cousin, the local Mayor of Paralimni, which led to me being granted a Cypriot ID card! So very handy, when, after three months as a tourist, one was classed as an alien.

To reside in the country after three months Cyprus had a strict sense of residential rules:
- You had to be self-supporting (bank statements on your monthly income had to be proven).
- You had to take out private health insurance.
- You had, in our case, to hold a valid UK passport.

The lack of these would see you off the Island. On production of these at the main police station, 'alien office', you were granted an Alien Certificate in a booklet for one year, thereafter renewable annually. Why the hell the UK don't adopt these rules? God only knows.

Life in Protaras was idyllic. At the end of our country road there was a small well-cultivated park, always full of pretty flowers and shrubs. A pathway from the park led up steps to the illuminated

264

church on a rocky outcrop. Newlyweds often used to have photographs taken in this area. At Parkside there was and still is the most super sandwich maker in the whole of Cyprus, with his own cooked joints and carved ham and pork, and a shaded seating area was provided.

We had not been in our 'Villa' long when the adjacent house was occupied for the weekend. We were introduced to Stavros and his family who lived in Larnaca, an hour's drive or so away and he was a close relative of our landlord. Stavros was a large fellow, over 6 ft in height, weighing a good 17 stones. I was amazed when he told us that he was the chief orthopaedic surgeon at Larnaca Hospital.

I had cause to remember after gardening one weekend. When walking, Stavros saw me limping. He said, 'Thomas, come here, you are limping.' He bent me over the property wall, gave me a twist and a thump and all seemed to come right.

Chris and I took to watering his garden plants during the week, as they rarely visited mid-week except when the school children were on holiday. One Saturday evening we were invited to supper with the family. Out of doors of course. Salads like no other, local bread, olives, roast potatoes, and out of the clay oven in the garden, carried on a large flat tray, was the meat dish of the day. I knew that it had been in the oven since dawn. It was a whole bull's head! Meat off the cheeks. Lovely!

Christine had the potatoes, salad and pasta dishes.

Awarded the MBE June 1991

What a surprise!

Whilst collecting our mail from the main post office at Paralimini on 14 June 1991, Chris and I received one of the surprises of our lives. There was a buff coloured envelope addressed to Major T. Godwin MBE. Inside was a signal telegram from St James's Palace, London. Reading as follows:

"Having heard the splendid news of your Decoration, I wanted to send you my warmest congratulations."

CHARLES
COLONEL-IN-CHIEF

The award of the MBE was published as a supplement to *The London Gazette* on 15 June 1991 on the occasion of the celebration of Her Majesty's Birthday. To Major Thomas Godwin (506253), The Parachute Regiment. We were asked later in the month by, Headquarters British Forces Cyprus, if we wished to attend an Investiture in Cyprus at Episkopi (Air House). We were given the option to fly to London at our own expense but to attend an Investiture at Buckingham Palace.

In due course we attended at The Palace having received a letter beforehand to arrive there between 10 and 1030 on Tuesday 3 December 1991.

This date could not have been better. We flew out of Cyprus early, stayed in Brecon by our younger daughter's arrangements and I was able to attend my Regimental Dining Out at Depot, Aldershot on the 29 November: my final farewell to The Regiment. The Host was General Sir Mike Gray, my former CO in 1 Para years ago.

Our younger daughter, Trudy, who at that time was the manager of The Castle Hotel, Brecon, arranged a night's stay for us at The Eccleston Hotel, at the rear of Buckingham Palace, the night before the Investiture on the 3 December. Our elder daughter Tanya flew in from New York, USA, the same evening and so we were all together at the Eccleston Hotel. We went out on the town and took in the theatre, to see 'Starlight Express'.

Tuesday 3 December saw us all attend the Investiture within the magnificence of The State Ballroom at Buckingham Palace, where I, in uniform, received the MBE decoration, pinned on by Her Majesty the Queen. Afterwards we drove out of the courtyard to return to Brecon, calling at brother Christopher's house for tea at Tongham near Aldershot. What a wonderful experience for our family to see the opulence of Buckingham Palace and to be in the presence of Her Majesty the Queen.

My MBE was awarded for services to the Parachute Regiment and in particular to services whilst in Berlin. I received many letters of congratulations afterwards but not only from my peers. What really pleased me were letters from 'The Toms' and my own serving fellow officers. Having retired some six months previous I really did think that the decoration had passed me by.

266

To Purchase 'The Village House' Kalo Chorio, Limassol

Whilst at Protaras, and realizing that we were in Cyprus for the long term, we kept an eye out at the local property market. We were conscious of not purchasing a property without title deeds. They were never forthcoming for new properties. This is a malady that seems to blight the Cyprus economy even to the present day. Thousands of purchasers of both new and old are without title deeds Many Cypriots prefer to keep it this way to halt the final purchase of property tax having to be paid to the Government.

Christine and I, in our travels around Cyprus, favoured Tochni Village, a few miles east of Limassol and about two miles from the very pleasant 'Governors Beach'. Chris fancied the renovation by a local builder, of a set of old goat sheds on a hillside overlooking the small town and river valley.

We even met up with the builder. A property in front would have restricted our view and so we were shown another property over three floors that was part complete. Thank God we were not tempted as we did visit the site a year later and the part build was a disaster. Water leaks everywhere and no vehicular access.

Going into Larnaca one morning to view a flat and an old build bungalow, we called on our 2 Para friends, Capt. Terry and Carole White. They had rather a nice bungalow rental not far from the centre of Larnaca. Terry knew the area well and advised us to call in on the local butcher, an ex-pat, who he swore made the best 'Cornish Pasties' in the whole of Cyprus. Ray, the Brit, married to a Greek Cypriot girl, was the manager of their family butcher's shop, owned by his Cypriot father-in-law. We made the visit, as the bungalow that we had viewed together with the estate agent was to the rear of the shop by a couple of streets. As well as having two most glorious pasties each (one to eat in the shop, the other to take-away), out of the blue we were given information that was to change our location within the month.

Ray Burden, the butcher, a past serving Senior NCO with the RAOC, had been employed as the garrison butcher and had as his supplies OC, a Major John Kenwright. This Officer, about to retire and newly married, owned a small house in the village of Kalo Chorio in the Limassol district and he wished to sell it.

Some days later and armed with a piece of paper on which was the location of 'The Village House', we were in the village to find 'Louis', the baker, the keyholder. He gave us the keys to the house and in we went.

Kalo Chorio Village, Limassol at 2,500 ft.

At just under 2,500 ft. and below the snow line, Kalo Chorio was a Greek Cypriot village of some 600 inhabitants nestling within the lower slopes of the Troodos Mountains, and some twelve miles north of Limassol town. The village had a Co-operative Shop and bank, a coffee shop, youth club, taverna, medical centre and visiting nurse with doctor on call. The village owned its own olive press and wine factory where grapes both white and red were pressed, and from the late pressing the famous Commandaria Dessert Wine was made. It was one of only three villages that had licence to export this wine. From the husks, a lethal brew of Zivania was distilled. This by law as sold to the government through the Keo Brewery Tanker collection. The Zivania from the grape husks was the basis of much alcoholic liquor made in Cyprus. Those villagers in the know had their own tipple from the odd illicit still! However, who was to know?

The village had its own mountain water supply for drinking and for crop irrigation. Many villagers were self-sufficient on crops, fruit and veg and the annual olive harvest. Goats and sheep were kept, but outside the village. Bee-hives of old oil drums were at the village boundary to the south.

There were two well attended 'St George' Churches.

The village lads made up a second division soccer team, top of their league in the early 90s and the local girls and young men made up a traditional dance troupe to take a part in the Annual Limassol Folk Festival, all in traditional dress.

Within the village, in addition to the Co-operative, could be found a small village shop run by Mr Vassillis and his wife Elani, and they seemed to sell a variety of goods, everything from frozen chickens and fish to petrol in cans and even cement! Many of the younger inhabitants would travel to Limassol Town to work, the elders normally working the fields. There was never a shortage ever though within the village of a plumber, carpenter, tiler or electrician.

The small village of Louvaras some two miles south east had a similar configuration as did Ayious(?Agios) Pavlos to the north east but only a quarter of the size.

The village was 1/4 mile south and off the main Limassol to Agros Road and Louvaros Crossroads. At this junction before one dipped down into the village 'B' road, was a well sited police station and super café come local produce shop.

The village boasted of one, 'master builder' Michael. Well used and always well employed by the ex-pat elements of the village, totaling, in the early 1990s, about 30 inhabitants. A happy Ex-Brit Community.

'The Village House', so called by its owner Major John Kenwright RAOC, was a derelict 19th century building renovated by himself, as labourer to Michael the village builder, mainly on weekends. It stood off the through village road, on a corner between the village water supply pool and the frontage of the Co-operative Bank. Three storeys high, the sitting room was on the first floor leading to an outside cover patio and a double door entrance. The patio level overlooked the road below and once inside the sitting room, glass doors opened out onto a balcony looking outwards towards the church. The sitting room had a spiral staircase in one corner that led down into a blue stone clad double bedroom with en suite shuttered windows opening onto the ground floor village road.

Back into the sitting room with corner fireplace, a swing door led into the kitchen and shower/toilet separate room, with windows to let in light. At the kitchen entrance a stairway led to an upper bedroom under beams, with leaded light windows at the far end. The kitchen had a refrigerator and Calor gas cooker. The shower room held a washing machine. All electrics were in, with 2 x chandeliers in the main room. Solar panel heating was to be had and the electricity sockets were ample. We were impressed on opening the door and in particular with the location of the house.

We were not looked into as there was a large, flat shop roof opposite and below, and yet we were well overlooked by the terraced houses on the hillside across the way, some 100 yards away. We were never to get the feeling of obtrusion as we had open views from a lofty perch.

The patio outside was tiled, held a large Webber barbecue, a small fridge and enough comfortable seating for six. The patio could be washed down and out through the side stairs at will.

We had much of the view of village life as it unfolded! The hourly bus to Arakapas, livestock passing below, villagers to the Co-operative or to the main church and those villagers drinking coffee on the patio of the Village Club some 50 yards away. One could say that the 'Village House' had the vantage when it came to what was seen to be going on. As a rural village property it certainly ticked all the boxes!

Without much ado and after a tour of the area to Kakomallis Mountain at another plus 1000 ft. we decided that it was for us. Three further visits with measuring tapes to The Village House saw us in negotiation with John and Val Kenwright over the purchase of the house and of some contents. We were fortunate as John actually had the title deeds to the property and after not many weeks we had bought the house and moved into Kalo Chorio on the 11 November 1991.

Kalo Chorio and Village Life 1991-1999

I did keep most of a diary of events: a visitors' book, photographs by the hundred and books of plants & flowers and maps and charts of the Greek southern coastline, a record of which deserves additional writing. However, that is not to be, as this book as written is to leave a record of Cyprus and Kalo Chorio as life left its memory on *us* in Cyprus. Apart from immediate family I will not mention the various visitors, both past and serving, whose company we enjoyed and who we went out to meet. Numerous lunches were taken on our patio, whole turkeys roasted within the Webber and countless bottles of Keo Beer and village wines quaffed at our tables. Lovely Jubbly.

Christine's Mum, Lois, came out on holiday from England, as did my brother Christopher and his wife Anne. They also came later to the Limassol Wine Fest.

Early into our second year saw our younger daughter Trudy from Brecon bring out, for the first time, our grandson, Thomas Oliver. Thereafter they were frequent visitors, both to the village and to the Curium Beach and Ladies Mile Beach off Limassol, almost every

270

day whilst on holiday. The village to the lovely Curium Beach, four restaurants and the Roman Amphitheatre for band concerts, was but 30 minutes away. Later and also to Fig Tree Bay and Konnos Bay in East Cyprus came Trudy with daughter Thalia as an addition to the family. The children were loved in the village.

Christine's sister Susie and her daughter Helen had two weeks with us at Protaras during May 1991 but never made Cyprus again and therefore didn't see Kalo Chorio. Phil, my brother-in-law, and Linda his wife visited us in June 1992 whilst on holiday and thereafter we saw them on occasions through the years at Ayia Napa. They loved the beach life. Our elder daughter Tanya and hubby Tony Chateauvert flew in from New York to holiday with us for a couple of weeks. Apart from taking them up Troodos Mountain walking, in January 1994, at 5000 ft. plus, we gave Tony a culture shock eating fish heads at a famous Limassol Fish Tavern. Peter the owner served, dressed in his vest! His armpit looked like a Grouper. To soften the shock and to add a little culture I bought them both boat tickets for an on board trip to Israel and an onward return journey into Jerusalem. Christine and I had already done the trip to The Holy Land the year before, and how wonderful it was, although in our time one could go to Bethlehem and into the Church of the Nativity.

Mention must be made of two almost family friends of ours who always played host to Christine's Mum. Al and Laurie MacConnell, who had a super bungalow at **Pyla** near Paphos. We were all, always, invited for dinner on many occasions. We had known each other for years as neighbours in Aldershot Married Quarters. Alaister as a SNCO in the Scots Guards whilst I a SNCO in the Paras.

Their daughter Julie, a police inspector, was often at their house at Paphos. It was always like family to see them.

271

Easter in the Village: Bonfire and Donkey Race

More is made of Easter than is made of Christmas within the Greek Cypriot villages. The village comes to a standstill during Easter weekend as festivities are centred around church life. In the UK we had the burning of Guy Fawkes. In KH they burnt a similar effigy, but that of Pontius Pilate, on a large bonfire within the church grounds.

Beforehand the youth of the village, by agricultural vehicle, Landrover, dumper truck etc. used to take off from the village square, klaxons blaring, to leave for the woods to collect old timbers from which to build the substantial bonfire pile. Hours later, early evening, the convoy would return.

On the Saturday the annual donkey race would be run through the village. A half-mile race over the tarmac road between the old 15th century church and new church. Through two bends streamside, to finish at the youth club building opposite the large concrete freshwater holding tank. The one below our house that was occasionally used as a swimming pool, 15 yds x 15 by 5 feet deep.

During our first Easter in 1992 I was persuaded by the lads of the village (mainly the soccer team) to take part in the donkey race. As I was somewhat bigger than the average Cypriot, the village wits decided to import an ASS, up from Limassol for me to ride! Dressed in Vraka, waistcoat, long boots and Tyrolean Hat I was ready at the start at 2pm. All I remember of the 'Beast' is that it was tall and had long ears. Five other donkeys were lined up, with on one, jockey Georgeous, the tavern keeper to my right. Stavros the plumber to my left. On a whistle being blown my steed refused to move so someone hit its backside with a plank of wood and we were off! No saddles, just a bridle, no stirrups just limpet legs. I came 4th when eventually brought to a halt at the ice cream van near the youth club. The Ass was still attached!

It was tradition that the jockeys after the race were thrown into the village irrigation pond. Two of the village lads came to pick me up to heave me over the shallow concrete lip but could not lift me at about 14 $\frac{1}{2}$ stones in weight. I elected to jump in and did so. They were not to know that I had a cunning plan. Being an excellent swimmer, I jumped in, then sat on the bottom of the pond for a

272

minute.

I could hear shouting, 'Mr Thomas, Mr Thomas'. Then a number of bodies dressed in shirts and slacks came in to find me. I shot to the surface, laughing, and they had been fooled.

So into the club for a few beers. What a day. The Ass had an ice cream and was taken back to Limassol.

Mr Vassillis, local Shopkeeper

From our Village House balcony I could see the roadside entrance to Mr Vassillis' Village Shop some 50 yards away. We had not lived there more than a week or so when I realized that once a week the shopkeepers open truck was there to be unloaded late morning. All manner of goods seemed to come from it, in no particular order except that cans of petrol were to the rear. Some with wooden bungs! There were cement bags, dry goods in boxes, frozen chickens and fish, cans by the dozen, bolts of cloth, cases of beer, wines and soft drinks etc. etc.

Seeing the unloading being done by Mr Vassillis, who was well into retirement age and with the help of his somewhat aged wife Elani, I decided to go and give him a hand to unload. This led to a liaison that lasted for years. He asked me if I would travel with him to Limassol once a week, in his vehicle, to pick up his weekly shop and then back in the village help him unload. Lunch and beers were offered and having checked with Christine, whenever possible, once a week, I was his man.

The first journey that we made together was never to be repeated. He drove and after twelve miles through the hills into Limassol, around 52 bends he nearly killed us both on the way. Mr Vasillis in the truck overtook another vehicle on a bend, side by side until the vehicle travelling toward us, with nowhere to go shot off our tarmac road onto an uphill track. After that we had cause to be stopped by a policeman on traffic duty at a crossroads who had his back to us. His arm was out to the side as a 'Stop' signal and Mr Vassillis had the truck hit it, before he stopped! The policeman came to me to give me the bollocking! That did it! Future journeys made by me in that truck were driven by me.

Our liaison was a super one. I got to know Limassol like the back of my hand; shops and stores still run in an old fashioned way. Much on trust with a central controller manager. What was promised was obtained! If not this week certainly next. I met Mr Vassillis' daughter, son-in-law, grandchildren and his sisters for coffee and cakes, and the stop at his favourite kebab shop where we always stopped for Kebab and Greek Coffee. 'Metrio' for me – no sugar.

Within the village, Christine and I went for lunch to his house to meet Elani's father, Mr Christos, now in his 90s who had fought for the British as a muleteer during the Second World War. He was a delightful gentleman. He always wore a trilby hat and waistcoat when out in the village. Indoors, he took more or less the same lunch: tomatoes, salad, sardines, village bread and chips, two glasses of red wine at each sitting and three fingers of Zivanier, the local mountain hooch. As he always said, 'To drive the bugs away.' He still worked out on the vines on the lower hillside slopes, in wellies!

'The Agnes Martha'

What else but a Sailing Yacht moored in Limassol Marina. She was a 9 metre Jeanneau, single masted, single fin keel craft, owned by Peter Rothery, a long term resident of Kalo Chorio Village. Peter and his wife Anne had hit it off with us when Christine and I first came to live at The Village House in November 1991. In fact they were lunchtime guests at our very first party on the patio.

Peter, an ex-Royal Signals Officer of some years ago, had on retirement worked on BBC communications in Cyprus as an engineer, where he had developed his love of sailing. He was a member of the Limassol Sailing Club. He had purchased the Agnes Martha in Cyprus. Then the boat was under another name. He had it transferred though to the name of his Grandmother! (Long departed, but now still with us).

Peter never had a regular crew to sail with but a number of pals who sailed on the odd occasion. The yacht really was more at berth than at sea, until I came along. Chatting over Christmas during our first in the village, Peter and I discussed regular sailing on a weekly basis. Thereafter that's how we did it. Depending on the BBC weather forecasts, no matter what day. If the wind was to be westerly pm at Limassol Bay, force 3 to 5, we were on our way out of the village at 9am. We could be out of the marina by 10am and into Limassol Bay.

The girls were not much interested and in the years that followed I can recall them joining us on no more than a couple of occasions. Probably happy to get us out of the way weekly, the die was cast. The Aggie Martha, a comfortable four berth craft or six persons up top, on a day sail, had a comfortable turn of speed. Up to six knots against the wind, more downwind. It was a very stable safe boat and a good fishing platform when needed. We had inboard cooking, three-day water supply, and a Sat Nav and self-steering system. The sails, a full complement, had to be hauled up and taken down by hand and really that's where I came in. On the odd occasion and a long sail, we set a large orange spinnaker.

We had an efficient 2 1/2 HP Diesel Engine and a standby outboard that in the main powered the four berth dinghy. An ice compartment kept our beers and gin and ice bags. A small fridge the foodstuffs and Peter's '4 minute eggs'. Not a second more! We sailed together for years, certainly from 1992 to 1999 taking many friends of both our families out to sea; off Limassol to Governors or Ladies Mile Beaches, usually during the daylight hours 10am to 7pm.

Peter's son, my brother, grandson Thomas Oliver, daughter Tanya and son-in-law Tony from America, all came aboard, as did friends from our village.

Once a year we did a longer sail, and as the years progressed we turned the voyages into three or four day sails, east and west around the Island. The first, as I recall, took us from the marina in Limassol, east past Larnaca Harbour, to seek shelter for the night before we reached Ayia Napa. We put in at the Romanza Restaurant Fishing Shelter, and only because I had once spearfished within and told Peter the Skipper that the harbour could easily take our Keel. The restaurant/harbour owner was delighted as we were the first private yacht to have ever put in there.

A few beers, a lovely restaurant meal - then after Peter's 4 minute breakfast egg we were off the next morning, past Ayia Napa resort around Cape Greko to drop anchor 200 metres off Fig Tree Bay, Limni, in 30 metres of water. We stayed on board after supper ashore and decided to have a night sail direct back to Limassol

Harbour. We set sail about 10pm. On a stiffish easterly breeze and with the help of the diesel engine we made it back to Limassol by 8.30am. Interesting on the way to pass through an inshore fishing fleet off Larnaca, looking out for their boats' riding lights. We arrived at Limassol Marina with an addition. On a trolling line I had caught a 14lb Yellow-Jack Tuna off Cape Greko. We had trailed it on a short line tied to the Agnes Martha to keep it fresh. On arrival back in the village, Thomas Oliver, grandson on holiday with mum Trudy, was most impressed with the fish.

Yet another voyage on another day saw us sail west to go around Akrotiri Peninsular and the RAF Station across Curium Bay to anchor for the evening in Pissouri Bay. A meal at the 'Aussie' restaurant saw us back on board watching the stars under gin & tonics.

Off the next day to berth within Paphos Harbour and to stay for the night moored in the police berth at no cost. We returned the next day on a force 5 westerly direct to Limassol. Peter had the laugh on me as he loved to sail downwind. I hated it as I much preferred sailing into or off the wind, for the spray. I always told him that the 'Armchair' sailing was for the old folks.

Another four-day sail saw us once again go west but past the port of Paphos, having spent the night at Pissouri, onto or just off the deserted beach at **Lara**. We anchored 100 metres offshore and not until dark did we jolly boat onto the beach and to one deserted tavern for supper but afterwards we spent hours in the sand dunes watching the **turtles** come ashore onto the flat beach to lay their eggs. Afterwards, and by dawn they had all gone.

The next morning saw us round the Akamas Point to sail into Polis Harbour. On rounding the point and having a rod and line out with spinner I caught one hell of a fighting fish. A King Barracuda. 2 $^1/_2$ Kilos. In Polis we took the fish to 'Petra's' Fish Restaurant where much was made of it, in fillets with salad and Cyprus Potatoes.

I was to catch one other Barracuda as I recall, off the Keo Brewery outlet in Limassol Harbour. Whilst sailing together Peter and I had many laughs. I usually fished with a sturdy rod with a line always of over 50 lbs breaking strain and I said to Peter, 'I'm fishing and you never know.' Once whilst sailing together my rod did get broken and it all disappeared! This led us one day to catch a wind-surfer! Two surfers racing offshore, Next to even though we were two miles out. One decided to race inshore of us to gain an advantage. I was standing at the stern, rod out as this clown came steaming past. Despite my waving, shouting, pointing at rod and line he kept coming! The next second, and he must have been doing 25 knots, he executed the perfect somersault as my line broke. I had never seen anything as funny or so sudden in all my life. Nor had Peter. We left them far behind.

Another occasion saw me hook a dinghy! Once again warned, klaxon sounding but to no avail.

My party piece when anchored off Ladies Mile and at rest during siesta 1-3pm, was to swim the anchor rope looking for flatties as the anchor chain disturbed the soft sand. If nothing was forthcoming to the spear gun I would place this on board and swim out some distances around the other moored boats. Being somewhat offshore by a mile or two other boat crews would often wonder what I was doing. (They were not to know that I was a Bay to Bay competent swimmer in my own right and, indeed, always swam under a diver's quartered swimming cap). They would shout and ask if I was OK. To which I would reply, 'I could do with a beer.' Sometimes I was thrown a beer, not often was invited on board to drink a beer and on the rare occasion was invited on board for lunch. This always had Peter in fits; in particular as we had beers on board.

Once each second year Peter had the Agnes Martha lifted out of the water at the marina. Up on blocks she would be steam cleaned. Then over a week we would repaint and re-varnish the old girl. He cleaned and painted all above the water line, I below, keel and all - a labour of love.

In 2002 Peter sold the old girl to a Greek couple who took her to Athens where she is still going strong. He did ask me if I wished to buy her but we agreed, we were wind and wave expired, with some regret I add.

New Year's Day Lunch 1996
'Over the Edge'

New Year's Day saw Chris and me invited with village friends Peter and Anne Rothery to a lunchtime party at Lofou Village. The village was a good 20 minute drive through the Troodos foothills to the west of Kalo Chorio village, but the journey throughout was on the same contour height but mainly on unmetalled roads.

The Lofou Taverna was a legend for food and hospitality and so it proved to be. Our hosts were Peter and Shirley Whitwam, residents in Cyprus, and Joe and Jean their personal friends. The local villagers made up the party and we had violin and mandolin music, dancing and food and wine aplenty. It wasn't until well after 4pm that the party broke up and we said our farewells in the car park.

On the journey back to our village of Kalo Chorio, Peter Rothery drove their Ford Escort Estate car. It was between the village of Ayios Mamas and our village, with about two miles to go along the mountain road when the New Year's Day would never be forgotten! At the time I was the front seat passenger, and Christine and Anne Rothery were in the rear seats, with a dog.

In front of us, as we went around a wide left hand bend, in the headlights of the car was a loose dog running toward us. Peter swerved the car to the right, the edge of the soft road surface gave way and the car went over the edge and into the stream bed 60 ft. below.

I remember clearly the nose of our vehicle turning to toboggan down a scree slope, coming to a halt, turning over nose to tail 360 degrees then we landed with a crash, on rocks in the stream bed. Having twisted on the way. The rear window on the car was shattered. The engine was still running and with lights still ablaze I shouted for Peter to kill the engine. I was very much afraid of fire and a burst petrol tank. Peter switched off and there we were in complete darkness, a miserable evening and drizzle.

The roof of the car on my side being stove in, the door had sprung open and I was able to kick my way out. Peter having the help of the steering wheel as a lever was able to do likewise. We pulled the girls out of the rear compartment and the dog shot out of the rear window.

The next task of course was to find our way up the slope, and I

278

took our belts off and, by much tugging and heaving, we made our way up to the dimly lit track. Once on the track we shook arms and legs, checked necks and, although sore and bruised, had suffered no major injury. I, being the younger and fitter made best speed (sober) back to our village on foot to pick up our car, put the kettle on, and return along the track for Christine, Anne and Peter.

The car was a write off and took three days to recover with a heavy duty scammell vehicle.

Cyprus 1996: In and Out

Chris and I had the urge to leave our Island Paradise on the realisation that both our daughters were pregnant and due to give birth late April or early May.

In the half-year up to our wedding anniversary on the 25th June we decided to take a rather extended holiday to see as many family as possible in the UK. This idea took us to England, Scotland, Wales and the USA.

Manchester Airport saw us to Shafton in Yorkshire to Christine's mum's and from there, using brother-in-law Ian's Jeep, we drove to Gullane on the North East Coast of Scotland. We drove up. Stayed a night.

At Gullane a golfing holiday house was owned by daughter Tanya's former employer, Mr T B Remsen in Bedford, New York; and daughter had informed us that he was looking for a new housekeeper and caretaker, and that the proposition was worth a look if ever we should decide to return to the UK. Having seen it and having toured the dour area that it was when compared with Cyprus, Chris and I both agreed that it was not for us.

So back to Yorkshire, then a journey down to Wales to see daughter Trudy and to take our four year old grandson to school during the week and to the park and to look up old friends. Trudy at the time being noticeably pregnant.

We returned to Yorkshire to be taken to Manchester Airport to board a $7^1/_2$ hour flight to the USA in the hope of, during a two week or so stay, to be at the birth of our second American grandchild.

Christine and I arrived at JFK Airport, New York to be met by Tanya who was heavily preggers, hubby Tony and our young grandson, Henry, aged two.

Within a day or so we had caught up with the whole Chateauvert Family and once again were at supper with in-laws Betty and Wally at the beautiful Shore Club, West Chester. Tanya and Tony, having moved out of Pleasantville since our last NY visit, were now living in a super on course bungalow on Bedford Golf Course, where Tony worked as the head professional. I was fortunate to be introduced to the chairman of the club, an old WWII ex-colonel who addressed me as 'Major' and gave me the full run of the course, the clubhouse and the invitation to play or practice any time.

The middle weekend there saw us help host a drinks party for members on the lawns, all a part of the hospitality game. It seemed as though most guests were drinking out of bottles, as is the modern practice. Not for me, as I only drink from a glass. I saw a lady looking at my glass with what I thought was envious eyes and so without further ado I asked her if she would prefer one. She said, 'Yes, please' in perfect 'English', English. She had been born in England and was the widow of the film magnate and producer Wolf Mankowitz! We hit it off in how things had changed! 'Drinking from Bottles,' indeed.

Tanya's former employers, Laura and Ted Remsen had a most beautiful house overlooking the golf course and we were fortunate to be invited to supper and to make use of their pool. I played golf with Ted, but he, a lower handicap golfer than I, and on his own course, was the master.

We had days out on Long Island Beach and at Fire Island, viewed the famous 'Bedford Oak', went into China Town, New York and into 'Little Italy' for lunch, all with a very preggers elder daughter. So much so, it was soon off to the Yonkers Hospital, New York to view our new granddaughter Sophie, weighing in at 8lbs 2oz to a radiant mother. Visitors bounded in! Betty and Wallace Chateauvert, the other grandparents; Tony's sisters Amy and Julie, Tony's brother Paul and wife Sue and Tanya's English pal Pam from the trainee pharmacy days at Bournemouth, England. We all ended up at a champers breakfast at a restaurant in Yonkers. Back at the Bedford clubhouse I was there to witness Tony receiving a 'Baby Present' from Benny in the men's locker room from the staff members.

In the days to come Tony and I took in the Intrepid Aircraft Carrier, a floating Naval Museum moored on New York West Side and also went on board the submarine 'The Growler'. We viewed one of the first Polaris Missile Torpedoes.

'Moran's' Bar on the West Side was a must, where I thought that the minder/barman was standing on duckboards until all 6'8" came from behind the bar to stand with us.

On a lovely day out we played golf at Piping Rock Golf Club where Ian was the exiled Scottish golf pro. Afterwards his lovely wife Liz invited us to their super house on Long Island.

It was then farewell to Bedford, to Betty and Wally and a whole host of friends and off from JFK to the UK and to Brecon in Wales, there to see our new granddaughter at home in Trefecca, who had been born on the 6th May whilst we were in New York.

Of course, making ourselves useful to our new mum and daughter Thalia we were in no hurry to dash off home to Cyprus. We took grandson Thomas a day out to the Brecon-Talybont Railway, to school and on one occasion I encouraged Chris to climb with me, once again, Peny-Ffan on the Brecon Beacons. The Para Paradise.

It was then off to Yorkshire and to Christine's mum's house at Shafton, and on the way we made a detour to call in at Tongham, Aldershot to stay with brother Christopher and his wife Annie. Beers in the garden watching the deer jump the fence.

Then soon off to Yorkshire and the busy holiday continued. Brother-in-law Phil, who was the chief executive of Leeds Metropolitan Council, was a part of The Civic Welcome Party at the Elland Road, Leeds United Football Stadium and, as hosts to the Spain v Bulgaria European Soccer Match, Phil invited me to make up the host numbers. What a cracking evening. Sunday 9 June.

We didn't neglect Mum but took her for a day out into the Yorkshire Dales and to one of our past favourite watering holes, The Red Lion at Burnsall. River walks, trout to be seen from Burnsall Bridge and if one was lucky, up river and near to the church, kingfishers were to be seen.

The day was complete sometime later when calling at the world famous and original 'Harry Ramsden's Chippy' at Guiseley, where the ladies still served under chandeliers, dressed in black and white: pinnies, cuffs, collars and hat.

281

'Haddock, chips and mushy peas please with tea, bread and butter.' Tea served from the pot!

Another day saw us visit our sisters at Wakefield and Ossett, Melanie and June with niece Helen, and whilst in the area we had an afternoon at Nostel Priory, home to a super '**Adam Fireplace**' and to a Queen Victoria gigantic doll's house.

A final day out at Whitby saw us sniff the east coast of Yorkshire air, visit the harbour, Capt. Cook's House and the town beach. I could not resist calling at 'Fortunes' Whitby cured Kippers Smokehouse, for a pair. Established in 1872 they really knew how to smoke 'em dark or light! So the drive out of Whitby saw the end of a most memorable holiday.

It was then back to Manchester Airport and to return to Cyprus and home for a rest in time for our wedding anniversary at Angelo's Restaurant in Beachside Limassol.

A couple of months later in August 1996, grandson Thomas Oliver came out to holiday with us on his own under a BA charter of children under supervision on holidays. Naturally we were the named grandparents whom he recognised at Larnaca Airport as he ran toward us in the arrivals hall. What the BA Staff at the time failed to do was to have us sign a body receipt for one male juvenile passenger! We had a frantic call the following day from the BA office in Larnaca to see if we had him? All was well, he spoke with them.

Mother Trudy followed the week after, having been given the all clear to take new baby Thalia, on holiday by air. Thalia's first holiday of many to Cyprus.

Small Village Memories Kalo Chorio
The Bat Cave

Half a mile out of the village and in a rocky re-entrant there was found to be a cave and tunnel, mined in the past by repute in the 15th century for iron ore. Black smelted ore was found in shiny rivulets along the re-entrant bed, where smelting fires had once been set up.

Peter Rothery and I, together with seven-year old grandson Thomas, decided one day to go cave exploring. Armed with powerful lamps, me with a camera, and with Thomas standing guard

282

at the tunnel entrance, we made our entry into the cave. The tunnel opened beyond. There was no sign of roof slippage, dampness, musty smells, roof falls or loose rocks and so I encouraged Peter to go on. He believed my past mining experience, and so on we went but no more than 80 yards or so when, in the lights of our powerful lamps, a black cloud came toward us! Camera at the ready, I was filming! Whoosh, it was past. We heard a scream at the tunnel entrance and on making best speed back to grandson, we found him shaking with fear. He said that hundreds of BATS had passed him flying out of the cave. So it proved to be by my camera prints, dozens were filmed in flight past Peter and me and yet not one had touched us. We did re-enter the cave but met a solid volcanic rock wall on what we estimated was under a hundred yards.

Bay to Bay Swims in Cyprus

Each year the military bases at Episkopi and Akrotiri, and the Sovereign Base at Dhekelia, mapped out an offshore sea swim course of one Nautical Mile, 1852m. On the day, swimmers of all ages and abilities swam the distance for charity. At Episkopi we swam from Cape Aspro to Tunnel Beach, usually on a mid-morning westerly, up to 200 swimmers, flanked by canoeists and a couple of offshore inflatable safety boats.

My best time, as I recall, was 34 minutes to come in 21st. Not bad for a 55 year old and the chap I beat wore fins and I have a photograph to prove it. At Dhekelia the course was a figure somewhat U shaped, out and back to the safe jetty, graded and covered in coco matting. Here within Dhekelia Bay the sea was always calm.

One year, I took the 1st place for the 'over 40s'. So pleased, as I had cheerleaders from our village on a day out! John and Maggie Kennish and Brummie and Mary Walsh, as well as Christine my wife. On reflection, everyone came for the on base fish, chips and mushy peas! English style and known to be the very best on the Island.

On the swimming theme and at the present day in 2014, here in UK, I swim Monday, Wednesday, Friday and complete 40/50 lengths at the local pool. Once a year I take part in the SWIMATHON sponsored by Duncan Goodhew and the Marie Curie Cancer Charity. 5km or 200 lengths of the pool. What used to take me under two hours now takes me almost three! No sweat! It's the swim that matters.

Orchid Hunting and Mountain Walks

Throughout the years in Cyprus, and often with our visitors, we took a day bag and were off for the day as the seasons took us. The circular contour walk around Mount Olympus at Troodos, at over 5000 ft., was most spectacular in winter. The trail was well marked from Troodos Village, clockwise past the Islands only ski slope and down to Platres passing the Caledonian Falls. The Troodos pines at over 5000 ft. were most peculiar. All had flat tops as if they had been struck by lightning, as indeed they probably had. The smell of the pines was like no other - overpowering. East of Troodos at the same height was a ridge walk, out and back of about two miles to look down to the scarred landscape of the old Amiantos Copper Mine now worked out and having left acreage of multi coloured shale and awful pools of water over this vast area.

The mountain water dams in this area of Spilia and Prodromos were well worth a visit as one could go trout fishing. The dog Sam loved his swim!

In our time we took in and visited most of the monasteries of **Kykkos** and **Trooditissa**, Stavrovouni in the East, overlooking Larnaca and Apostolos Andreas at the extreme panhandle of Northern Cyprus.

Nearer to home, and around our village of Kalo Chorio, we had a circular walk through the hills to Louvaras that took us through the old abandoned village of Athracos. We mapped more than one way the two-mile uphill struggle to Louvaras and found hidden plots of cultivated opium poppies and vines.

February and March saw us orchid hunting, these are only found at this time of the year and sometimes up to Easter. They were usually found on hilly slopes, in grassy areas, or sometimes on stony patches, in our experience around our village hills, on northern facing slopes.

The wavy-leaved Monkey Orchid with tallish stem was 20-40 cm tall, flowers packed tight, pink to white in colour, with flowers much like little monkeys; the 'Bee Orchid', found in similar places but smaller, was harder to spot. Once seen though never forgotten. A green split tuber, covered in what one would swear were bees! Yellow and black, and with eyes. The flowers looked as if they could fly off. The 'Serapias' or long lipped orchid had deep pink flowers in a spike up to 10" tall. All orchids were protected and were so pretty and uncommon that we never ever disturbed them. There was the joy in photography.

We did buy books on the flowers of Cyprus and on the plants of medicine, and we had the greatest of pleasure in trying to find those that were most uncommon. The Wild Garlic, French Lavender, Poppy Anemone, Wild Asparagus, Capers, Crown Daisies, Cyclamen, Fig, Fennel were all in profusion but the Peony, Sea Daffodil and Monks Cowl were a devil to spot.

The Island at times was a carpet of flowers and in particular after early rain showers.

Farewell to our Island Home

During the late 90s and into early 2003 our family circumstances changed with Christine ever more so back in the UK. We were called upon to help our younger daughter Trudy who had suffered a lower back injury, and mum-in-law Lois who was in constant poor health.

Our retirement dream was over but with no regrets. The Island was changing fast and it was, as has been proven, it was time to get out.

The exchange rate was awful and we even saw our English Pound at 93 Cypriot pence, drop to 69 at one point. The Cypriot political class had sold themselves out to the EU to be a cosset member of the Big Boys Club. Even in our village no-one wanted to work in the fields and on the vines anymore. Shoddy tourist building in particular on the coast was beginning to make the place look like Legoland and we had enjoyed the very best that the Island had to offer for a decade.

We sold the Village House to an English couple who wished to purchase it for their daughter as a retreat. We regarded our move as

'Au Revoir', nothing permanent. We have been back, with the grandchildren and, God willing, will continue to do so.

Chris and I did enjoy our 50th Wedding Anniversary there and we did swim in Fig Tree Bay. We ate at Fernandos at Derynia and sat at the tables below the Church of Limni/Protaras, the host of the finest sandwich maker in the whole of Cyprus.

We left with no regrets, having really lived a decade of a retirement dream. We had been blessed with good health together, cushioned by the Cyprus Sea, sandy beaches and Zivanier.

I have decided to end this journal and bring the tales to a fitting conclusion within the parameters of Pit, Police, Para and Pension.

We took up accommodation in England in Hertfordshire within a bungalow sourced by The Officers Association in their Leavesden Garden Homes. It's 2014 now and we are in our tenth year here. We live in a twelve bungalow estate on a private two acre site on the start of The Chiltern Hills, thirty minutes by train to London, thirty minutes by car to The Thames – life goes on.

Regimentally I keep in touch with 2 Para, now at Colchester and a part of The Air Assault Brigade. I was fortunate in January 2014 to be a Guest of The Warrant Officers' and Sergeants' Mess, I was at the informal dining in of their new Commanding Officer.

Sixty years since I joined The Parachute Regiment at Maida Barracks, Aldershot at the start of training. Supported throughout most of the years by my most charming wife Chris and, in the Company of the very best of the best of Airborne Forces, I have been truly blessed.

father and Mother
Brighouse Yorkshire 1936

Uncle Stan Newman trainee pilot 1942

PC GODWIN 1948 floods

P Sgt Godwin with Jean Taylor 1954

Grandparents with Christine, Tom, Annie, Andrew Babe in arms

brother Christopher's wedding
day 1960's

Grandfather George Walton with
Tanya 1963 Brighouse

Crown Hotel Ossett with Charles
Wilkinson Butcher 1960s with father
the landlord

Alice Godwin 1960s
Mum at the Crown Inn

With family Crown Hotel 70's Christopher, Melanie, June and Tom

With Queen Aldershot1974 after presentation of new colours.

Tanya in wedding dress 1986

presented to HRH CHARLES 1978

2 Para with Mail 1982—Falkland campaign

last Hercules Para drop Belize 1983

Cyprus 1 mile sea
swim won over 40's
when over 60

Daughter Tanya with
Georgeos tavern keeper

daughter
Trudy
Limassol

Tuna Limassol

Disabled officer's garden homes Leavesden Hertfordshire

Tom in retirement Para Playground Pen-y-Fan

Sister June, Major Tom and Chris in Russian Memorial park in Berlin

Chris and Sam 1975

Daughter Trudy with the Red Devils

Mayor Tom & Sam the Lab